Tupaia

Tupaia

Captain Cook's Polynesian Navigator

Joan Druett

PRAEGER

AN IMPRINT OF ABC-CLIO, LLC
Santa Barbara, California • Denver, Colorado • Oxford, England

Copyright 2011 by Joan Druett

Library of Congress Cataloging-in-Publication Data

Druett, Joan.
    Tupaia : Captain Cook's Polynesian navigator / Joan Druett.
       p. cm.
    Includes bibliographical references and index.
    ISBN 978-0-313-38748-7 (hard copy : alk. paper)
    1. Tupaia, d. 1770. 2. Explorers—French Polynesia—Tahiti (Island)—Biography.
3. Cook, James, 1728-1779. 4. Oceania—Discovery and exploration. I. Title.
    G246.C7D78   2011
    910.92—dc22 [B]   2010034689

ISBN: 978-313-38748-7

15   14   13   12   11   1   2   3   4   5

Visit www.abc-clio.com for details.

Praeger
An Imprint of ABC-CLIO, LLC

ABC-CLIO, LLC
130 Cremona Drive, P.O. Box 1911
Santa Barbara, California 93116-1911

This book is printed on acid-free paper ∞

Manufactured in the United States of America

Contents

Contents

List of Illustrations

Introduction

⌒◟◞◞⌒

For more than two hundred years a painting of a Maori in a flax cloak and a European in gentleman's dress exchanging a lobster for a piece of cloth has been the subject of puzzled speculation. Carried to England in 1771 by Joseph Banks, who sailed as a scientific passenger on Captain James Cook's *Endeavour*, the work is now iconic. As a symbol of first contact between native and westerner, it is so evocative that it has been reproduced many times, though the identity of the artist remained unknown. Held by the British Museum and then the British Library after Banks's death, it was catalogued simply as the work of "The Artist of the Chief Mourner," because of another strangely compelling watercolor by the same painter.

Then the mystery was solved. In 1998, Harold Carter, the biographer of Joseph Banks, described a letter he had found in the Banks collection, dated December 1812, which reads, in part:

> . . . Tupia the Indian who came with me from Otaheite Learnd to draw in a way not Quite unintelligible The genius for Caricature which all wild people Posses Led him to Caricture me and he drew me with a nail in my hand delivering it to an Indian who sold me a Lobster but with my other hand I had a firm fist on the Lobster determind not to Quit the nail till I had Livery and Seizin of the article purchasd . . .

The lapse of forty-three years had misled Banks into remembering that the piece of cloth he had offered for the lobster had been a nail. Despite this, it was now clear that "The Artist of the Chief Mourner" was the extraordinary Polynesian who sailed with Captain Cook from Tahiti, and acted as the Europeans' go-between in dangerous first contacts with the Maori people.

His name was Tupaia.

Tupaia, a gifted linguist and a devious politician, could aptly be called the Machiavelli of eighteenth-century Tahiti. In June 1767, when the first European ship, HMS *Dolphin,* arrived at the island, Tupaia became Tahiti's foremost diplomat. He took on the same role soon after the *Endeavour* dropped anchor in Tahiti in April 1769, and then, when the ship departed, Tupaia sailed with them.

He was not afraid—Polynesians were never afraid to voyage. Over the next two centuries thousands of fellow Polynesians would sign onto European ships with the same confidence and courage, to work side-by-side with British sailors and American whalemen. Tupaia was special, though, because in his own culture he was a master navigator, highly skilled in astronomy and navigation, and an expert in the geography of the Pacific. In normal times he would have kept his privileged knowledge a deadly secret, never revealed to anyone outside his select group. But, as an exile . . . and a man who had narrowly avoided capture and sacrifice by his enemies . . . he was willing to share this sacred lore.

Yet Tupaia, for all his generosity and brilliance, has never been part of the popular Captain Cook legend. This is largely because he died of complications from scurvy seven months before the ship arrived home. Once he was gone, his accomplishments were easily forgotten—indeed, by removing Tupaia from the story, what the Europeans had achieved seemed all the greater. James Cook could have resented the fact that Tupaia had been hailed by the Maori as the "admiral" of the expedition. Seemingly, too, the sacred gifts that Tupaia had received from New Zealand chiefs had proved useful for presentation to monarchs and museums. It was also important that Tupaia should be forgotten when James Cook received his medal from the Royal Society—for the remarkable feat of never losing a man from scurvy!

Partly because of all this, the biography of the unacknowledged Tahitian who contributed so much to the success of the *Endeavour* voyage has never been written. Polynesia relied on oral histories, and so what we know about the eighteenth-century Pacific comes from the diaries, journals, logbooks, and memoirs of European witnesses, and the record has been too one-sided for a rounded account. Lately, however, folklorists and anthropologists, by paying attention to Polynesian myths and memories, have added immensely to our understanding. By consulting this new, rich literature, as well as the journals and memoirs written by the men who dealt with Tupaia on land and sailed with him at sea, the story of this "extraordinary genius" can at last be told.

CHAPTER 1

❧

In the Beginning

At the instant of his birth, Tupaia's life hung in the balance. Infanticide was widely practiced on his native island, Raiatea, partly because of overcrowding, and partly because of social pressure. The father might not want to acknowledge the child. The moment a chief's heir was born, he ruled as his son's regent, and was no longer an *ari'i* in his own right, and so he might order the child to be smothered.

Once Tupaia let out his first cry, however, he was safe. Indeed, he was looked after very well. A new baby was considered highly sacred, and for a while Tupaia could not be held by anyone except his mother. After cleansing herself in a sweat bath, followed by a dip in a stream, she showed the infant to his father, who recognized him as his son by making an offering at the *marae*, where a priest buried the umbilical cord with appropriate prayers. Then Tupaia's mother secluded herself, as she had been infected by his sanctity. Anything he touched became equally dangerous. Shrubs he brushed against had to be cut down.

These hampering prohibitions were gradually removed by profaning the baby or making him *noa*—ordinary—in a series of rites called *amo'a*. As the months went by, his father was able to hold him, and after another interval Tupaia was introduced to his uncles, then the rest of his extended family. Finally, he was tattooed with a special mark on the inside of each elbow, and proclaimed an ordinary human being, free to play and experiment with the world.

This world included the sea. Tupaia was able to swim before he could walk. By the age of five he was listening to stories of epic voyages that did more than entertain, introducing him to the mysteries of navigation. Within a year, he was being taken along on voyages, to learn that the ocean was not just a great, formless expanse of water with the occasional reef or island passing by, but a web of distinct and well-traveled seaways. Soon, he would know what distance to expect to cover on an average day's sail on each route, and could recognize the dusk-time, shore-seeking flights of different kinds of seabirds. As the months went by, he learned the patterns of currents and swells, and absorbed an impressive knowledge of star bearings. Great directional stars and constellations—*Matari'i* (the Pleiades), *Ana muri* (Aldebaran), *Ana mua* (Antares), and *Te matau o Maui* (the hook of Scorpio)—became as familiar to him as friends. He was an expert fisherman, too, able to forecast changes of wind and weather, and their effect on schooling and spawning.

At home, young Tupaia surfed with his playmates, wrestled, practiced the noble sport of archery, and fought mock battles with a club like a quarter-staff. At the same time he learned traditional crafts by watching and assisting carpenters, canoe-builders—and priests, as he grew older. A small number of outstanding boys, who had to be intelligent, tall, flawless in looks, deft, and sure-footed, as well as high-born, were chosen to go to schools—*fare 'aira'a upu*—which were presided over by priestly teachers, and Tupaia was one of these.

The place of learning he attended was in the south of Raiatea, at the greatest *marae* in all Polynesia, Taputapuatea at Opoa, by the sea. There, by rote, recitation, and chanting in unison, he and his classmates learned history, geography, and astronomy. Tupaia was an outstanding student, "distinguishing himself very early by his inquisitive disposition"—or so the first missionaries were told. As his spiritual power was recognized, he was taught sacred lore and ritual, and learned to recite ancient prayers without stumbling over a syllable. He was fated to become a *tahua*, or priest, in constant communication with the gods who had so lavishly endowed him, his specialty being the highly respected art of navigation.

When Tupaia reached the age of 12, there were further rites to come—*tatau* and *tehe*. In the first, a well-paid practitioner used charcoal to mark a pattern on his skin, tapped it in with a stick armed with finely sharpened bird bones, then dyed the perforations with candlenut soot. As it was extremely painful, getting tattooed was a gradual process. Over time the buttocks might be entirely blackened, while artistic designs covered the legs, arms, feet, hips, and torso, though the neck and face were almost always left undecorated. In the second puberty rite, another specialist slit the upper part of Tupaia's foreskin with a shark's tooth knife, and stanched the flow of blood with ashes. This freed him to explore and enjoy the world of the opposite sex.

Sometime during these teenaged years, Tupaia served a three-year cadet-ship in the *arioi* society. An ancient guild of traveling artists and entertainers, the society was going through its greatest flowering at the time, akin to the Renaissance in Europe. While anyone could apply to join the guild, mem-bers were chosen for their good looks, their perfect bodies, their intelli-gence, artistry, oratory, and acting ability. They were also ardent lovers, with no restrictions in the practice of the amorous arts, apart from incest bans—and the ruling that any progeny should be put to death, as only the highest ranking *arioi* were allowed to have children. Lesser members who allowed their infants to live were dismissed.

Tupaia was inducted into the third order of *arioi*, *taputu*. This was distin-guished by a special tattoo made up of a pattern of lines radiating from the base of the spine, spreading and curving around the hips, and meeting again in the small of the back, and gave him the right to wear girdles, wreaths, and garlands of sweetly scented ginger leaves. Then, after the festivities that welcomed him as an accredited member of the society, he commenced his voyaging, serving as a wayfinder, like his father and grandfather before him.

During his apprenticeship, Tupaia had been taught to keep a mental ship's log, complete with details of the courses steered, and the patterns of wind, weather, and sea, so he could retrace his voyage in his mind, and know the exact position of the place he had left. It was an accomplishment a European navigator would have recognized as a remarkable feat of dead reckoning. Not only did he have a very clear idea of his departure point, but he also knew from memorized knowledge the whereabouts of his target, and the details of the seaway that would lead him to it—even if he had never been there before. Now, he was honing these learned skills with hands-on experi-ence, by watching the direction of ocean swells, sensing the presence of unseen islands by interruptions in the currents and the winds, looking for the reflected green of distant lagoons in the bellies of clouds, detecting subtle changes in the color of the water that betrayed the presence of reefs, and noting the drift patterns of seaweed and the flight paths of birds, all of which helped him keep track of their course. He did not steer, paddle, work the sails, maintain the canoe, or oversee stowage and rationing of provisions. His entire responsibility was the crucial one of navigating the canoe.

As a star navigator, Tupaia was considered a hero, distinguished by a deep double-crease between his brows, and a distant, unfocused look in his eyes, the result of many concentrated hours of watching the far horizon. Tall, straight-backed, commanding in presence, and dressed in flowing robes of pristine white, he could have been an intimidating figure. Yet master way-finders were not overbearing, particularly those of the pleasure-loving *arioi* cult. Confident of their status, they were relaxed enough to be laughing,

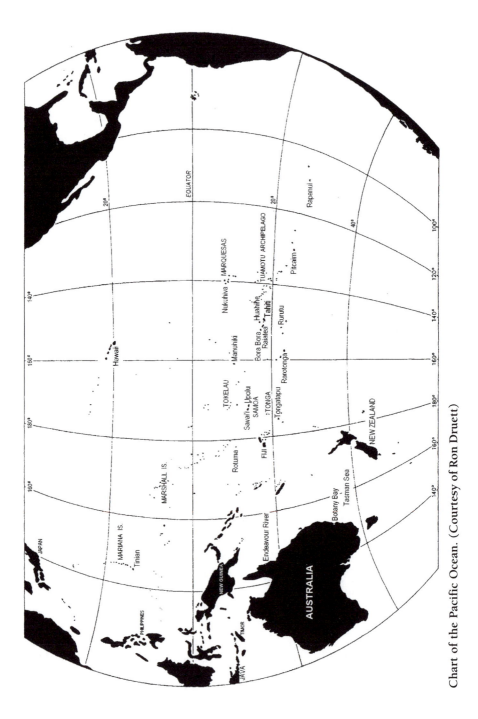

Chart of the Pacific Ocean. (Courtesy of Ron Druett)

outgoing, and kindly, great favorites with the children because of the wonderful tales they told.

If Tupaia became haughty and arrogant later, it was because life made him that way.

Wayfinders like Tupaia were the inheritors of a long and impressive tradition. Their remote ancestors were skilled sailors who had burst into the western Pacific from the archipelago of Southeast Asia more than three thousand years earlier, to settle in the islands of Fiji. About a thousand years before Christ was born, they colonized Tonga and Samoa, where Polynesian language and culture developed. Fifteen hundred years passed by, and then, perhaps because of overcrowding, perhaps because of the pressure of war, or perhaps just for the excitement of adventure, men and women sailed out from this ancestral cradle, fanning out across the broad Pacific, and exploring more of the Earth's surface than anyone ever before.

It was a feat made possible by the evolution of the double-hulled canoe into a stable voyaging vessel, capable of freighting a heavy load of plants, animals, provisions, and people. The big, graceful craft ranged as far east as Rapa Nui (Easter Island), and are very likely to have made a landfall in South America, either introducing the *kumara* (sweet potato), or carrying kumara sprouts back to Polynesia. At a time when sailors in the Mediterranean were just starting to experiment with the fore-and-aft sail, Polynesian canoes powered by lateens made the tough twenty-five-hundred-mile voyage to Hawaii, and then back again, battling cross-currents, the doldrums, and contrary trade winds. Two hundred years before the era of Columbus, Magellan, and Drake, Polynesians crossed two thousand miles of storm-tossed ocean, reaching far south to find the mountainous, deeply embayed islands of New Zealand.

The *marae* Taputapuatea at Opoa on Raiatea became the hub of a voyaging network that extended from Fiji, Tonga, and Samoa, to the Marquesas. There was a certain amount of trade, particularly between high, mountainous, fertile islands like Tahiti, and flat, almost barren atolls like those in the Tuamotus, and what are now the northern Cooks. Pearls were freighted from the atolls, plus, incredibly, iron spikes and nails, a trade that probably started after the Dutch ship *African Galley* wrecked on the Tuamotus in 1722, and was pulled apart for its iron. All these were bartered in the high islands for breadfruit, taro, yams, cooking bananas, tapa cloth, and volcanic rocks, essential for heating earth ovens. Manihiki, in the northern Cook Islands, exported pearl shell, used in sacred ceremonies. Tonga was a source of highly valued red feathers from the heads of tropical parakeets.

And then there was Raiatea's intangible export, religion.

All Tahitians were very religious, deferring to any of a number of gods before even the most mundane activities, but in Tupaia's time the veneration of one particular deity, the war-god Oro, was predominant. The cult of Oro originated on the Taputapuatea *marae* at Opoa, and was carried to other islands by the *arioi*, who, like brightly colored flocks of birds, voyaged from Raiatea in spectacular fleets. Their graceful double canoes—*pahi*—flew long albatross-feather streamers from the tips of their tall, narrow, elegantly curved sails, which were woven of matting and extended far above the tops of the masts. Though the leading *taputapuatea* canoe carried a sacred image of Oro, and the mission was to promote his worship, the atmosphere was festive. Platforms linking the twinned hulls were crowded with gaily dressed men and women, their faces rouged, their beautiful bodies gleaming with perfumed oil, and their heads and breasts garlanded with scented flowers and leaves. As Tupaia, or a wayfinder like him, guided the *taputapuatea* canoe to a safe landing, the chief *arioi* emerged from his small thatched house at the stern. Sharkskin heads of drums were beaten, nose flutes shrilled and whistled, singers ululated, and dancers revolved. The instant the curved prows loomed over the beach, the vivacious throng leapt ashore in a surge of color, noise, and movement, ravenous after their voyage.

They arrived like a plague of locusts, but were welcomed with great excitement. Villages emptied out as the local population raced to meet them, then rushed to prepare a great, pillared hall, the *fare arioi*, for the banquets and dramatic entertainments to come. After visiting the local *marae*, where the idol of Oro was placed in safekeeping, the visitors bathed in a secluded, shady pool, oiled and decorated their bodies, and dressed in fine garments. Then everyone gathered in the hall, where the chief *arioi* gave splendid presents (always including a fine pig) to their host, the district *ari'i*, who responded with gifts of his own, such as vast lengths of dyed tapa, which were wrapped around the *arioi* women so extravagantly they sometimes fainted under the weight of cloth. After that, a lavish feast was served, the best the district could provide. Normally, men did not eat with women, and women were not allowed certain fishes and meats, but these restrictions were abandoned when the *arioi* were in town. Once every man (or woman) had stuffed themselves with as much food as he or she could hold, the *arioi* presented their entertainment, a program that often lasted all night, and which included an extensive repertoire of music, drumming, singing, erotic dances, and satirical comedy.

Several libidinous nights later, the *arioi* made their departure. Local orchards and gardens were stripped, and the local chief was temporarily impoverished, but his reputation was greatly enhanced. If they ever came again, the *arioi* would be just as welcome. The idol of Oro was ceremoniously replaced in its special chamber in the *taputapuatea* canoe, and Tupaia resumed his responsibilities as sailing master. Then, after navigating the fleet safely to Raiatea, and taking the idol home, he returned to his estates in northern Raiatea until his seafaring skills were called on again.

In 1757, when Tupaia was about thirty, this glamorous existence fell apart. Warriors from the neighboring island of Bora Bora invaded Raiatea. In the course of one of the bitter life-or-death battles Tupaia was speared in the back with a particularly deadly lance tipped with a stingray barb—as Joseph Banks wrote a decade later, "a spear of his countrey headed with the bone of a stingrays tail" went right through his chest and protruded just under his breastbone. Luckily, Tupaia managed to escape the battleground, as otherwise he would have been sacrificed by enemy priests. But still he was close to death.

Penetrating wounds of the thorax have been common ever since men first joined in battle—Homer recorded men being speared in the chest in *The Iliad*. Death was the usual outcome, and still today thoracic trauma is considered extremely serious. Many victims die of shock; those who do survive are put immediately into intensive care. If the wound is a sucking one, it has to be sealed before the lungs collapse from the pressure of the outside air, causing instant death from compression of the heart. Oxygen is administered, along with antibiotics to prevent infection. A tube is inserted to maintain negative pressure in the chest. Open chest surgery might be needed, to inspect damage, and repair vital organs such as the heart or lungs. Where penetration was low in the thorax, as it was in Tupaia's case, the stomach or liver might also be involved. There could also have been damage to his diaphragm. Another complication was that his wound was contaminated with fragments of the brittle, toothed sting.

Friends carried Tupaia to a wound dresser, who was another kind of priest. As the stingray spine was barbed, the spear had to be drawn out from the front of Tupaia's chest, adding agony to shock. The dirty fragments had to be washed out thoroughly, or surgically removed, because of the grave risk of infection. If Tupaia had not been a strong, healthy man in the prime of life, he would have died quickly. Instead, over the following months, with the application of herb poultices and a great deal of clean, cold water, he recovered so well that in 1769 Banks was able to record the "scar is as smooth and as small as any I have seen from the cures of our best European surgeons."

The battle Tupaia had been forced to leave fared badly. In 1760 the Raiatean forces were routed. The *ari'i rahi*—sacred chief—of Opoa was vanquished, and his son, the source of his political power, was killed. As many Raiateans fled their homeland, the priests worked feverishly to save the cult of Oro. A copy of the god's image was forged, and entrusted with Tupaia.

His instructions were to secrete it on board a canoe and flee to Tahiti with Maua, grandson of the sacred chief.

It was a daunting assignment, as the new effigy carried a dangerous potency, transmitted from the master god of the *marae*. The priest who fashioned the new idol began with a wooden staff that was shaped like a belaying pin, tapering from a broad end to a point. This *to'o* was tightly bound with twisted coconut fiber, into which the shafts of red and yellow feathers were inserted, row by row, until it was completely covered with color, earning it the name of "feathered god" by the missionaries later. Then it was wrapped in layers of fine tapa cloth, and carried to meet the master god at Taputapuatea *marae*, where more priests were waiting, having spent the night in fasting and prayer. The great god and the new image were both reverently unwrapped, and the chief priest, after receiving the new idol in his hands, exchanged its ordinary, *noa* feathers for the sanctified feathers on the master image—feathers that had become intensely holy through years of close association with the great god. After this ceremonious transfer of power was completed, both idols were rewrapped, and the new god, now as taboo as the master god, was given into Tupaia's care.

He was also entrusted with a second highly sacred totem: a *maro ura*, or royal loincloth. It was modeled on the breechcloth that all male Tahitians wore, except that, like the new god, it was covered with feathers, and tapered from a blunt end to a point. During his coronation, a new paramount chief stood on a hallowed stone, and this feathered girdle was ceremoniously wrapped around his naked loins. Though the ritual could be likened to the placing of a crown on the head of a new European monarch, the symbolism was much greater than that, because the wearing of the *maro ura* affirmed the new *ari'i rahi*'s direct connection with the gods.

It was its preparation for this ceremony that made the *maro ura* so dangerous. Each time a new great chief was proclaimed, it grew a little longer, as a new flap, or lappet, was sewn to the blunt end. The base material of the lappet was the finest bark cloth, strengthened with a network of fine, strong flax, and closely perforated with little holes. The shaft of a small, glossy feather was set in each little hole, caught at the back in a lock stitch, then turned and smoothed against the feathers next to it, so it looked like the plumage of a bird. A man was sacrificed to Oro for the first perforation. Another human sacrifice was carried out for the first stitch, sewn with a long, polished needle, fashioned of human bone, that was never taken out of the work. The final sacrifice was made for the lappet's attachment.

Thus, the ancient loincloth Tupaia carried to Tahiti had demanded hundreds of human victims over the long history of its gradual creation. Naturally, it was regarded with horror and awe.

Tupaia navigated the canoe safely to Papara, in the southeast of Tahiti Nui—the larger bulge of the figure-eight-shaped island of Tahiti—where he found sanctuary with Maua's great-uncle, a chief by the name of Amo Teva-hitua. Tupaia quietly installed the feathered god in Amo's family *marae*, and after that his prospects improved. Understanding his potential as an astute politician, and recognizing his prestige as the custodian of the idol and the girdle, Amo made him his advisor. Then Tupaia enhanced this position by becoming the lover of Amo's wife, Purea.

Purea, whose full title was Te Vahine Airoro atua i Ahurai i Farepua, was a statuesque, good-looking woman with a compelling personality, about the same age as Tupaia, a little over thirty. Noble Tahitian women were able to inherit property and rank, and Purea, who was an Ahurai princess with kin connections to the most powerful clans of Tahiti and Moorea, wielded power independently of her husband. She had given birth to a son, and had gone against her husband's wishes by allowing the child to live. Amo consented to acknowledge the boy, named Teri'irere, but was so displeased with Purea that he turned away from her, and took a mistress.

His wife retaliated by openly recognizing her advisor as her favorite, stabilizing Tupaia's political position. It was now that he could aptly be called the Machiavelli of Tahiti; not only did he greatly influence the policies at home, but he was an advisor in dealings with great warrior chiefs. Tupaia also completed the island's conversion to the worship of Oro, with the result that by June 1767, seven years after he had landed at Papara as a humble refugee, he was Tahiti's highest priest.

Then the canoe without an outrigger arrived.

CHAPTER 2

☙◦❧

The *Dolphin*

The arrival of the British ship *Dolphin* should not have been a great surprise to the Tahitians. In ancient times the demi-god Maui had warned of the arrival of a *vaa ama ore*—a canoe without an outrigger—and similar predictions had been made within living memory. In Tahiti a prophet named Paue had forecast that a *vaa ama ore* was coming, crewed by men who were closely covered with cloth from neck to knee. New manners would be adopted in the land, he said, and the tapa, or cloth-beating, mallet would go out of use. Three days later, while his prediction was still being hotly debated, Paue dropped dead.

In Raiatea there had been another prophesy, one that Tupaia probably witnessed. During the invasion of Raiatea, the Bora Boran warriors hacked down one of the sacred miro trees bordering the Taputapuatea *marae*, and a priest named Vaita was shocked into a trance by the desecration. When he finally opened his eyes, he announced that Maui's ship without an outrigger was coming, crewed by men who were completely covered with garments, and the old customs were doomed. "And the sacred birds of land and sea will come to mourn," he intoned.

So the auguries were not good.

Yet, when the cloudlike sails of the *Dolphin* loomed on the eastern horizon, hundreds of islanders paddled out eagerly to meet her, to be received by the Europeans with joy.

On board the canoe without an outrigger, otherwise known as the sixth-rate, twenty four-gun frigate, HMS *Dolphin*, the sailors were in desperate straits.

When they had left Plymouth, England, on August 21, 1766, hopes had been high, but nothing had worked out as expected. While the *Dolphin* was a fine, copper-bottomed ship that had successfully circled the world once already, both her consorts (a store ship and a sloop) were unseaworthy. The store ship had turned back after springing a leak, and the sloop was lost from sight in a fog on April 11, the day they entered the Pacific.

Since then, the lone frigate had traversed a vast area west of Cape Horn, but had discovered nothing but a handful of atolls, which yielded just a handful of the fresh provisions the vitamin-starved sailors desperately needed. On this date of June 19, 1767, the state on board was critical. Thirty were confined to their hammocks by scurvy, that dreadful scourge of long voyages at sea, which could only be cured with fresh fruit, and both the captain, Samuel Wallis, and his first lieutenant, William Clarke, were very ill with some kind of bilious fever. The second lieutenant, Tobias Furneaux, was nominally in charge of the deck, but needed all the help he could get, so was forced to rely on the ship's master, George Robertson, a large, confident man with a dashing history as a pirate-hunter.

The rank of master was a hangover from the days when captains and senior officers were warriors, not seamen, and needed someone to navigate the ship into battle, and trim the sails so they could make best use of their cannon. This man—the master, or sailing master—was a petty officer with a great deal of experience and mathematical ability. Not only was he a fine pilot, but he knew exactly how the sails should be set to take advantage of every vagary of the breeze. In Robertson's case, he was a racy journal-keeper, too.

Considering the state of health on board, it was only natural that the sight of tree-clad mountain-tops looming above a bank of morning fog should fill him "with the Greatest hopes," as he wrote. At eight in the morning the mist blew away, and Robertson saw a rocky peninsula, graceful palms, a gray reef with growling breakers—and a multitude of outrigger canoes paddling furiously toward them. He and Furneaux sent for the captain, who staggered out onto deck, looked around, then gave orders to haul aback and take in sail as an invitation to parley and trade. Yards were hauled around by gangs of seamen, and the ship stilled as her sails rippled, working against each other.

The canoes slowed and stopped, too. The paddlers sat staring "with great astonishment," while their leaders held some kind of consultation. Trying to entice them closer, the *Dolphin* sailors leaned over the rail, dangling beads and ribbons in their scarred and tarry hands.

Finally the headsman stood up in the leading canoe. Holding up a leafy plantain shoot, he made a long speech. Then he threw the sprout into the water. Evidently this was a signal, as a "fine brisk young man" jumped up from the head of his canoes and into the mizzen chains, then clambered lithely up the shrouds of the sternmost mast, and reached the wooden awning that shaded the poop. There he perched, laughing at the Europeans, who gathered at the bottom, beckoning and calling out. Finally, he jumped to the deck, accepted a few trinkets, and was shown how to shake hands, which he found even more hilarious.

Encouraged, a few friends threw peacemaking plantain shoots over the rail, then clambered up to join him. The young men were a fine, healthy sight, straight-limbed, golden brown, tall, and stalwart. They were naked except for white breech-cloths, their long black hair tied up into topknots or trailing over muscular shoulders. They had black designs on their legs, arms, and buttocks, which the Englishmen thought were painted. They all had strong, white, even teeth, which they showed in very broad grins, particularly when the British sailors, desperate to convey their need for fresh food, "Grunted and Cryd lyke a Hogg, then pointed to the shore," as Robertson reminisced; while others crowed "Lyke cocks, to make them understand that we wanted fowls."

Showing them the few scrawny animals in the shipboard pens proved more useful. Though the natives were amazed to see sheep, turkeys, and geese, common fowl and pigs were familiar to them, and when the seamen indicated they would give spikes and nails in exchange for livestock and fruit, their visitors suddenly became very cooperative, signing that they would fetch lots of fowls and pigs from shore, and coconuts and bananas, too. The British sailors were surprised the natives knew about iron already, but happy that nails had proved to be such a handy item of trade—life, for the *Dolphins*, suddenly looked much more promising. Even the ship's goat took part in the fun, butting one of the islanders in the bottom. Turning, the lad took one horrified look at the strange horned beast, and sprang precipitately overboard. Everyone laughed.

Then the atmosphere turned nasty. Seamen noticed some of the visitors pulling at the ironwork about the ship, trying to yank it free, and when they were stopped, the islanders became aggressive. The fleet paddled closer as voices rose. A panicked officer ordered a cannon to be loaded and fired.

The natives on the deck watched with interest as the lashings holding the squat iron gun in place were cast away. Down the barrel went a flannel bag of gunpowder, then a nine-pound cannonball, followed by a wad. Hurriedly, the loaded weapon was pushed to the gunport, and its muzzle thrust out as far as it would go.

"Stand by . . . and FIRE!" shouted Lieutenant Furneaux. Powder exploded with a mighty roar. A cloud of smoke gushed, the cannon bounced back against its ropes with grumble of wheels, and the cannonball screamed over the assembled canoes. It cleared them all by just a few feet before bounding along the surface of the water.

The shocked natives had already dived overboard, though a particularly saucy fellow had enough presence of mind to snatch a gold-laced hat from Midshipman Ibbott's head as he went. Twenty yards off, he turned in the water, flourished the hat, and tauntingly put it on his own head. The marines angrily pointed their muskets, but the youth did not understand. Instead, he laughed, delighted with his own daring. Emboldened by his example, the islanders were coming back, paddling vigorously to surround the ship. The *Dolphin* fled to the open sea.

It was impossible to go far. Sailing for the nearest known port, Tinian in the Marianas, four thousand miles away, was a virtual death warrant. They would all succumb to scurvy long before they arrived. Orders were given to stand in again, and sail northwest along the bulge of land. Longingly, the men saw plantations of fruit-bearing trees, thatched houses, and many beautiful valleys straggling up into the mountains. Warm scents of fruit and flowers drifted seaward with every breeze. The shore was lined with multitudes of people, but no canoes came out to trade.

In the mid-afternoon the lookouts found a break in the reef. The ship was hauled aback, and a cutter was lowered. John Gore, an American master's mate, was in command of this, with a crew of heavily armed sailors. His orders were to sound the lagoon to see if it was deep enough for the ship to sail inside.

Before the boat even reached the reef it was surrounded by canoes. Again, there was panic on board the *Dolphin*. Another nine-pound shot was fired. As the cannonball whistled overhead the canoes hesitated, and Gore seized the chance to tack about, and race back to the ship. The paddlers in the canoes took up the chase, throwing stones as they came. Gore stood and fired his gun, blasting a native in the shoulder. The wounded man jumped overboard, followed by his companions, causing confusion in the rest of the canoes, and so the cutter escaped.

As the sun lowered they continued their coasting, keeping a safe distance from the reef. A fleet of great double voyaging canoes was raised, racing in from the northwest. Closer they came, closer—and then they were gone, still heading south, with no attempt to contact the *Dolphin*.

Against the bright horizon, their fleeting silhouettes were magnificent.

When dawn broke, the sea was empty. Late in the afternoon, another promising bay was sighted, so the *Dolphin* lay off and on outside the reef all night, ready for going in at dawn. This time, two boats were lowered, one commanded by Gore and the other by Robertson. Both were crammed with well-armed, exceedingly nervous men. As they pulled away from the ship great numbers of canoes could be seen setting out from the beach.

Coming up with the boats, the men in the canoes angrily waved them away, but the situation on board was desperate. Both the captain and first lieutenant were too ill to get out of their berths. Several seamen were close to death. Gore and Robertson ignored the islanders, sending a signal to the *Dolphin* that a harbor had been found. The ship entered the gap in the reef and anchored two miles from the shore.

The two boats were hoisted back on board, and the *Dolphin*s waited to see what the natives would do. Slowly and hesitantly one canoe came out to the ship, and then others followed, loaded with coconuts, fruit, a few fowl, and some pigs. The islanders proved to be sharp traders, refusing to hand over their goods until they had received their nails, often demanding more than the previously agreed number. Fists were lifted as their demeanor became increasingly insulting, but at last the ship had a supply of fresh food.

Drinking water was another priority. The boats were put out again, and Robertson and Gore were sent off to search for a suitable stream. By the time they were in the surf, which was running high, they were surrounded by a hundred-strong fleet. The men inside them hooted in challenge and warning. Thousands of yelling people thronged the beach, many contemptuously beckoning, daring the men to come on shore.

Robertson and Gore decided to retreat, but found they had left it too late. Before they were a third of the way to the ship, both boats were attacked. The double canoes racing up to them were equipped with fighting platforms on the foredecks, where warriors armed with war clubs were standing ready for combat. Gore's men fought back, hacking and stabbing with their bayonets, and managed to beat off their attackers. Robertson, however, was forced to order his marines to fire.

A rattle of muskets. Two natives fell into the water, one dead, the other mortally wounded. Their companions dived overboard and hoisted them back into the canoe. Then, with growing puzzlement, they tried to make the dead man sit up. By the time they had worked out that somehow, mysteriously, he had been killed from a distance by the stick that spat fire, Robertson's boat had escaped.

For a while it looked as if the islanders had learned their lesson. When canoes came out to the ship to trade, thieving or cheating was swiftly stopped by pointing a musket or even a spyglass at the offender. The surf was still too high to go on shore and find fresh water, so natives were bribed with nails to fill some barrels and bring them to the boats. However, two of the irreplaceable kegs were stolen. When Robertson and Gore angrily demanded their return, the islanders brought a bevy of attractive girls instead.

The girls pulled up their calf-length sarongs to reveal the nakedness underneath, and "made a thousand antick tricks to entice them on land," wrote Captain Wallis in his logbook, after hearing about it. The native men laughed at the sailors' half-scandalized, half-fascinated reaction, and when the boats beat a prudent retreat, the women disdainfully pelted them with fruit. The next day, another attempt was made to get fresh water, but again casks were stolen, and again the girls tormented the sailors. The decision was made to try to find a better anchorage by coasting still farther west. And so the *Dolphin* arrived at Matavai Bay.

They called it Port Royal. It was the most promising haven yet, with an extensive lagoon, surrounded by tree-packed hills. Canoes were drawn up on the beach, but there was no scurry to push them out to stop the *Dolphin* from coming inside the reef. The *Dolphin* had a brush with a rock coming through the gap, but eventually an anchor was dropped. A better mooring beckoned, abreast of a stream of water running to the east of a tall hill crowned by a particularly large tree. Dark was falling, but at dawn they could easily warp her there by taking out anchors in the boats, dropping them ahead, and pulling on the lines with the capstan.

As night fell, the dark was punctuated by a multitude of flickering lights on the reef. The men on watch were issued cutlasses and pistols, and the gun crews assembled. And so the nervous hours wore on.

At sunrise, all seemed peaceful. After breakfast, the seamen began working the ship up to the chosen anchorage. Captain Wallis was confined to his cabin with his bilious fever, and Lieutenant Clarke was just as badly off. Again, Furneaux was in charge, with Robertson as chief officer. When Wallis looked out of the window of his toilet in a quarter gallery, he became uneasily aware that about three hundred canoes paddled about the *Dolphin*, with more coming all the time. The first arrivals proved to be loaded with pigs, fowls, and fruit, though, so it looked as if trading would go on as hoped, with the natives haggling shrewdly for their nails, and the sailors watching to forestall cheating or theft.

Then another wave of canoes came up to the side, this time with girls who stripped naked and gyrated their hips to the fast, provocative rhythm of drums. Titillated, the British seamen clambered onto the bulwarks and up into the rigging, to get a better view. While they were raptly staring, another fleet of canoes slid near—large double canoes, crewed by men who, according to Wallis at the gallery window, were blowing conches, playing flutes, and singing hoarsely. He sent for Furneaux, and ordered him to have gun crews stationed by the two quarterdeck cannon.

A stately, elaborately caparisoned double canoe was at the head of this new fleet—"with several of the Principle Inhabitance in her," as Robertson reminisced later, adding, "we afterwards found out that the King of the Island and several of the Grandees was in this canoe." An imposing figure sat cross-legged on a canopy, almost level with the deck of the ship. Leaves and flowers wreathed his turban, and he had more garlands about his neck. In his right hand, he held up a tuft of red and yellow feathers.

Wallis felt relieved. At last he was to meet a native monarch, a man with whom he could negotiate trading arrangements, and make a treaty for annexation of the island. Leaning out of the toilet window, he politely gestured for the king to come on board. To his great surprise, instead of rising from the canopy the chief passed the bunch of feathers to a seaman, making signs that he should carry it to the captain. Wallis went to the door of the Great Cabin to receive it—with no idea that it was a *ura-tatae*, a fetish meant to focus the malign attention of the gods onto the ship.

He was happily "preparing some presents" to be given to the king in return for the pretty object, when he became aware that a deathly silence had fallen on the waters outside. On deck, the seamen saw the ceremonial canoe paddle some distance away, then come to a stop. Momentously, the chief on the awning drew a red mantle about his shoulders. John Gore saw him pick up a staff wrapped about with white cloth, and thrust it high in the air.

It was a signal. With a universal roar warriors leaped onto the fighting platforms of the big canoes, which charged the ship headlong. A hail of stones hammered through the rigging of the *Dolphin*, and crashed onto the decks. Seamen tumbled down from their exposed positions, many bruised and bleeding. The sergeant bawled an order, and the marines leveled their muskets. The crackle of a volley was answered by more warlike shouting from the Tahitians, and another hail of stones. Panicked orders, and the snouts of the two quarterdeck guns were run out. A roar of, "Fire!" Powder exploded. The air rang with the double concussion.

The surface of the lagoon became the stuff of nightmare. The two stern cannons had been armed with grapeshot—bags of small iron balls, which burst apart when fired. These were not warning shots, but deliberately aimed at boats and people. The water was frantic with desperately swimming natives. As Wallis recorded later in self-justification, "I believe there was not less than three Hundred Boats about the Ship, and on an average

Two Thousand Men, besides some Thousands on the Shore and boats coming from every quarter."

More orders were bellowed, and the great guns were loaded, some with grapeshot, and others with cannonballs. The appalling blast of a broadside crashed out, to be followed by another and yet another, this time aimed at the people who packed the beaches. When the guns silenced, the bay echoed with screams of pain and fear. Bodies floated past the *Dolphin*, caught in reddened eddies. "Saw an Indian Woman floating athwart our cut-water, having received a Shot in her Belly," wrote one of the midshipmen, George Pinnock.

Five hundred yards away, more double canoes gathered about the chief's craft, as if for an urgent conference. A fraught pause, while the *Dolphins* waited to see what would happen next. The surgeon, John Hutchinson, and his mate, Robert Saunderson, moved about the decks, binding up the cuts of those who had been hit by stones. There were none gravely wounded, and no British dead.

Hoisting white streamers, the big canoes made another dash for the *Dolphin*, the warriors throwing stones from slingshots as they came. The ship was heaved around so her broadside bore down on them, and a hail of iron seared the oncoming fleet. The ship was hauled around some more, and the two cannon in the bow were aimed at the admiral's canoe. Shouted orders, two deafening explosions. The ship rocked with the concussion, sending ripples across the lagoon.

When the smoke cleared the canoe was broken in half. The other canoes were beating a panic-stricken retreat, though a handful of brave men hung back to salvage the two pieces of the king's craft, and carry its wounded and dead away. On shore, the people were fleeing for the hills and disappearing into the trees. Then they were gone. The sun was high in the sky, and the waters of the bay were as empty as the beaches.

Chapter 3

❦

The Red Pennant

The ship Tupaia and Amo Tevahitua studied from the top of the hill must have been pretty, once. Since she had left home, though, she had had a rough time. Exposure to the elements had discolored the expensive blue paint on her upperworks, so it was mottled in parts, and greenish in others, and her varnished hull with its deep black streak at the waterline was stained with rust from her chains. Her sails were blotched with mildew.

But still she was impressive. A yellow ocher stripe ran along each side, squared off with gunports, and a great rank of windows gleamed mysteriously in her stern, flanked with graceful galleries, also glazed. Her three masts rose high, with the noon sun pointing up their white-painted tips. Many of the islanders had thought she was a floating island when she had first come into sight, because her cloud of billowing sails reflected the color of the sea on their lower surfaces, as a cloud above an atoll reflects the color of the inner lagoon. Now, those sails hung loose, revealing themselves as huge sheets of fabric, drying in the gentle breeze.

Undoubtedly, Tupaia studied her with curiosity inspired not just by her foreign shape and sails, but by the strange actions of the men she carried. The strangers had quickly made it obvious they wanted to trade iron for chickens and fruit. Not only was it incomprehensible that any man should want to exchange anything so rare and valuable for goods so readily obtained and easily replaced, but it was strange there was any barter at all—for the foreigners had also made it plain they were determined to get what they wanted, and that they had powerful weapons to back up their demands. They could so easily march ashore and seize it all, covered by their great guns. Yet, instead, they were offering bribes. This was something very novel—that men should offer death and destruction with one hand, and riches with the other.

Her weaponry, while terrifying, was fascinating, too. Everything about the technology was new: the spurt of flame, the smoke, the very idea that fire could be used to hurl missiles. Inevitably, Tupaia, who had lost so much when the warriors of Bora Bora had invaded Raiatea, pictured the effect of broadsides of cannon on the war fleets of his Bora Boran enemies. It must have been a most enticing vision.

At two in the afternoon, three boats swung up from the struts that crossed the amidships deck, and were lowered onto the water. Ripples spread as men jumped down into the bobbing craft. Many were wearing red coats, and holding muskets. The oarsmen wore motley, mostly blue. The young officer in command of the force was clad in a splendid blue coat, white silk breeches, and a gold-buttoned cocked hat. As the boat was rowed to shore the sun glittered on his buttons and lace.

The officer clambered out of the boat, followed by eighteen seamen, three midshipmen, a marine sergeant, and twelve marines, who all waded ashore. The marine squad lined up on the beach, and then, as usual with naval landing parties, they commenced to carry out exercises, presenting their muskets and then shouldering them again as their sergeant barked orders, each time with a stamp of boots. The intention, of course, was to impress and intimidate the natives. Here, their audience numbered in the hundreds, watching silently from the other side of the river, just a pistol shot away.

A twenty-year-old master's mate, Robert Molineux, was left in charge of the boats, which were kept floating ready for a quick withdrawal, if necessary. A dark young man with a cadaverous, intent face, he ordered his men to train thick-barreled musketoons on the crowd. Because so many of the Tahitians were holding peacemaking plantain sprouts, the gathering looked like a human forest. Yet the ship's big guns were aimed at them, too.

Lieutenant Furneaux made signs to the Tahitians for a representative to come over and parley. There was a pause as a messenger was sent to the top of the hill. According to the story the Tahitians related to the missionaries later, Amo Tevahitua was hiding behind a tree, paralyzed by fear. Now, too frightened to descend to the beach himself, and unwilling to send Tupaia, his senior advisor, into danger, he ordered a lesser chief named Fa'a to communicate a message of peace.

Fa'a, a venerable fellow with a long, white beard, fearfully waded over to where Furneaux stood. He was carrying a plantain shoot and a small pig, and was flanked by two equally elderly friends. Talking volubly and unintelligibly, he laid down the pig, and put the branch on top of it. Furneaux made an incomprehensible speech of his own, and gave the old man some nails and "toys," worthless things like beads and ribbons. He then made signs asking permission to take water from the stream, and Fa'a waved an arm, inviting him to take as much as he wanted.

While seamen filled casks at the clear, fresh river, another sailor planted a tall stick in the soil of Tahiti. Then a solemn ritual commenced. Furneaux flourished a document Captain Wallis had penned, and in sonorous tones renamed Tahiti "King George the Third Island," proclaiming it a British possession "by right of Conquest." A pennant was ceremoniously hoisted, and the marines fired a salute of guns. A toast of brandy mixed with good Tahitian water was drunk, and three hearty cheers were roared from British throats. Birds wheeled high in the sky like shadows of the offended gods, and the massed Tahitians trembled.

The *Dolphins* had not noticed the general distress. When several men hurried across the river with offerings of pigs, fruit, and plantain sprouts, and hastened back without waiting for payment, Furneaux merely assumed a supply of provisions was now guaranteed. After leaving more nails and toys on the sand, he boarded his boat, and led his marines and sailors away. It was not until he was back on board that he finally paid attention to the Tahitians' strange reaction to the flag.

The mark of a British vessel in commission, the pennant Furneaux had left flying was long and narrow, tapering to a point. Apart from a white rectangle with the scarlet cross of St. George at the blunt, or hoist, end, it was completely red in color. Not only was it the same shape and size as the *maro ura* Tupaia had carried when he fled from Raiatea to Papara, but it was the sacred red of Oro.

Not knowing this, Robertson was mystified when he saw the old man and one of his friends approach the flag "with as much ceremony as if it had been a Demi God." After casting some boughs at the foot of the post, they recrossed the river, to return with a dozen men, all carrying plantain shoots, who humbly crept toward the flag, taking one slow step after another. The wind gusted, and it flapped with a crack like thunder. Terrified, they ran off.

When a handful of islanders bravely returned, they were bearing two live hogs. These were laid down at the foot of the staff, as if in propitiation. The pennant hung still, so after some praying and dancing they carried the hogs to a beached canoe. Fa'a clambered inside, and was pushed into the water. Alone, he paddled the canoe to the side of the ship.

There, visibly trembling, he stood, held up some plantain shoots, and made a long speech. At the end, he handed over the pigs, and after refusing to accept anything in return, he hurriedly paddled away. The *Dolphins* watched the old man arrive at the beach, abandon the canoe, and scurry across the river. He disappeared into the trees, and then there was perfect silence. All the people were gone; it was as if the island was deserted. The sun set in tropical scarlet and gold.

Then, as night fell, there was movement. "At night we heard the noise of Many Conchs, Drums and wind instruments," wrote Captain Wallis. The British watched a multitude of lights progressing along the coast. Closer they came, closer, the torch-fires blowing in the wind, the chanting and drumming growing louder and louder. Scared by the solemnity of the procession, the *Dolphins* jumped to the conclusion that the Tahitians were bringing firebrands to burn the ship. Two cannon were set on the forecastle, facing the beach with its parade of lights, and each was loaded with a bag of seventy musket balls. And so the nervous night wore on.

When dawn broke there were still no canoes in the water. The beaches were as deserted as the lagoon. Everything looked as it had the night before.

Except that the red pennant was gone.

The uncanny silence was broken as three boats were lowered into the water. Sixty men jumped into them. Naturally, everyone was nervous. Furneaux was still the only officer fit enough to command the landing party, leaving the master, Robertson, in charge of the ship, with master's mate Gore to assist.

No one materialized from the groves of trees, but the marine squad kept their hands on their muskets. The routine of collecting fresh water began. Empty casks were trundled to the river, and pushed under the water with their open bung holes upmost. After they had filled and sunk, the bungs were rammed hard home, and the casks, much heavier now, were rolled back to the boats. Ferried to the side of the *Dolphin*, they were laboriously muscled up over the rail and down into the hold, using the mainyard as a hoist.

For two hours, the work went smoothly. Then, at 8:30 A.M., a fleet of canoes was glimpsed approaching from the southwest point of the bay. At the same time a procession came into view, winding down from the top of the hill. At the head of the parade a tall man held the *Dolphin's* red pennant high on a pole. Many in the crowd behind him were carrying long staffs. To the alarmed *Dolphins* they looked like spears.

"It was no longer a doubt that their intentions were to try their luck with us a second time," wrote Wallis. He staggered out onto deck, shouting, "All hands to quarters!" Drums rattled. The boatswain and his mate piped on their silver calls, the shrilling noise they made echoed by the urgent thump of running feet. Gun crews cast away lashings keeping great cannon housed up tight against the side of the ship, then hauled on rope tackles to heave them back for loading. Then the iron snouts were run through the gunports, as far as they would go. Using spikes, the crews forced them round, aiming at the procession slowly wending down the hill.

The little jolly boat had been launched. The oarsmen shouted warnings to Furneaux as they rowed frantically for the beach. The watering party had already glimpsed yet another host of natives creeping through the trees. These unarmed men were hunched in the same cowering pose as the day before, when they had crept toward the flag, but Furneaux was too panicked to take chances. There were plenty of stones by the side of the river, and for all he knew, they had been piled up in readiness. The watering party splashed out to the boats and tumbled inside.

The natives straightened and ran out of the trees, making a beeline for the abandoned casks. At the sight of his barrels being rolled away, Captain Wallis ordered a warning shot to be fired into the woods—but, as Robertson recorded, that did not have the desired effect, which obliged the *Dolphin*s "to fire a few round & Grape amongst the thickest of them." The islanders broke and ran as a lethal storm of shot screamed through their ranks. Arriving at the top of the hill, the survivors joined the hundreds of women and children who were watching.

By this time the fleet of canoes had arrived at the river mouth, where they drifted to a stop. Robertson saw the chiefs of the leading craft send a small party of men up the hill, apparently for instructions, and then a council being held after the messengers ran back. Wallis, from his limited vantage at the gallery window, had not seen the men leave and then return, and thought the canoes had paused to take on more warriors. When the fleet began to move again, paddling slowly and ceremoniously toward the ship, he ordered a broadside fired.

A rolling roar, closely followed by the ripping sound of released grape-shot. The hail of iron was briefly visible against the sky, then the air was fouled with billows of black, roiling smoke. The paddlers turned and fled. Some made it past the point, but most of the canoes were abandoned on the beach. Their occupants ran for the woods, but found no refuge, because another barrage was fired into the trees. Torn branches crashed around their heads. They scrambled up the hill—and stopped at the top, in the supposed safety of the massed crowd, imagining they were out of range.

It was time, Wallis decided, to teach these turbulent islanders a lesson. Ordering the cannon let down from their carriages at the back, so that their snouts pointed as high as possible, he ordered four shots fired at the crest of the hill.

Two huge explosions, and then two more. The balls soared high. Without moving, the islanders watched the first pair fall short, but then the next two bounced lethally along the ground, cutting furrows toward the tree where Amo was hiding. Terrified, all the Tahitians fled, disappearing in a panicked mass down the far side of the hill. As Wallis recorded with satisfaction, the realization that the ship's guns could maim and kill from such a great distance "so affrighted them that in two minutes time there was not one to be seen."

Silence descended. The smoke drifted slowly away. When it cleared, there was no movement on the hill, or on the beach. The only sign of the alleged attack was the canoes left helter-skelter on the deserted beach, or grounded in the shallows.

To prevent them being launched against the ship in the night, Wallis sent Furneaux, with marines, to stand guard while the carpenter and a gang methodically destroyed every single canoe, including craft that might have great ceremonial significance. As one of the ax-wielders, John Nicholls, described, "two in particular were of a larger size than common, with very pretty carved work on them, much resembling the Doric Order of Architecture."

It was a cruel and deliberate assault on Tahitian pride. These canoes had taken thousands of hours to build, from the careful selection of trees to the ceremony of launching, every stage blessed by priests. And apart from its psychological effect, the vandalism was pointless, as the Dolphins knew very well it was impossible to destroy every canoe in Tahiti. They could even see a dozen large canoes getting under sail beyond the point.

It was the remnant of the Paparan fleet, with Amo and Tupaia on board. As they left, a few brave warriors could be seen running down the hill in a doomed attempt to stop the desecration, to be driven off by musket fire. Then the canoes found a gap in the reef, and fled to the open sea.

CHAPTER 4

❧

The Queen of Tahiti

By running away, Amo had chosen what he considered to be the prudent path. Hundreds had been killed—as many as a flock of birds or a shoal of fish, the Tahitians said later—and Amo wanted nothing more to do with the murderous outsiders. Undoubtedly, they would ravage the countryside in revenge before they sailed away, and then the age-old process of repairing war damage would begin. Purea, Amo's wife, thought quite differently—according to what the missionaries heard later, in Amo's place she would have stayed "to meet the wrath, or enjoy the favor of the foreigners." In this, she was undoubtedly influenced by Tupaia, who emphatically believed that an alliance with the rich and powerful strangers would prove politically and economically profitable.

Amo might have left this golden opportunity to his rivals, but there was one consolation. Tupaia had brought the *Dolphin's* pennant away with him, so was able to carry out a highly symbolic ritual. First, the rectangle with the cross of St. George was cut off the blunt end of the pennant, and patched onto a white streamer destined to be flown from the stern of a *taputapuatea* canoe. Then the scarlet length of the tapering part of the *Dolphin's* pennant was sewn to the sacred *maro ura* Tupaia had carried to Papara.

Tupaia made history when he took the emblem of British imperialism and mated it with the royal insignia. There were European precedents for this. In Roman times an emperor might seize a defeated general's gold laurel wreath, and add to his prestige by attaching it to his diadem. In the same way, by attaching the pennant to the icon he guarded, Tupaia was empowering himself. It also enhanced Amo's standing, serving to repair some of the damage done by the defeat at Matavai Bay, and his cowardly withdrawal.

Even more importantly, by sewing the pennant to the feather girdle Tupaia had fixed the *Dolphin's* arrival into the context of Tahitian history. The *maro ura* chronicled decades of important events—not in words, because the Tahitians had no knowledge of writing, but in memory-triggers. As well as the brilliant red feathers from the heads of parakeets, the girdle was embellished with pale feathers from sacred doves, and black feathers from man-of-war birds. There were bright yellow feathers, too, and the occasional attached bobble. Any of these served as an aide-mémoire for a well-educated priest—a man like Tupaia, who could read the *maro ura* like a book—to recount an important and stirring episode that might have happened a hundred years before. So, by adding the red length of the pennant to the *maro ura*, Tupaia stitched the arrival of the *Dolphin* into the tapestry of Tahiti.

Ritual was a consolation. Undoubtedly, though, he kept on thinking about the politically profitable pact with the foreigners that would have been possible, if it were not for Amo's cowardice.

Ten days after the debacle at Matavai Bay, Tupaia learned that there was still a chance to make an alliance with the strangers. Fa'a had left the river to make a journey upcountry, carrying a hatchet, some nails, and a coat as evidence that he was still the middleman for the Europeans, and the news that none of the northern nobles had managed to contact the paramount chief of the ship.

The peacemaking ritual had not progressed as hoped, though the locals had done their best. As soon as the *Dolphin's* boats had returned to the ship from their canoe-smashing exercise, great heaps of conciliatory gifts had been delivered to the Europeans' landing place, including hogs, fowls, fruit, Polynesian dogs (a delicacy usually reserved for chiefs), and six large bales of white tapa cloth. After depositing these, the chiefs' emissaries had returned to their side of the river, and then had waited for the Europeans to respond in the proper manner.

For a while, it had looked as if it would go to plan, as boats dropped over the side of the ship, and pulled to where the pile of peace-offerings lay. Much to the watchers' confusion, the strangers turned the dogs loose. Worse still, they rejected the cloth. They took the pigs, chickens, and fruit away, leaving iron in exchange, but declined the tapa, leaving the bundles lying forlornly on the sand. Yet the acceptance of the sacred gift of tapa was an essential part of the peacemaking rite.

The manufacture of tapa was a labor intensive process, involving the whole community. The men's work was the planting and cultivation of paper mulberry trees, and then the harvesting of the thin, rod-like saplings. At that stage, the women took over, stripping off the bark, soaking the inner fibrous pulp in a running stream, and then hammering it flat with special beaters. This resulted in long, narrow strips of cloth, which were pasted together and then beaten again, until the felted piece of fabric was a yard or more wide and up to thirty feet long. Finally it was bleached to a luminous white, and the very best cloth was dyed.

Because it represented the strength, spirit, and enterprise of the entire village, tapa was the supreme gift, reserved for momentous occasions. By making a ceremonial presentation of tapa, the losers in a battle acknowledged the superior might of the victors. When the fabric was accepted, the power of the conquerors was symbolically captured, just as the spiritual might of a feather god was contained by being wrapped. But the Europeans, in their ignorance, had spurned this crucial rite.

Furneaux was not an imperceptive man. Back at the ship, he noticed that the Tahitians were milling about in agitation, and realized he had blundered in leaving the cloth, which the ship did not need, and he had thought the natives could not easily spare. To the joy of the local people, the boats returned, and the bundles were collected. But it was still a bad augury, confirmed when trading commenced.

The Europeans set up a tent for their sick, guarded by marines and sailors, and at the entrance of this the gunner, William Harrison, traded nails for provisions. It did not mean that any man with fruit or hogs to sell could approach Mr. Harrison, though. The gunner would deal only with Fa'a, the one Tahitian allowed to cross the river, except for a few occasions when the loads were heavy and he was helped by a young man, considered by the *Dolphins* to be his son. Fa'a inspected what the traders had to sell, and then waded over to Harrison's tent and bargained on their behalf. Once a deal was struck, he returned to the other side of the stream, picked up the goods and carried them across, then brought back the agreed-upon price.

Not only did this system put a heavy burden on one old man, but it was slow, greatly reducing the amount traded. Worse still for the local nobility, it meant they had no chance to meet the gunner, and start the process of establishing a politically useful alliance. The chiefs gathered hopefully on the far side of the river, but Harrison ordered the guard to threaten them with muskets if they so much as put a foot in the water, which was not just an unprecedented insult, but also very frightening.

Harrison was not being stupid: he was just following instructions. When he had been put in charge of the market, it was with orders from Wallis "not to Suffer any to Straggle or trade with the Natives but himself." Nothing about it was easy. While he had to harden his heart to limit his dealings to old Fa'a, he also had the problem of the *Dolphins* in the camp, who were becoming restive and amorous. This included the rapidly recovering scurvy sufferers, as well as the sailors and marines on guard—all of them, once they spied the pretty bare-breasted girls, wished very much to "straggle."

The same day the tent was set up, June 30, Captain Wallis noted in his private log, "the Women particularly fond of prostituting themselves." The men (much more joyfully) agreed—"The Women were far from being coy," remembered Henry Ibbott, the young man who had lost his midshipman's hat. Initially, however, the situation was not as sordid as Wallis considered. Though the girls, like all Tahitians, were as fastidious as cats, they found the hairy, gap-toothed, bad-smelling Europeans sexually attractive, being particularly fascinated by the contrast between their white bodies and their mahogany-tanned faces, hands, and forearms. Getting a present of a nail was a bonus to an interesting experience.

The first sailor to escape the gunner's watchful eye, as Robertson recounted, was "a Dear Irish boy," one of the marines. A distinct drawback to Paddy's conquest was having to perform in front of an audience of highly interested islanders, who passed comments in their native language. He also got a thrashing from his shipmates for making such a rude exhibition of himself, but, as he confessed to the master, he was too keen to attain "the Honour of having the first" to care. The agreed-on price was a four-inch nail (called a thirty-penny nail because four-inch nails cost thirty pence per hundred), and before long so many four-inch spikes had been pried out of the hull that the ship was in danger of falling apart.

"Got only two Fowls, the Inhabitants all making signs for large Nails; in looking around the Ship the Carpenters found that all the belaying cleats were Ripped off," grumbled Wallis, going on to relate that he, "Ordered all hands up and endeavoured to find out who had been the thieves, then told them if they would not discover it I would put a stop to their going onshore." To his frustration and alarm, however, the thefts continued apace. The girls were demanding bigger, longer nails (a phallic symbol that eventually led to a lot of hilarity in the taverns of London), which inspired a lot of sailor ingenuity in the way of prying important pieces of gear off the hull, in order to get at the spikes that secured them.

This busy trade in sex also meant that Fa'a had trouble finding provisions to barter with the gunner. Now that the islanders had another source of iron, they were much less eager to sell what they would normally be eating themselves, and, because no chief had formed an alliance with the Europeans, there was no one to order them to go short or gather more. To complicate the situation still further, the Matavai men were asking higher prices for the food they did consent to trade. As Wallis meditated, the traffic in women "was productive of a double mischief; damage to the ship, and a considerable rise at market."

The *Dolphin*s were in trouble, and it was all their own fault.

For Tupaia, the news that the northern nobility had not managed to make a connection with the Europeans' leader was energizing. Amo was still not interested in trying for an alliance, but Purea saw reason, so Tupaia at once made preparations for a well-provisioned fleet to sail to Matavai Bay. On July 8, Robertson noted in his logbook, "This Day a Great Number of large Craft Come Round the SW point of the Bay, with Red & White and Blue Streamers flying." The big double canoes were packed with people, and loaded heavily with provisions. "I am yet of a loss what to think of this fleet," he wrote, unaware that he was probably witnessing the grand entrance of Purea, with Tupaia and her attendants.

Because of her clan connections, Purea was able to commandeer the local *fare hau*, or conference hall, a magnificent pillared building that also served as an *arioi* theater. Then, accompanied by Tupaia, she crossed the river, casually waving the muskets aside. Where the local nobility had quailed and failed, imperious Purea, Te Vahine Airoro atua i Ahurai i Farepua, was bound to succeed.

Once they arrived in the European encampment, however, they were faced with a problem. Who was the paramount chief of the ship? Which man should they approach? Tupaia's only clue was what the Europeans were wearing. It was easy to see that the Europeans wore different types of coat, waistcoat, breeches, and hats, which presumably denoted status, just as clothing did in Tahitian society. The difficulty was to decide which coats, waistcoats, breeches, and hats were superior.

After some discussion, Purea and Tupaia accosted the sergeant of marines, Nicholas Gallagher, and Purea presented him with ritual offerings of foodstuffs and tapa. It was a natural mistake, as Gallagher's frockcoat was a splendid scarlet, the color of authority, sacred to Oro. Understandably, too, none of the locals had realized that the sad little figure occasionally glimpsed at the windows of the quarter galleries was the captain of the *Dolphin*. Gallagher then committed his own blunder, failing to recognize that the red color of Purea's cloak denoted nobility in Tahiti, or that the tall, white-robed man with her was a figure of authority. When Purea refused to accept payment for the gifts, he simply sent the food and cloth on board without bothering to consider the implications. It took John Gore, and one of the young men in his gang, to understand that Purea and her advisor were people of importance.

John Gore, a red-haired, thirty-seven-year-old American, was known for his quick temper and his sharpshooting. He was also very intelligent, a man who had passed his lieutenant's examinations in 1760, but still had not been commissioned. He had joined the first discovery voyage of the *Dolphin* as a midshipman, under Captain John Byron, been promoted to master's mate within three days, then had stayed with the *Dolphin* for this second circum-navigation under Samuel Wallis. Here, in Tahiti, he had been put in charge of a wooding party, with the job of collecting firewood.

The first time he had sallied out at the head of his gang the islanders had become agitated, thinking he had come to cut down their breadfruit trees, one of the traditional ways the victors in a tribal war wreaked revenge. Gore placated the owner of the first tree with a seven-inch spike, and since then had devised a tactful method of buying the right to cut down a tree by tapping a spike into its trunk, and waiting to see if the owner would take it out. If he did, then the tree was bought, and the woodsmen cut it down.

On the morning of Friday, July 10, Gore took his party to the northern side of the river, having spied a few likely old trees. As usual, he stuck a spike in one specimen, the elderly owner took it out, and the tree was cut down. Then came trouble. According to the tale Gore told Robertson, a man who was apparently a local chief strode up, and arrogantly appropriated the nail. The owner of the tree put up a vigorous protest, but rank prevailed, and the old man went off to his house to sulk.

Then Purea arrived, accompanied by Tupaia. Informed what had happened by some native witnesses, she sent for the owner of the tree, "who immediately appeard before her trembling," and mumbled his side of the story. Purea turned and spoke sharply to the offending chief, who, according to Robertson's recounting of the story, "gave up the nail to the old man, and walkt of seemingly in great fear." Then, having delivered justice, Purea calmly continued her stroll, disappearing into the woods with Tupaia, "the man who came down with her."

One of the men in Gore's party was a nineteen-year-old seaman, Francis Wilkinson, who thoughtfully noted in his journal that this lady was a woman "whos Power seems to be equal to that of A Queen." Wilkinson was very observant, and also mathematically minded. The first time he found the *fare hau*, he measured it, finding its dimensions to be "367 foot long 36 foot broad and 20 foot high." Not only was the great building "ingeniously con-trived," but it had been "the Inhabitants of one of their Kings." By logic, therefore, Purea, the current resident, was a queen.

When Gore, Wilkinson, and the rest of the gang of wooders returned to the ship for their midday dinner, they brought two islanders with them.

Robertson wrote that one "appeared to be a Chieff," because his companion (the young man who assisted Fa'a) paid him so much respect. This "fine, well-made" fellow was about thirty years old, and obviously intelligent, managing with facial expressions and hand signs to express a great deal of curiosity about the ship. Robertson cooperatively led him on a tour of the very large poop, which extended from the stern almost all the way to the amidships main mast, and formed the roof of the afterquarters. Partially sheltered by a wooden awning, this was where the helmsman stood at the ship's wheel; it also served as the quarterdeck for the captain and officers, having a commanding view of the sea around and the open deck below.

Having given the Tahitians a good opportunity to gaze raptly at the lofty web of rigging, Robertson took the chief and his friend to dine in the officers' wardroom (called the gunroom by Robertson), which housed six massive iron cannon, and was pierced with gunports. This was beneath the poop, and forward of the Great Cabin, where the captain reigned. Guaranteed to be drafty, in tropical Tahiti it was a pleasant, airy space, if rather cramped and cluttered with cannon.

Intrigued by the news of the Tahitian guests, Wallis and Clarke left their sickbeds to join them at the table, and a good dinner of roasted meats and vegetables was laid out, accompanied by pies, bread, puddings, and fruit. Before sitting down, the chief picked up the chair, and examined it from every angle. Then he set it down, sat on it, and gave the plates, knives, and forks the same close inspection. After taking note of how the Europeans handled the strange cutlery and attacked their oddly cooked food, he coped very well, considering he had always used his fingers to eat. "He tasted of every dish that was given him," Wallis noted, but eat only the "Yams, Plantain & apples," the last being a native fruit (*Spondias cytherea*), that was a favorite with the sailors. Various wines and beers were offered, but after a sniff and a taste the chieftain rejected them in favor of water, though he enjoyed the ritual of touching glasses before drinking.

It was usual at the time for gentlemen to wipe their mouths with their pocket handkerchiefs before sipping from their glasses. Robertson, a practical joker, noticed that the chief was uncomfortable about this, having no handkerchief about his tapa robes, so solemnly handed him a corner of the tablecloth. The Tahitian fell for the trick, and lifted it to wipe his lips, offending the first lieutenant, who growled at the poor fellow for his gross behavior, shaking the cloth for emphasis.

Though embarrassed by his mistake, the chief recovered fast. Exhibiting a robust sense of humor, he made it plain he would fetch a girl to sleep with Clarke, to atone for his unintentional rudeness, and improve the officer's unpleasant mood. According to Robertson, Clarke exclaimed, "Well done,

Jonathan!" The lieutenant was probably being sarcastic, as "Jonathan" was current English slang for an unsophisticated yokel, usually applied to an American colonial. It was a turning point in Anglo-Tahitian relations, however, as for the first time a nickname was bestowed on a native of the island. "This man we called Jonathan," wrote Captain Wallis in his logbook. Robert Molineux recorded that Jonathan's friend, the man they considered to be Fa'a's son, was given a nickname beloved by all sailors—Jack. And, with that, the *Dolphins* were content, having no interest in finding out what the Tahitians were really called.

Wallis tried an experiment, showing Jonathan a number of coins, and inviting him to take his choice, but the chief simply shook his head, as they had no value in Tahiti—"shewed him silver Gold & Brass but he knew nothing of it & preferred Iron before them all." They handed him a looking glass, and when he stroked his beard, Dr. Hutchinson handed him a pair of tweezers. Understanding their function at once, Jonathan plucked the hairs from his upper lip, "as dextrously as any of us cou'd do," marveled Robertson. The surgeon followed this up by producing a miniature of a pretty English-woman, signing jocularly that if he came to England with them, "he should have one of them always to Sleep with." Enraptured by the idea, the Tahitian delightedly caressed the portrait, while his hosts watched with condescending amusement.

Undoubtedly, their visitor found their behavior equally funny. At sunset Jonathan was landed on shore, to be received by a large crowd, and Robertson heard their roars of laughter as he delivered a hilarious account of his adventure. He was as good as his word, too. The following day, a canoe arrived with Jonathan and his friend, both wearing very broad grins. The presents they brought were a big roasted hog, and *two* young women for the disconcerted Clarke.

Because of Jonathan's tale, Tupaia understood the British chief lived on the ship and never came on shore, and that to establish a political alliance it was necessary to go on board. Giving up on the imperceptive Gallagher, he and Purea accosted the gunner and chief trader, William Harrison, and after presenting him with tapa, hogs, and fowls, let him know they wished to be taken onto the *Dolphin.*

Impressed by their confident bearing, and the obsequious way the locals treated Purea, the gunner had no hesitation in obeying. A boat was summoned, and Purea and Tupaia, with two attendants, were ferried to the *Dolphin*, then ushered up the ladder of battens nailed to the ship's side. Leading the way through the gunroom to the lobby, Harrison announced their presence to the marine standing sentry, who tapped at the Great Cabin door, went in, clicked his heels together, and informed Captain Wallis that he had visitors from shore.

Wallis was at his desk at the time, irritably estimating the number of nails stolen from the ship, and writing up a reward for their recovery: "found several of the Large Belaying Cleats drawn & the Nails taken away and many Nails in places drawn—Searched but could find none of them, offered a reward," he wrote in his logbook that day. Sick, feeble, and sorely tried, he was quite unprepared to receive royalty. Then, as he recognized Purea's "very majestic Mein," his exasperation turned to relief.

Samuel Wallis *needed* a Tahitian monarch. Liberal ideas were popular in western Europe, inspired by revolutionary thinkers like Rousseau and Voltaire in France, and Franklin and Jefferson in the American colonies; newspaper writers and coffeehouse debaters were convinced that civilized man was emerging from centuries of ignorance into an era of reason, science, and a respect for humanity—a humanity that included the "Indians" who had met such harsh treatment in the Americas and the Spice Islands from England's traditional enemies, the Spanish and the Dutch. As Wallis was acutely aware, his taming of the "Indians" of "King George's Island" by hammering them with his cannon would not be received at all well in London. He could plead he had been forced to counter treachery with violence, but was uneasily conscious that taking possession of the island by right of conquest would not earn him any accolades. If he could find a native sovereign who would *give* him the island by right of treaty, it would make his annexation respectable, but up to this moment, he had thought there was no native sovereign available, as the king had been killed when his canoe was blasted in two. Now, registering Purea's regal demeanor and the attentive way Tupaia treated her, he jumped to the wild conclusion that the king had left a widow to succeed him, who was none other than this imperious-looking woman.

It was a convenient assumption, but also very wrong. Purea's husband, Amo Tevahitua, may have played a major part in the disastrously one-sided battle, as his canoe was at the head of the fleet from Papara that joined the local flotilla, but otherwise Wallis's reasoning was well off the mark. Not only was Amo alive and unscathed, but he was not the king of the island: Tahiti did not have a single ruler, being divided into a number of districts, each with one or more *ari'i* in charge, many of them rivals.

For the unknowing Wallis, however, Purea was the perfect model of a native monarch. Not only was she dignified, statuesque, and handsome, but her draperies strongly resembled the imperial toga of a Roman emperor. Her outer cloak was dyed a regal red. Underneath was a *tiputa,* a poncho made of a broad length of tapa with a slit cut lengthways down the center, so it could be easily dropped over her head, to fall gracefully fore-and-aft. This was cinched about her waist with a long feathered sash. Underneath, she wore an ankle-length sarong, the *pareu,* fashioned of white tapa patterned in yellow, which looked to Wallis like a petticoat. Her abundant, curly hair, cut short, was bound with another piece of dyed tapa, and decorated with tropical feathers and flowers.

Confronted with this eye-catching vision, it is little wonder that he scarcely noticed Tupaia, her chief minister, who was certainly murmuring advice into her ear. Instead, he searched his mind for an appropriate gift for this very well-timed queen—and was struck by divine inspiration. He called for a generous length of the blue broadcloth that was commonly stocked as trade goods, then draped it about Purea's shoulders, and lashed it about her middle with blue ribbons.

Wallis could not have chosen better. By enfolding Purea, he had quite unconsciously recognized her *mana*—her prestige—in a distinctively Polynesian way: not only had he presented her with cloth, but he had acknowledged her sacred power by wrapping her in it. At the same time, he had managed to give her something excitingly novel. When Tahitians decorated their tapa, they were confined to red, yellow, and brown dyes, but this mantle was *blue*, the color of rare and beautiful butterflies, birds, and fish. Never before the Europeans' arrival had the Tahitians seen the color of the sea and sky captured in cloth.

Even more remarkably, the presentation somehow communicated Wallis's strange conviction that Purea was the Tahitians' queen, for from that moment on she behaved exactly as Wallis expected a Tahitian queen to behave. This can certainly be credited to Tupaia, who somehow, by an amazing leap of understanding, deduced that the captain's deferential attitude was quite different from the condescension Jonathan had reported after his dinner on board the ship. A bonus was Purea's natural sense of theater. Once Tupaia had described the role she had to play, she played that part as if on the stage.

For Tupaia, it was even easier to guess his own role in the drama—the mundane business of procuring the provisions Wallis needed. And he, too, played his part to perfection. "When she landed," the relieved captain wrote, "she sent off Hogs enough for one day for the Ships Company—who from this day never wanted a fresh meal."

CHAPTER 5

⟡

The State Visit

Before she left the ship, Purea extracted a promise. According to Wallis's journal, "she taking noticed that I had been ill pointed to the shore," which he took to mean an invitation to visit the *fare hau*, which he assumed was her palace.

The weather turned breezy and heavy rain threatened, but he arrived at the landing place the next morning, as arranged, accompanied by "severall officers," including Clarke, the purser, and Dr. Hutchinson. The sight of an English captain in gold-laced knee-length coat and white silk breeches immediately attracted an enraptured crowd, but to Wallis's relief Purea and Tupaia arrived before he was suffocated by the attention. She imperiously waved her hand, the crowd reluctantly backed away, and Wallis and his officers, trailed by a squad of marines, tramped to the *fare hau*, assisted over running streams by Purea's powerfully built attendants.

At the great pillared hall another inquisitive crowd was waiting. Purea paused to make a long speech, gesturing with a banana leaf. Then various notables were beckoned forward, and instructed to kneel and kiss Wallis's hand, while his officers loitered awkwardly, and his bodyguard of red-coated marines stood rigidly at the rear. This was the moment Wallis had been waiting for—according to the story he told in London later, this was when the queen formally surrendered her island. It was just a convenient fiction, however. Not only did Purea not have the right to cede Tahiti, but the Europeans had not a notion of what was being said.

In reality, everyone went inside, to commence confusing each other. Wallis, as fascinated as Frank Wilkinson by the immensity of the hall and the ingenuity of its structure, paced out the measurements of the building, making it 327 feet long and 42 feet broad, and, as he wrote, "raised upon 39 pillars on each side, and 14 in the middle." Settling down, he made a scale drawing of it, while the puzzled Tahitians politely watched. Then Purea and four beautiful young female attendants took hold of the bemused captain and the sick officers, and firmly undressed them. Each man was given a healthful massage—the real reason Purea had invited them here. After half an hour of kneading their thighs, sides, and necks, the women dressed the men again, though naturally they were awkward, and even more naturally, the men were embarrassed.

The surgeon introduced a comic note when he removed his wig to wipe his sweating head, striking the entire Tahitian assembly dumb with astonishment. (As told in London later, they could not have been more amazed if he had unscrewed a leg.) Recovering from the shock, Purea "ordered some Bundles to be brought, and took from them some Country Cloth, which is like paper," according to Wallis. With her own hands, she cut a *tiputa*, and ceremoniously lifted it over his head. Wallis tried to stop her, not understanding the significance, but finally consented to be wrapped, "not choosing to offend her."

And, with that, the strange visit was over, though getting back to the boat was yet another foreign experience. To Wallis's discomfiture, every time they came to a muddy patch he was heaved up by the queen herself, who carried him as easily as a child.

Five days afterward, on July 18, the weather was much improved, and one of the master's mates, Richard Pickersgill, took a stroll through the woods with his friend, Sergeant Gallagher. Pickersgill, only eighteen years old, was a lively character and a talented seaman, with a knack for drawing beautiful charts and coastal outlines. A lusty young man who loved women almost as much as he loved a beaker of grog in convivial company, he was also very good at telling a tale. As he related to Robertson later, he and the marine sergeant blundered across a long, grand building, "where," as Robertson wrote, "the Queen of the Island lives."

Purea was sitting on "a very fine Matt," in the middle of a ring of people. She signed to Pickersgill and his friend to make themselves comfortable, and they settled down to watch. Servants carried in "Severall Dishes of Different sorts of Meat drest after the Country Manner," and everyone washed their hands in coconut shells of fresh water. The man who sat nearest to the queen (undoubtedly Tupaia) was served first, then the rest of the men in descending order, according to their rank. This done, two young women brought in more dishes, set them down in front of Purea, and squatted down, one to each side of her. To Pickergill's surprise, they began to feed her, taking turns to poke choice morsels into her mouth. It was very cleanly, because the two attendants washed their hands between each serving, but never once did she touch her own food.

Even more puzzlingly, while those who were also partaking of the meal were eating with their own fingers, all of them were men. When the queen had finished her dinner, her two maids took their own meals aside, and as if it were a signal, all the women began to eat. And, though Pickersgill estimated there were five hundred or more people there, no one spoke a word. Naturally talkative, the natives quietly waited their turn, then attacked their food in uncanny, single-minded silence. Purea made signs to Pickersgill and Gallagher to help themselves, but, being nervously aware there were customs and rituals in operation that were beyond European comprehension, they played safe by plucking fruit from the overhanging trees.

It was not until a final washing of hands that normality returned. A babel of talking began, and Purea stood up, brushed down her robes, and demanded with imperative signs to be taken on board the *Dolphin*. Pickersgill and Gallagher did not even consider refusing the royal request, though Captain Wallis was too ill to receive visitors. Robertson was in charge of the deck, and perfectly capable of hosting Purea, Tupaia, and various courtiers, and so they escorted the noble Tahitians to the shore, and summoned a boat to carry them to the ship.

George Robertson was delighted to meet the famous queen. Jovially leading the party into the gunroom, he sent for food, and though Purea declined, the men with her managed to do hearty justice to the meal, despite having just eaten. Like Jonathan, they rejected rum and brandy, preferring water, but appeared to like Madeira. They also contrived to express curiosity about how the strange food was cooked, so after dinner was cleared away Robertson and Pickersgill took the Tahitians to the galley, which was at the foot of the foremast, under the shelter of the forecastle deck.

A wonderful aroma wafted out to greet them, because a pig and two hens were being roasted there. This intrigued the Tahitians, who were used to leaf-wrapped meat steamed in an earth oven. One tried his hand at turning the spit, while the others examined the two immense copper cauldrons, which fortunately had been cleaned to a brilliant shine. After foiling an attempt to pry off a piece of the copper, Robertson ushered the party to the quarterdeck, to show them the ship's fowls in their coops. Features of the rigging were then pointed out, "which Surprized them the most of anything."

"In my oppinion the whole was Smart Sensable people and very cureous in observing everything which they saw, but the Queen was rather more so nor any of the rest," Robertson continued in his logbook, going on to describe Purea as "a strong well made Woman about five foot ten Inches and the strongest made Woman that I ever saw." Though she wore no footwear or headdress, her costume was splendid, Robertson relating that her robe was "Red, which was the Mournings, which she wore for her Husband, who was killd in the Great double Canoe which gave the Signal for the Attack." Despite coming to the strange conclusion that red was the color of mourning, he expressed no surprise that the supposed widow "appeard very cheerful and merry all the time she was Onboard." Her "Attendance," he added, "was Drest in White."

At sunset Captain Wallis sent orders that the queen and her retinue should be taken on shore in the barge. As he was feeling a little better, he decided to go along too, and as the evening was mild, they rowed about the lagoon for a while. When they finally landed, Purea seized the chance to further demonstrate to the locals that the *ari'i rahi* of the ship was her particular friend. As Wallis noted in his logbook, "she harrangued the People taking me & the Officers in her arms & shaking us by the hand & pointing to the ship." Robertson testified that "not a Whisper" could be heard as she spoke.

Two days later, again according to Robertson's reminiscences, the queen and "one of her principal attendants"—unmistakably Tupaia—paid another visit to the *Dolphin*. They arrived at 8 A.M., and were ushered into the Great Cabin, where Captain Wallis, who was feeling a little better, ordered a breakfast set.

When the food arrived, Tupaia stood up to say prayers. He made a long speech, gesturing about the cabin, and then went into a quarter gallery, looked out the windows, and spoke to the sun. His oration ended with a ritual offering to the gods: sitting down at the table, he plucked up some butter in his long nails, and cast it down in the traditional manner. Lieutenant Clarke, who had been waiting impatiently, snatched the dish of butter away, considering it dirtied, and ordered the captain's servant to bring a fresh one, an insult so offensive that Tupaia sat stiff and silent from then on, refusing all food.

To mollify Purea, who was also greatly affronted, Robertson took her below for a tour of the officers' accommodations, making her a present of anything that took her eye, including a fancy ruffled shirt. He helped her put this on, pulling it over her head and showing her how to put her arms through the sleeves, an intimacy that, as he flattered himself, "gaind her heart." When he delivered her back to the Great Cabin, as the master reminisced after getting back to London, she formally approached Wallis, "looking upon him as our King," and asked him to "Signe a Treaty of Peace in order to settle all Differences betwixt her Maj^s people and ours." This could not possibly be true, as not only did she have no command of English, but Tahitians had no concept of writing, let alone the legal value of a signature. Robertson explained away the lack of a signed treaty by claiming Wallis had a paralytic disorder of his writing hand, but no such document existed. His story was part of the *Dolphins'* myth of English possession of Tahiti, designed to appeal to the audience back home.

More convincing is his claim that Purea decided to check his muscular frame for tattoos. Being proud of his physique, Robertson happily bared his legs and arms, and then his chest, which she was amazed to find was furry. Impressed by his size, she called Tupaia to come and feel his muscles, "which I allowed him to do, and he seemd greatly Astonished as well as She." The two Tahitians discussed it for a while, and then Purea turned to Robertson, put her arms around him, and tried to lift him up. He foiled her by making himself a dead weight, so her advisor "made a Sign for me to Lift her," which Robertson did, effortlessly carrying her around the cabin, much to her delight. As he went on smugly, "this is the way the Ladys here trys the men, before they Admit them to be their Lovers."

Wallis was not well enough, so Robertson was ordered to take the barge and escort Purea and her companion to her house, "but not to stay any time, as he and both the Lieut⁵ was in a bad state of health." The usual crowd was hanging about at the landing place, and Purea introduced Robertson to the local dignitaries, showing them how to shake hands with him: "We then set out Arm in Arm for the Palace, and all the Principal part of the Inhabitance came after us." At the *fare hau* the procession was received by yet another crowd. Speeches were made, and food cooked, ready for a feast. An elderly noblewoman was enticed to feel Robertson's muscles and run her long fingernails through his chest hair. "Oh! Oh! Oh!" she exclaimed, impressed. Purea cut a *tiputa*, threw it over Robertson's head, tied it with a sash, made a short speech, and presented him with sixteen yards of tapa.

Remembering the captain's instructions, Robertson turned down an invitation to stop and dine. The unintentional discourtesy took the old woman so greatly aback that she made "very plain Signs" that Purea would be his bedmate that night, if only he would stay. Both women smiled understandingly when the master declined, but his appearance of gentlemanly virtue was quite ruined when he stopped to flirt with a particularly fair maiden on the path to the beach. Purea, obviously miffed, drew him away, and firmly saw him into his boat.

"This day the Queen came Onboard again, & insisted on going to her House," noted Wallis in his logbook on Wednesday, July 22. It was an unwelcome interruption, as he was having trouble with his crew.

The previous evening, Robertson, while standing on the forecastle deck above the galley where the men were waiting to collect their suppers, had overheard some of them accuse six sailors of spoiling the trade in sex by giving bigger nails to the girls. The sextet spiritedly defended themselves, claiming they got double value for double-sized spikes, and the argument turned into a brawl. Robertson jumped down and broke up the fight, but after consultation with the officers it was decided that one of the six—a hapless fellow by the name of Francis Pinkney, who had been found guilty of prying off a wooden belaying cleat to steal the nails that secured it—should serve as an example for the rest by running the gauntlet three times around the ship.

At noon next day Robertson ordered the men into a double line, facing each other and armed with nettles (light ropes used in sailmaking). Pinkney was launched into a dash between the two rows, while the men flailed feebly at his back. As the master swiftly discerned, the reason for their "merciful" play with the nettles was that Pinkney had staunchly refused to implicate any of the others. Robertson gave him a couple of solid thumps that jerked a few names out of him, and led to a much harder drubbing on the next run of the gauntlet.

It was obvious, however, that the problem of thieving important nails out of the ship was only going to get worse, and so Samuel Wallis, being a sane and sensible captain, had come to the firm conclusion that it was high time to sail away from this over-amorous isle. Nevertheless, when Purea came on board to insist on another call, he summoned his best manners, paid attention, and agreed.

As before, he joined her on the riverbank with a retinue of officers, this time carrying "a hansome present of Hatchetts BillHooks knives buttons threds needles scissars—a Shirt a Piece of Broad Cloth and many other things." Again, Purea had them carried over the river, and again, "she made me the Two Lieut^s & Purser who had been all ill sit down & called a Number of her attendants & they Chafed our Legs thighs sides & Necks for near half an Hour."

What followed was new, and very solemn. Signing to her guests to be seated, Purea removed their cocked hats, and sanctified them by securing tufts of sacred feathers to the upturned brims. Then she bound their bared heads with fine cords made of human hair—a powerful gesture, as she made signs "it was her hair & her own work." The head of any person was considered *tapu*, being the seat of their spirit, but because of a chief's close connection with the gods, anything to do with his or her head was encompassed by some of the most intense and terrifying taboos of Polynesian society. Undoubtedly, Purea was playing out her own act of possession, using her sacred hair to bind the Europeans to Tahiti and to herself.

There was more to come. After they had arrived at the landing place she beckoned to some servants, who came forward bearing "a Large Hog & a Sow Big with Pig," symbols of a fruitful partnership. She had already given the men the intricately patterned mats they had been seated on, a gift as significant as the presentation of tapa. As these were loaded into the boat, Tupaia—who certainly had orchestrated all this—must have felt a sense of a ritual completed, and a diplomatic alliance confirmed.

Then Captain Wallis ruined it.

They would sail in four days' time, he firmly communicated. Horrified, Purea made signs of her own, urging him to come to her district, Papara. As Wallis noted in his log, she "pointed to the Country, & shewed she was going there & made signs for us to stay Twenty or 15 days but on my shewing her that four days was the time she sat down & cryed very much."

Collapsing to the ground and dissolving into tears was a theatrical way to make him change his mind, but Purea's grief was sincere. On Tupaia's advice, she had invested a great deal of political capital in the *entente*, and it was important that Wallis should make a formal visit to her own territory. While Amo might be terrified to see the British ship with its broadside of cannon heave to off Papara, it would also impress and intimidate their rivals. Samuel Wallis ignored the outburst, however. It was time to set sail and take his sexually sated and increasingly combative men away, and so, while his journal testifies that he felt guilty enough to send her "two Turkeys, Two Geese, three Guinea Hens, a Cat big with Kitten," and an assortment of useful things like bottles, ribbons, scissors, and seeds, he was adamant in his refusal.

It was a lapse of understanding on his part that was to have grave political consequences not just for Purea and Amo, but for Tupaia, too.

The weather turned squally, with rain, but preparations for departure forged ahead. Anchors were weighed until the *Dolphin* was held by only one, and the topgallant masts and yards—the most lofty parts of the rigging, which had been struck (taken down) and stored while the ship was at anchor—were sent up again. So many hogs, pigs, and hens were brought on board that the ship sounded and smelled like a barnyard. Spare bins in the holds were packed with hay the men had cut and dried, along with other fodder.

On July 25, while all this was going on, Wallis belatedly remembered orders from their Lordships of the Admiralty to "obtain a complete knowledge of the Land or Islands supposed to be situated in the Southern Hemisphere," with particular attention paid to anything that might reap riches for England in the future, such as ores or spices. He summoned John Gore, and sent him off with a party of forty seamen and Fa'a as a guide, to penetrate as much of the hinterland as he could reach before nightfall, and then return the next day. As Robertson reminisced later, "This was the first and Last Attempts that we ever made to discover the Inland Country."

Robertson was busy with another project. The purser, John Harrison (no relation of the gunner), a remarkable man of astronomical bent, had worked out a surprisingly accurate position of the island, finding its longitude by "taking the Distance of the Sun from the Moon and working it according to Dr. Masculine's method which we did not understand"—as Captain Wallis (like everyone else in the ship) frankly admitted. Harrison was able to do it because he had a pre-publication copy of an ephemeris compiled by the Astronomer Royal, Dr. Nevil Maskelyne, this being an almanac tabling the daily positions of important heavenly bodies.

The previous evening, while leafing curiously through the book, Robertson had noticed there was an eclipse of the sun due next day, and applied to Captain Wallis for permission to go on shore and take observations. This was given, so at daybreak Robertson and John Harrison set out with a telescope fitted with a dark glass, and Midshipman Pinnock to assist. Just as they had ended their observations and made their calculations, Purea and "one of her chiefs"—evidently Tupaia—arrived to see what they were doing. Robertson offered them the telescope, and they both looked at the sun. The master enjoyed their open amazement, so after removing the dark glass he refocused the instrument on various parts of the bay, and handed it over so the two Tahitians could marvel at the enlarged views. Then Tupaia wanted another look at the sun. Allowing his rough sense of humor to get the better of kindness or good sense, Robertson deliberately neglected to put back the dark glass before aiming the telescope at the full sun and beckoning Tupaia to have a look, "which almost blinded the poor man." To confuse him still further, Robertson studied the sun himself (after surreptitiously replacing the glass), "then Looked him full in the face as if I hade been Surprized at his not being able to look."

The following afternoon Gore and his party had not come back, so Purea and her attendants were invited on board the *Dolphin*. Wallis had an ulterior motive for this, writing in his journal, "I thought by securing her and some of the Principal People there would be no danger to the Party." In effect, Purea, Tupaia, and an unknown number of other chiefs were being kept hostage against Gore's safe return.

There was another, even darker, reason for this. Suspicions had been expressed in the gunroom that Purea was anxious for them to stay because she planned to attack and seize the ship. Robertson was furious, expostulating, "what reason my Shipmates has for this unCharitable Conjecture I know not," but Wallis and his officers felt their suspicions were justified, as the natives were restless.

Frank Wilkinson had been the first to note that "The Indians suspecting that we Ware going Away" were assembling in multitudes on the beach and the overlooking hills, and becoming agitated at the prospect of losing the source of so much gossip and iron. According to Wilkinson's shipmate, George Pinnock, the gunner "sent word off that ^{y}e natives began to grow very Numerous, verry obstinate & troublesome." Captain Wallis promptly ordered Gunner Harrison to strike the trading tent and come on board with his party. No sooner had they arrived than the gunner was given yet another order, to load and ready the cannon, just in case force was needed. It was then, as an added precaution, that Wallis invited Purea and her attendant chiefs on board, on the pretext of a farewell dinner.

Though future events make it certain Tupaia soon realized they were being held hostage, it is doubtful Purea even noticed. While the chiefs with her "eat very hearty" (though without touching the wine or grog), she was doing her utmost to prevail on Wallis to stay just ten days longer. When he doggedly refused, she cast herself across an arms chest, her varicolored robes flowing gracefully across the floor as she wept.

Understandably, Samuel Wallis felt both awkward and embarrassed. Finally, in desperation, he gave an earnest (and completely false) promise to come back very soon, which helped stem the flood of tears. About five in the evening, much to his relief, Gore and his party materialized on the beach, and he was able to put Purea and the other captives ashore. It was not even as if Gore's excursion had been worth all the fuss and bother. He had brought back a small quantity of ginger and turmeric, plus a few black rocks that just might hold some sort of mineral, but otherwise had little to report, save that the accessible land up the river was heavily inhabited and closely cultivated, and it was very hard going once they got into the foothills.

Next morning, as Robertson noted in his logbook, Gore "found the old Lady on the Beach." She and her attendants had slept there—for fear, Robertson said, "of not seeing us before we Sail'd." Accordingly, she was able to do a last service for the ship. Wilkinson was sent in charge of a boat's crew to fill a few last barrels with water, but was fearful of landing, because the beach was so packed. Purea saw his predicament, and banished the crowd to the far side of the river. When Wilkinson was about to pull off again, she tried to bribe him with some large hogs to carry her in his boat, but his instructions were not to take any islanders to the ship, so he shook his head and rowed away.

Accordingly, Purea, with Tupaia and several others, boarded a large canoe. They arrived in good time to hear the shouting from the officers as men were ordered to the capstan, then rhythmic chanting as brawny fists shoved the capstan bars round, and the ship eased up to the straightening anchor chain, until the anchor was a-peak, on the verge of leaving the bottom. More shouts, and more seamen, fit from five weeks in Tahiti, scrambled up the rigging, and side-stepped along the yards to loosen the sails. Loud rattles as the great sheets of canvas dropped and took the wind. The ship began to glide forward, plucking the rest of her chain as she came, and up the anchor surged, in a sudden scent of seaweed and saltwater, dripping black Tahitian sand.

"The Queen came alongside in a great double Canoe with many of her Atendants," wrote Robertson. Leaning out of the gunports, the men and the officers threw them presents, "but the good old Lady took very little notice of them, but Cry'd continually." The wind was very light, forcing the *Dolphins* to lower three boats and tow the ship through the gap in the reef. Then at last the sea breeze gusted. The boats were hoisted aboard, and the yards were squared for the open sea.

Sails rippled and snapped, then billowed and tautened. An incoming swell lifted and dropped the ship in a farewell curtsey, and the *Dolphin* was on her way.

It was July 26, 1767.

CHAPTER 6

❧

Tupaia's Pyramid

Pa'ipa'i i te rima ia huha
A fava ei pua'a tote!
Auaa i ape au nei i te rao!
Clap the hands on the thighs
Rush headfirst as a hog enraged!
I do not flinch at a fly!

—*Tahitian war chant*

At the beginning of April 1768, a little more than eight months after the departure of the *Dolphin*, two European ships hove into view off the eastern coast of the larger bulge of the hourglass-shaped island of Tahiti. It would be little wonder if the Tahitians thought it was Captain Wallis returning, true to his promise, this time with a companion. Not only did they appear in the same place, but both ships looked a lot like the *Dolphin*, being three-masted, square-sailed, and with the same dull yellow stripe along each side, checkered by gunports. Accordingly, a young chief (whose name was Ahutoru) sallied out at once in a double canoe, enthusiastically waving a plantain sprout.

He hailed the smaller ship, probably because it was closest in size to his memory of the *Dolphin*. "*Taio!*" he cried—"Friend!" A sailor threw him a rope. The young chief grabbed it and hauled, bringing the big canoe up to the side with an impressive show of strength. Bracing his palms on a chain plate, he sprang into the chains, then vaulted over the bulwarks onto the deck. Gesturing to the men in his canoe to pull away, he strode up to the tallest officer, assuming that he was the *ari'i rahi* of the ship because he looked the best fed, and presented him with the plantain shoot.

The officer replied in a language no Tahitian had ever heard before, which was probably the moment it dawned on Ahutoru that the ship was not the "brittane" one he expected. Instead, the vessel he had so blithely boarded was the storeship *L'Étoile*, one of the two ships of a French discovery expedition, the first scientific exploration of the Pacific in history. The officer, who was just the second lieutenant, was trying to correct Ahutoru's social blunder by introducing him to the real captain of *L'Étoile*, François Chenard de la Giraudais. The captain of the other ship, the frigate *La Boudeuse*, was Nicolas Pierre Duclos-Guyot, and the expedition as a whole was commanded by a thirty-nine-year-old military veteran, Louis de Bougainville.

Ahutoru, who was blessed with the same cheerful aplomb as Jonathan, was not at all embarrassed by his mistake, though he did turn pale and exclaim "*Pou! Pou!*" when he sighted the muskets and cannon. He readily exchanged his tapa garments for European clothing, and was not surprised to see his reflection in a mirror. He hunkered down on the deck to share soup with the seamen at mess-time, and was equally at home when he sat at a table and used a knife and fork to eat supper with the officers. Like Jonathan, he sniffed or tasted all the dishes, but preferred water to wine. Exploring the ship, he demonstrated a lively interest George Robertson would have recognized. His only surprise was that there were no females on the ship, indicating that more Tahitian girls came on board the *Dolphin* than Wallis might have suspected.

Then, however, Ahutoru spied the valet of the botanist, Philibert Commerson. "*Vahine!*" he exclaimed, with expressive gestures, and for the first time the French sailors understood that M'sieu Commerson's servant, "M'sieu Jean Baret," was female. There had been a lot of comment about the valet's effeminate looks, that "he" never shaved, removed "his" shirt, or relieved "himself" in public, and that "he" slept on the floor of "his" employer's cabin. However, it was not until Ahutoru, who (like all Tahitians) judged gender by stance and shape, and not by what a person wore, cried out that word "*vahine*" that they realized the sensational truth.

Enchanted, Ahutoru did his utmost to seduce the girl. The Tahitians on shore were equally beguiled by the novel prospect of sex with a European woman. After Bougainville had found a beautiful but "detestable" anchorage in a coral-studded lagoon off the eastern village of Hitia'a, Jeanne Baret and Commerson went botanizing in the hinterland, only to have this innocent pursuit abruptly cut short when they were waylaid by a group of inquisitive and playful young men. Partly as a joke, and also because they were curious, the islanders demanded the same favors of this white girl that their women were granting the sailors. Jeanne had to be rescued by a squad of marines, who were summoned by Commerson's panic-stricken shouts.

Otherwise, the Tahitians were both friendly and cooperative. Though Bougainville had not guessed that another European nation had beaten him to the "discovery" of the island, he was benefiting greatly from the visit of the *Dolphin*. The Tahitians had been made to understand cannon and muskets, and the Hitia'a people were determined to avoid violence, if possible. The district chief, Reti, having heard about the endless greed of Europeans, also tried to limit the time the ships would be visiting his shore, but in the meantime an abundance of foodstuffs was provided for barter. The women were equally generous. To the northwest, in the country around Matavai, an imponderable number of half-European newborns were being stifled to death, but there were plenty of available girls here.

The French, however, were forced to face the same problem as Robertson's "Dear Irish boy." Perhaps because the Tahitians had learned from watching the *Dolphins* that European men preferred to make love in private, they enjoyed the consternation of the ardent *matelotes* when they found they were supposed to carry out the act within a circle of deeply interested spectators. After being coaxed into a thicket by a pretty girl, Bougainville's cook was seized by an inquisitive crowd, stripped of his clothes, and minutely inspected. Once curiosity was satisfied, he was invited to carry on while everyone watched. Instead, thoroughly demoralized, he fled back to the ship with his breeches gripped in his hand, and never ventured on shore again.

A noble passenger, the Prince of Nassau, was one of the mightier ones to be offered public sex. Caught in the rain, he took shelter in a house where he was welcomed by six beautiful damsels, who undressed him and beguiled him, while a crowd looked on and a musician serenaded with a nose flute. Bougainville himself was offered three girls. While he was refusing in the most gallant manner possible, an achromatic glass was stolen from his cabin.

The Tahitians had returned to the "thievish" habits Wallis had stemmed with firepower. The first object to disappear had been a pistol the Prince of Nassau had used to amaze chief Reti by firing at a bird. This was soon returned, Reti being a timid man who was easily cowed, but a book of astronomical observations followed Bougainville's achromatic glass into the void, along with other knickknacks and valuables. This puzzled Bougainville, since Tahitians never stole from each other. What he did not reckon with was the adventurousness of young Tahitian men, and their enjoyment of a challenge—the same spirit that sent them out into the unknown ocean. The stolen items were often handed back quite readily, after inspection. It was the daring appropriation that was admired.

As thefts became more brazen, they were countered with brutality, which meant that their first formal visitor had chosen a very bad moment when he arrived on the morning of April 10. This was Tutaha, a tall, impressively muscular man in his late fifties who was regent of the Pare Arue district (immediately to the west of Matavai Bay) during the minority of his great-nephew, Tu. He had great ambitions for both himself and his ward, which, if his plans worked out, would lead to the domination of all Tahiti. His rival, Amo's wife Purea, had forestalled him in making an alliance with Captain Wallis, but he was determined to out-maneuver her with this new set of Europeans.

Tutaha began with the usual ritual, presenting Bougainville with hogs, poultry, fruit, and tapa cloth. After exchanging names as a sign of brotherhood, he invited him to sleep with one of his younger and better-looking wives. Unfortunately, however, this pleasant friendship-making process was brought to an abrupt halt by the news that a Frenchman had shot a Hitia'a man dead.

None of the sailors would confess to the crime, and no one came forward to identify the murderer. More violence followed. An islander was paid for a pig with a beating, and when his neighbors swarmed around in protest, they were bayoneted by panicked marines. Villagers fled, taking their possessions with them, and the trade in provisions faltered. At the same time, Bougainville was finding out what a terrible choice of anchorage he had made, with the ships in constant danger of falling onto coral outcrops, and anchor cables parting. One was cut deliberately. He decided it was time to leave.

Chief Reti gave vent to ceremonial tears, and made generous last presentations of livestock and fruit, but was undoubtedly delighted, as his people were demanding, "*Taio, taio, mate?*"—"Friends, friends, why do they kill us?" Tutaha's reaction is unrecorded. He went on board *Boudeuse* to present Bougainville with some pigs before beating his own retreat, but without doubt he was annoyed that his chance of a political coup was thwarted. Certainly, too, he had been hoping to inspect, and procure, if possible, some of the Europeans' guns.

Strangely, despite the conflict and killing, Ahutoru decided to sail away with the violent strangers, to see what France and Frenchwomen were like. Charles Félix Pierre Fesche, a volunteer officer, thought it was a terrible idea, writing, "I am firmly of the belief that this poor wretch will long regret his foolish action, as I consider his return to his home to be impossible." Bougainville, apparently, felt no such qualms. Dubbing his new passenger "Louis de Cythère" after the name, "New Cythera," he had given the island when claiming it for France, he shipped the young man on board, and sailed with him for the western Pacific, after just nine days on Tahiti.

Perhaps, like Robertson, Bougainville saw the benefits of carrying an intelligent Polynesian. As the *Dolphin's* master remarked in the final write-up of his journal, if the young chief they had nicknamed Jonathan had come with them to England, "I dare say he would have soon learnd the English Language, and being a sensable fine smart man, he certainly would have been able to give us a mutch fuller account both of his own and the Adjacent Countrys then it was posable for us to learn." Jonathan, however, had chosen not to make himself available. On July 13, while Wallis was paying his first call to Purea's house, Jonathan had brought his friend for a third visit, and though the *Dolphins* did not suspect it, it was in farewell.

Furneaux, who had been left in charge of the ship, joined them at the table, and on a whim he and Robertson rummaged in their sea chests and "Drest the young chief and another after the European manner," as Frank Wilkinson phrased it. The two Tahitians were puzzled by the breeches, never having had to pull a garment up their legs before, but once they were clothed in their European dress they promenaded the deck just as proudly as Ahutoru, similarly outfitted, promenaded the deck of *L'Étoile* later, and when taken ashore they signaled to their friends to carry them through the surf and across the river, to keep their new dress clean and dry.

Then Jonathan disappeared into the trees . . . forever. "What became of this Jolly young fellow afterwards we know not," wrote Robertson, "as we neaver saw nor heard anything more of him."

Another candidate for a Tahitian passenger had been the lad they nicknamed "Jack," the young fellow who had helped Fa'a carry the trade goods across the river. Five days before departure, Wallis noted in his log that the gunner hoped "the Old Man will let his son go with us, as he seems inclined so to do and the Boy very willing." Jack had not been on the beach when they sailed, though, and so he, too, had missed the chance of an adventure.

Tupaia, the most intelligent and learned Tahitian encountered by any of the early English visitors, would have been ideal. There is no record of any such suggestion having been made, however, or of Tupaia displaying any desire to sail on the *Dolphin,* as tempting as the idea of acquiring European guns must have been. The disrespectful treatment he had received from Lieutenant Clarke and George Robertson's rough humor would have deterred him. Nor is there any evidence of him showing any interest in the visit of the *Boudeuse* and the *Étoile*. Despite Tutaha's approach to Bougainville, which surely Tupaia recognized as a political challenge, he and Purea made no attempt to travel to Hitia'a to pay a ceremonial call on the French.

Instead, as Arii Taimai, last chiefess of Papara, recounted, Tupaia, Purea, and Amo remained at Papara, "preparing for the great feast at which

Teri'irere i Tooarai was to wear the Maro for the first time in his great new
Marae at Mahaiatea."

At Papara, Tupaia was making history again.

The construction of a magnificent *marae* on a promontory named Mahaiatea
had begun about four years earlier. It was a huge project, because Purea's
ambition, fully backed by her husband, was to create the greatest temple
compound in all Tahiti for the investment of their son, Teri'irere, with the
red *maro ura,* which, when added to the yellow *maro tea* the head of their
clan wore by right, would proclaim him paramount chief. Not only would
the great *marae* be a fit setting for the coronation, but the event would spec-
tacularly pre-empt Tutaha's ambitions for Tu, the great-nephew for whom he
was serving as regent.

At the beginning of the building project, as hundreds of men arrived to
work as carpenters and masons, hundreds more were given the job of finding food and preparing meals. Stoneworkers spread about the mountains
and beaches collecting suitable rocks, many of which had to be grubbed out
of the deep water of the lagoon. All of these, despite their great size, were
manhandled to the work site. There, most of the boulders were arduously
hammered into square blocks, while a few chosen stones were shaped into
turtles' heads, to be set at regular intervals into the outer wall.

When enough material for the stonework had been collected, the ground
for a great pavement was cleared, and Tupaia, with his retinue of priests,
sprinkled it with seawater in a sanctifying ritual. Next, a cornerstone was
ceremoniously removed from another *marae*, and carried to the site. The
corpse of a man who had been sacrificed by moonlight was laid in the hole
where the foot of the stone would rest, so his spirit would guard the temple
for the rest of time. After that, another stone was set at the corresponding
corner, creating a real, as well as a symbolic, entrance.

Piles of stones were then distributed about the compound, according to
where they were needed. Slowly, according to Tupaia's directions, a great
stepped *ahu*—an elongated pyramid—took shape at one end, over 260 feet
long at the base, and extending seventy feet from front to back. The riser of
each of its eleven great steps was five or six feet, as it was not supposed to
be easy to ascend to the gods. Designed by Tupaia to be precisely aligned to
the axis of the stars Antares (*Ana mua*) and Aldebaran (*Ana muri*), the
eight-foot-wide top was a magnificent viewing platform for the rising and
setting of the Pleiades (*Matari'i*) and the tail of Scorpio (*Te matau o Maui*),
harbingers of the seasons, and crucial for the timing of religious rituals.
Constructed with no metal tools, and with volunteer labor, this giant

edifice would not have looked out of place among the great pyramids of Egypt.

The rest of the complex was paved level, to make an apron-like courtyard, and various slabs, altars, and thatched god houses were gradually added, with more sacrifices at particular phases. The result was awe-inspiring. When the investiture of Teri'irere with the *maro ura* was staged here, the visiting nobles could not fail to be stunned.

Meantime, Tutaha had been gathering supporters to his cause by accusing Purea of delusions of grandeur. It was a justifiable claim, because being treated as a queen would have turned any woman's head. A wily strategist, Tutaha took advantage of family rivalries, too, an important recruit being a woman who was both Amo's niece and great-niece. This was Purahi, whose paternal grandfather was the older brother of Amo's father, and whose mother was his oldest sister. Her claim, on behalf of her own son, was probably a just one, because she had seniority on both sides, but Amo—and Purea—dismissed her arguments as inconsequential. Crucially, however, Purahi was the wife of Vehiatua, an important chief of Taiarapu, the smaller bulge of the island (also called Tahiti Iti). And Vehiatua had a longstanding vendetta with Papara, because their clan had killed his grandfather.

Other family members who harbored a grudge were a sister-in-law of Purea's, Vavea, and Vavea's daughter, Itia. When Purea declared a *rahui* (a ritual ban against the consumption of choice foodstuffs, to conserve them for a coronation feast so lavish it would shame her rivals), first Vavea and then Itia tried to approach Papara, demanding the traditional welcome for important visitors, a procedure that would have broken the *rahui*. Purea turned them away, an intolerable affront, which added to the number of enemies she was driving to Tutaha's side.

Recognizing that the situation had become dangerously precarious, Tupaia urged Purea to have Tutaha assassinated. She spurned his advice, accusing him of callousness. Then, in December 1768, she and Amo fell into a trap of their own making. Their plan was to consolidate their son's claim as *ari'i rahi* of all Tahiti by sending the flag of Oro from *marae* to *marae* in an imperious summons to the coronation feast. By allowing it to pass through his district unimpeded, not only would each chief tacitly accept the invitation, but he would be recognizing Teri'irere's claim.

The flag used on this occasion was a "vane," which, like the pennant, had originally come from the *Dolphin*. A vane was a short tapering flag flown at an empty masthead, colored according to the group the ship belonged to—and in Wallis's case it was red, as the *Dolphin* was his independent command. By flying the vane, not only did Purea arrogantly demand that each and every chief bow down to her son, but she was flaunting her alliance with the powerful British.

Vehiatua was neither impressed nor intimidated. All the other chiefs allowed it a free passage, but when the vane came to Taiarapu, Vehiatua stalked forward, seized the staff from its bearer, tore the flag in pieces, and sent the rags back to Amo.

It was an unbearable insult. Amo declared war at once, expecting to take his enemies by surprise—another mistake, because Vehiatua had an army ready, plus a fleet of war canoes, and Tutaha had a standing force, which attacked from the other direction, the west.

The battle was short, bloody, and brutal. Despite their outwardly peaceable nature, Tahitians were ferocious fighters. Like Vikings, they worked themselves up into a murderous frenzy before the conflict commenced while priests stalked up and down the ranks, exhorting them with shouted incantations. When a warrior felled an enemy, he might beat the body flat, chop a slit through the middle, drop it over his head, and wear the bloody corpse like a *tiputa*. No quarter was given—any prisoners taken alive were delivered to the priests for sacrifice, so everyone fought to the bitter end.

The Paparan army was utterly crushed. The beach where they made their last stand became carpeted with their bones, and cuttlefish lived inside the hundreds of skulls that rolled into the lagoon. Heads of priests and nobles were carried off to join lines of whitened skulls on enemy *marae*. The body of Amo's younger brother, Ma'i, was profaned by cooking it in an oven.

Amo himself, with Purea and their son, escaped to a fortress in the mountains, to cower there while the victors rampaged through their district, slaughtering babies and children, and disemboweling women. There was looting, too—Wallis's gifts were carried off in triumph, and the sacred *maro ura* that had empowered Tupaia was seized.

Tupaia himself was long gone. As soon as Purea spurned his advice to have Tutaha assassinated he made his escape, knowing perfectly well that Tutaha would hear about it—"he, foreseeing the consequences, retired to the mountains, alleging that this retreat was necessary for the preservation of his life," recorded one of the midshipmen of the *Endeavour*, James Magra, after hearing Tupaia's story.

As Magra went on to relate, Tutaha, magnanimous in victory, opted not to take revenge on the man who would have had him privately killed—he, "respecting Tobia's understanding and sacerdotal character, afterward permitted him to return from the mountains in safety." This was Tupaia's carefully rephrased version of what happened. In reality, he changed sides—he joined Tutaha's court, after making a pact with the warrior chief.

His intermediary in this peace process was Purea's older brother, Tupura'a i Tamaita. An *ari'i* of Fa'aa district, in the northwest of Tahiti, who was also known by his title, Tepau Ahurai, Tupura'a was a middle-aged, sensible, good-natured man who had formed an alliance with Tutaha because he disapproved of the imperial ambitions of his sister and her husband.

He was not just Tupaia's negotiator, but his friend. They were together four months later, on April 13, 1769, when the bark *Endeavour* arrived in Matavai Bay. And they were together five days after that, when they both joined the crew of the ship.

CHAPTER 7

❧

The *Endeavour*

On May 18, 1768, seven months before the Paparan War, the *Dolphin* hove to off the port of Hastings, in Kent, to put Captain Wallis on shore. Wallis hired a horse, and rode to the Admiralty with his report, while the ship kept on her homeward course, under the command of Lieutenant Clarke. Early the next morning the ship anchored safely in the Downs (a roadstead in the English Channel, close to Dover), and journalists, scenting a big story, flooded on board.

For the crew, it must have been an intoxicating moment. They had been ordered to keep quiet about their discovery of an island paradise in the tropical Pacific, but when the newspaper writers surrounded them with their notebooks and questions, they could not keep their mouths shut. Not only did they have a grand new word—"tattoo"—to add to the English vocabulary, but they had amazing tales to tell: of bare-breasted, remarkably generous girls; of a country where no one had to work, as food could be plucked off the trees; of chiefs robed like Roman senators; and of an open-hearted island queen.

On May 23, *Lloyd's Evening Post* broke the news that the *Dolphins* had found "a large, fertile, and extremely populous Island" in the South Seas. "From the Behaviour of the Inhabitants, we had Reason to believe she was the first and only Ship they had ever seen," the writer declared, going on to impart the salacious detail that the Tahitian maidens "endeavoured to engage the Attention of our Sailors, by exposing their beauties to their view." The attack on the ship was described, along with the "disagreeable Necessity" of quelling this rebellion with cannon balls and grapeshot, creating such devastation that the islanders "now looked on our People as more than human."

The Tahitians bore no umbrage for the slaughter, because they were intelligent enough to realize "that we had only made use of those dreadful Engines against them when their Rashness had forced us to it." Nor did they seem to resent the appropriation of their country, and its rechristening as "KING GEORGE'S LAND." Much space was devoted to the "Queen," whose husband had been killed in the attack, but who nonetheless became so fond of the interlopers that "the last Thing she did was to take the Crown from her own Head, and present it to Capt. Wallace. It has been carefully preserved, and is to be presented to her Majesty of Great Britain."

Undoubtedly, the men got the same attention in the riverside taverns of Gravesend, when the ship anchored there for the night. From then on, however, everything went rapidly downhill. There was no formal welcome when the *Dolphin* arrived at the Royal Naval Docks in Deptford, and within days the ship was paid off. Captain Wallis was discharged with a £500 gratuity, while his men, on average, received just £24 each.

There was little hope for any of them of finding another job, as there was no war to fight, and merchant shipping had ground to a halt. The glut of seamen since the end of the Seven Years' War in 1763 had led to such intolerable conditions that the crews were rising up in rebellion. On May 5 bands of sailors had boarded the outward-bound ships lying at Deptford, to check the ship's articles for whatever awful rates were being paid to the crews, and then to strike the topmasts, making it impossible for them to sail—the origin of the word "strike." Thousands of sailors were out of work, and armed cutters were patrolling the inner pool of London.

The *Dolphins* wrote a petition begging Wallis to do his best for them. A good-natured man who treated his crews like a father, he carried the paper to Whitehall. He also took along many trophies of the voyage, including the wreaths of Purea's hair and her tufts of sacred feathers, "Instruments for marking their backsides," a drum, a flute, a "Conque," breastplates, a "Bow & Casquette of Arrows," fish and shark hooks, "a stone for bruizing their bread," a fishing net, and some "oars found on Osnaburg Island" (Maitea), plus a great deal of tapa, and a little fishing canoe they had stolen at Nukutavake in the Tuamotus.

All the Admiralty wanted, however, was the paperwork of the voyage, which was going to prove very useful indeed. Because of the precise observations made by the talented purser, John Harrison, the newly promoted Lieutenant James Cook—who, just days earlier, had been given command of a Whitby coal-carrier, bought for discovery purposes and renamed *Endeavour*—now had a precise location to steer for, and a known place for astronomical observations of the transit of the planet Venus across the face of the sun, which was due in June 1769.

The *Dolphins'* petition was of no interest to their Lordships, though they did remark that "it did me great Honour," as Samuel Wallis noted bitterly in his logbook, adding, "and this was all either they or I got by the Voyage but much ill health & fatigue." The men did not give up so easily. Led by Robertson, they petitioned King George for a reward, arguing that the crew of the previous voyage of the *Dolphin*, under Captain Byron, had received additional pay in recognition of the dangers of the voyage. They did not receive an answer until June 24, when they were summoned to Whitehall. "No such encouragement," they were coldly informed, had ever been promised, and Captain Wallis should have told them so. The best that could be offered was "to serve on board the guardships at the different ports."

Little wonder, then, that the old *Dolphins* did their utmost to sign onto the muster roll of the *Endeavour* for another voyage to Tahiti, where they expected to find the kinder patronage of an island queen.

John Gore was one of the lucky four who managed to get a berth. Not only was he shipped, but at last he was a commissioned officer, being listed as the junior lieutenant, next in rank to the senior lieutenant, Zachary Hicks. So, when Gore—now *Mister* Gore—arrived over the gangway of the ship where she lay at Deptford, he made a grand entrance in a blue frockcoat with white lapels and cuffs, white breeches, and cocked hat, which was the smart new uniform of lieutenants in the Royal Navy.

He found not just three, but *four* old shipmates on board, the fourth being Charles Clerke, a high-spirited, adventurous young man (now twenty-five), who had been with him on the first circumnavigation, under Captain Byron, and who had joined the *Endeavour* as a master's mate. Another master's mate was the sociable, lusty Richard Pickersgill, who, despite his age (just nineteen) was considered promising enough to be promoted. The master was yet another *Dolphin* hand, twenty-two-year-old Robert Molineux, while the mathematically minded Frank Wilkinson had re-embarked as an able seaman, though he was soon to be promoted to master's mate, too.

Gore changed his expensive clothes for more workaday gear, to take charge of the deck as the *Endeavour* worked down the Thames to Plymouth, where they lay for nearly two weeks undertaking the last of the preparations, including going over every inch of rope and canvas. It was now that it was brought home to him how different the chunky little 369-ton *Endeavour* was from the greyhoundlike 508-ton *Dolphin*. Even the standard-sized sails had to be made smaller—on August 16 he had to send the square-sails on shore, "to be reduced, being too large at the head for the yards."

It was more than a difference in size, however, for the *Endeavour* was an unusual ship altogether. She had been built as a collier—a virtual floating coal bucket—and originally a cavernous hold had taken up just about all of her bulging hull, save for great beams that ran from side to side about halfway down (bracing her so her sides would not collapse inward), and a couple of little mezzanine-like hanging decks for her crew. The accommodation deck in the stern was the "after fall," where the captain and one or two mates had lived, and the other, toward the bows of the ship, was the "foremost fall," where seven or eight seamen had slept in rough bunks. Back in the days when the collier was the workaday, though grandly named, *Earl of Pembroke*, she had had accommodations for no more than twelve. To become the discovery bark *Endeavour* she had to be made able to house a hundred.

For that reason alone, it was almost unknown for the navy to acquire humble colliers. Despite this, some inspired person in the Admiralty (or maybe even Cook) had seen advantages in her bulky strength, her comparatively shallow draft, her flattish bottom, and her capacity for storing much equipment, plus supplies to last three years. Not only was she a roomy sea-boat, the sturdy, reliable kind of vessel James Cook knew from his apprenticeship on coal-carriers, but her barrel-like shape meant she could be easily hauled up on a beach for repairs to be carried out on her hull before she was floated out again.

The problem was that for her discovery voyage the *Endeavour* had to carry a crew of seventy with their officers, and a squad of marines with their sergeant, in a ship that was just under ninety-eight feet long and slightly less than thirty feet wide at her broadest part. It meant big changes, obviously, and a major fitting out.

To make space for so much and so many, a new deck was built the length of the ship, horizontally dividing the vast hold, using the bracing beams as joists. Nothing could be done about the curved shape of her hull, or the immovable falls decks, which meant that the headroom varied drastically. Directly beneath the forward part of the after fall the ship's twelve marines slept in hammocks that brushed the floor, and had to walk doubled right over, or crouched like frogs.

Traditionally, the officers were much more comfortably off than this—and on the *Endeavour* the newly promoted Gore should have been very comfortable indeed. Rooms had been built for the commissioned officers, surgeon, gunner, and master on either side of the officers' gunroom (now properly a wardroom, as it held no guns), forward of the Great Cabin, and because this area was on the after fall, the ceilings were seven feet high. During the last throes of the fitting out, however, Cook received instructions to prepare to receive "Joseph Banks Esq. and his suite comprising eight persons and their Baggage, bearing them as Supernumeraries for Victuals only." A determined and very rich young man, Banks had not just lobbied relentlessly to be allowed to join the expedition, but had paid good money for the adventure, too, and so of course he wanted the best quarters.

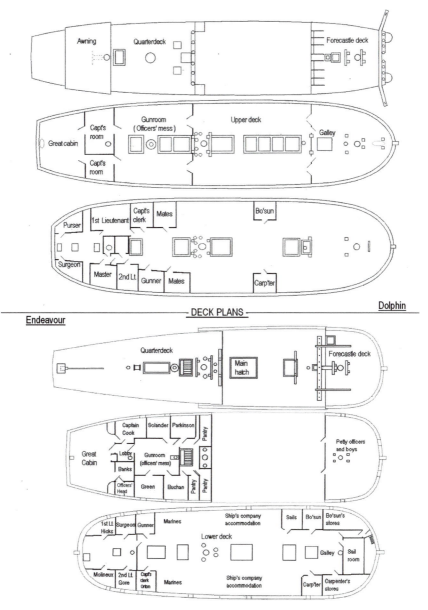

Ship plans, *Dolphin* and *Endeavour*. (Courtesy of Ron Druett)

Accordingly, the officers' rooms were renamed the Gentlemen's Cabins, and refurbished for Banks and his retinue. Gore, like the other rightful occupants of the upper deck cabins, had to move his sea chest. While he and his fellows still dined in the gunroom, they were forced to descend ladders to sleep in hutches off a little stern lobby on the berth deck. Unlike the cabins they had given up, these tiny rooms had no sidelights for sun and air. There were a couple of stern-ports in the lobby, but their cabins were guaranteed to be icily dank off Cape Horn, and stiflingly hot in the tropics. The headroom was a mere four-feet-six, so just moving around was tricky, and when the ship rolled and pitched there was a distinct risk of cracking heads on low beams, reputedly the reason for the high rate of insanity in the navy.

Despite his notoriously short temper, John Gore did not resent being ousted from his rightful quarters, though there was plenty of reason to envy and dislike the rich, arrogant usurper, as they came from such very different backgrounds. Gore, born in Virginia in 1730, and therefore a colonial, was a career seaman who had worked his way up through the ranks, having been sailing since a boy. After his apprenticeship on the Chesapeake Bay, he had joined the Royal Navy at the age of twenty-five, starting out as a midshipman on the *Windsor*, and then, after a spell on the *Bellona*, serving as a master's mate on the *Aeolus*, before starting the first of his circumnavigations under Captain Byron.

Joseph Banks, by contrast, had been born into the lofty merchant class. Though he was not noble, the shrewd business dealings of a series of ancestors had made his family very rich. Also, he was a leading light in the fashionable scientific community, an ardent botanist who had already been on a collecting trip to Newfoundland and Labrador. On the surface of it, they had nothing whatsoever in common. There is no evidence that Gore was interested in plants, and for him, animals were just moving targets. He had no wealthy relatives or important connections. He was also thirteen years older than twenty-six-year-old Banks.

Despite all these differences, over the voyage to Tahiti they became close friends. The developing comradeship must have been partly due to the fact that they were both very strong characters. Gore's resourcefulness and marksmanship had been very useful on the Wallis *Dolphin* voyage—during a month in Tinian on the way home, he had shot wild cattle, providing the ship with so much meat that he signed his journal, "John Gore, Master Hunter"—and Joseph Banks was a keen shooter, too. On the *Endeavour* Gore had unusual power, and Banks was drawn to influential men. Gore was often in charge of the deck. Four of the most important petty officers in the ship were his old shipmates; Gore, with Molineux, Pickersgill, Wilkinson, and Clerke made up a cadre of experienced Pacific hands, all of whom had circled the world before. Gore had made *two* circumnavigations, so knew more about the Pacific than anyone else in the ship—including Cook, who had never sailed in that ocean at all.

So there were several reasons why Banks should engage Gore in conversation. Not only did the American have great stories about America and the plants and animals there; and tales, too, about the many places he had seen, but he could answer countless questions about their destination. On this last count, all four old Tahiti hands were in great demand by the hands on board; and certainly, many colorful tales were told. Tahiti was spectacular, the natives had been tamed, and the fruit and pork were delicious. Most important of all, the young women were beautiful—and reliably generous with their affections. And then there was the charismatic queen . . .

By the time the mountains of Tahiti were glimpsed on the horizon on April 11, 1769, the expectations of all on board had reached a pitch of excitement.

It was cloudy weather, with outbreaks of heavy rain. Not until the sun was low did the dramatic outline become clear, a black tumble of peaks in the mists. At night, the offshore breeze brought evocative smells of damp dirt, fresh water, flowers, and vegetable growth, but when day dawned the ship was not much closer. There was little wind, the air was sultry, and the sea was gray and glassy.

Cook was navigating in the track of Wallis and Bougainville, so the precipitous hills and valleys of the eastern coast of the larger bulge of the island lay ahead. Canoes paddled out, crowded with natives waving plantain shoots and crying, "*Taio*," but though they circled the ship and tossed coconuts to the men who lined the rail, no one would come on board. Not only was the chunky little vessel very different from the *Dolphin* and the French ships they remembered, but marines, muskets shouldered, were lined up alongside gun crews who were standing ready at four-pounder cannon on the deck.

The *Endeavour* crept onward, her sails billowing briefly with every little puff, then flopping as the breeze died. It was not until the next morning that the gap into Matavai Bay was raised, and Gore was able to pilot them into the old anchoring place. Once they were moored dozens of canoes arrived alongside, packed with frond-waving islanders—but they were complete strangers. As Gore wrote, the only recognizable face was that of "the man who first ventur'd amongst the *Dolphin's* people after the skirmish," the one who "was known by the Name of the Old Man."

This, of course, was the long-suffering Fa'a. He clambered on board with confidence, much to the pleasure of Cook, who was keen to set up trading arrangements with the man who had been of such service to the *Dolphins*. A list of rules had already been made up for the crew, exhorting them to treat the natives "with all imaginable humanity," and forbidding them to exchange any "Sort of Iron" for anything but provisions; like Wallis, Cook wanted trade to be strictly regulated, with one man from the ship in charge. While he was trying to establish this with gestures and repeated words, he also asked the old man's name—the first European to trouble to do so. In response to his signs of inquiry, one of Fa'a's companions said, "O Fa'a," meaning "This is Fa'a," so the Tahitians' envoy was called "Owha" from then on.

A landing party was organized. Cook, accompanied by Banks, went in the first boat, with Gore as their guide. Another boat held a squad of marines, who splashed ashore, drew up in lines on the beach, and carried out exercises in the usual fashion, marching up and down, shouldering and presenting rifles, and stamping their boots, while the people gathered at the landing place watched them cautiously, and Gore studied the crowd in return.

He was feeling more perplexed than ever. As he said to Frank Wilkinson later, the throng was entirely composed "of the Meaner sort of Inhabitants." Everyone was half-naked. The men wore plain *maro* breech-clouts and the women wore short *pareu* skirts, and they were all dark-skinned from working in the sun. There were no statuesquely robed chiefs or priests in sight, let alone the famous queen. Everyone here was one of the lower, laboring class.

To find Purea and her court, it seemed, the party had to walk to the *fare hau*, so Gore led the way inland. To his dismay, only a few pillars stood to show where the great hall had been. Instead of the fine houses that had been dotted among the trees, "we found a few temporary huts with a few of the inferior sort of the inhabitants," he wrote, adding somberly, "Many of the Natives seem'd shy of us and but few would come near." As he exclaimed to Wilkinson, it was as if everything had been deliberately demolished.

Cook, who had been relying on the abundance of provisions Wallis had described, was disappointed, too, writing, "not so much as a Hog or Fowl was to be seen–no very agreeable discovery to us whose Ideas of plenty upon arrival at this Island from the report of the *Dolphin* was carried to the very highest pitch." Even the orderly and honest behavior that had followed Wallis's bombardment had lapsed. Next day, the ship was visited by a large number of strangers, and, as Wilkinson indignantly noted, "the Indians Commited Several Thefts in the Most Impident Manner on board."

These "Indians" had come on board with two chiefs, whose dress indicated they were "of a rank superior to those who we had seen yesterday," as Banks deduced. Their names were not given, but they are likely to have been two of Tutaha's courtiers, Nunahau and Tairoa. They were the first Tahitians seen close-up by one of Banks's two draftsmen, Sydney Parkinson, who had been hired to draw natural history specimens. A quiet, shy, twenty-two-year-old Quaker, Parkinson had led a sheltered life, so this was quite an adventure. Impressed, he wrote, "I never beheld statelier men, having a pleasant countenance, large black eyes, black hair and white teeth."

Though the two nobles made eloquent gestures apologizing for the behavior of their men, they were apparently quite unable to stop the stealing. Instead, they took off their tapa cloaks and enfolded Banks and Cook, then urged their new friends to visit their district, Pare Arue. Banks's assistant botanist, Daniel Solander, and Cook's astronomer, Charles Green, decided to come along too, so it was a party of four that boarded a boat with the two chiefs, who directed them to a bay a league or so southwest.

After landing, their guides escorted them through a raucous throng to a splendid longhouse, where a tall and remarkably muscular old chief, surrounded by attendant nobles, was waiting to receive them. Because of his impressive physique, Banks nicknamed him Hercules, but in fact this was Tutaha, the man who had allowed Tupaia to live. Here, in Pare Arue, he was the reigning chief (as regent for his great-nephew, Tu), and Tupaia was one of his courtiers.

Tutaha presented Cook and Banks with lengths of tapa, and Banks gave him a large silk neck cloth, which the *ari'i* immediately tied on. Communication was impossible, so the civilities ended, meaning Joseph Banks was free to explore the surroundings. A lusty fellow in the prime of life, he paid no attention to the pretty, bright-eyed children, or the older women with their enormous breasts and plump, deft hands, being lost in admiration of the graceful, doe-eyed girls, who were not backward in returning the compliment. Like the Frenchmen at Hitia'a, Banks was mischievously offered public sex, but, as he confessed, he was not up to the challenge of making love in houses that were "intirely without walls"—though, as he robustly pointed out, in other circumstances it would have been very different.

Plucked away from this interesting scene, he was ushered with the others to the thatched house of another middle-aged chief, who proved to be a cheerful but dignified fellow with thick, black, frizzy hair, and a beard to match. This was none other than Purea's brother, Tutaha's loyal supporter, and Tupaia's friend, Tupura'a i Tamaita, but no one asked his name. He gave the Englishmen a good meal of fish, then offered the scientist his wife, who was "ugly enough in conscience," muttered Banks, who had his eye on "a very pretty girl with a fire in her eyes."

His program of seduction, which involved lavishing her with every bead and knickknack he had about his person, was rudely brought to a halt when Solander cried out that his pocket had been picked. Everyone hurriedly checked their own pockets, to find that a snuff box and an opera glass were missing. Leaping to his feet, Banks banged the butt of his gun on the ground, and almost all the islanders, including the object of his desire, jumped up and "ran like sheep from the house."

Their host, who was brave enough to stay behind (with his wife, and "two or three better dressd than the rest"), tried to calm Banks by offering him a great deal of tapa. Banks angrily refused, and sat down on a mat, making it plain he would stay there until the missing goods were returned. So Tupura'a went out to find them. He returned triumphant, but the opera glass case proved to be empty, so the poor beleaguered fellow took Banks for a long walk to a hut where they might find a woman who knew the whereabouts of the glass. After some tortuous negotiation it was retrieved (earning Tupura'a the nickname of Lycurgus, a moderately famous Spartan lawyer), and the party returned to the ship.

Next day, a gang of seamen was sent ashore to prepare the ground for a fort, with a squad of marines to keep guard. Captain Cook negotiated with the locals for the use of a piece of land, with Fa'a and "one who appear'd to be a Chief," (as Cook phrased it) as his intermediaries. By the time a suitable site had been chosen and paced out, and the first tent pitched, it was too late to do much more, so the work party returned on board. Cook, Banks, Parkinson, Hicks, and Green went for a stroll in the woods with Fa'a as their guide, leaving nineteen-year-old Midshipman Jonathan Munkhouse and thirteen marines to guard the tent.

About two hours later, Gore, who was in charge of the watch on deck, heard gunshots, shouts, and the sound of running feet. He immediately ordered a boat manned with armed sailors, and sent it ashore "to Assist in case of need." At the same time Cook and his companions rushed back to the beach, to find the terrified natives fleeing in all directions, with the marines in hot pursuit. Wrote Parkinson, "A centinel being off his guard, one of the natives snatched a musket out of his hand, which occasioned the fray." The midshipman, losing his head, had ordered the marines to fire into the thick of the crowd, and "they obeyed with the greatest glee imaginable, as if they had been shooting at wild ducks." Several had been wounded, the thief had been shot dead, and all to no effect, as the musket was gone.

Back on board, the atmosphere was grim. Everyone was acutely aware that this awful and unnecessary execution had cost their budding alliance with the locals. Banks had persuaded some of the natives to return to the tent, where Cook had done his best to convey that though the crime deserved the punishment of death, the *Endeavours* still wanted to be friends, but the message was too complicated. Next day no canoes came out to the ship, and there was almost no one on the beach. Trust had been eroded on the English side, too.

The *Endeavour* was warped nearer the shore, so the guns covered the ground where the encampment was built.

Another crisis followed. At two in the morning of April 17, Banks's landscape painter, Alexander Buchan, died after collapsing in an epileptic fit. A well-liked and talented young Scotsman, he was going to be sadly missed, particularly by his employer, who was now reduced to one draftsman, Parkinson. More immediate was the problem of what to do with Buchan's body, as burying him on shore was all too likely to violate unknown local laws, and upset the Tahitians still further. So the corpse was stowed into a boat that was rowed well offshore, and Buchan was hurriedly interred at sea.

About noon, matters took an upturn. Tutaha arrived at the side of the ship with a retinue that included Tupaia, Tupura'a i Tamaita, Tairoa, and Nunahau. He obviously hoped to make peace, though was scared enough to approach with caution. His attendants were carrying two hogs and some roasted breadfruit, and plantain shoots were placed on the deck before they would come aboard.

Naturally, the ambassadors were welcomed with relief. After the nobles had been presented with hatchets, they were ceremoniously ushered into the Great Cabin, where Cook was busy, because it was the time of day when he posted the events of the past twenty-four hours in his log. This day, he also had to register Buchan's death in the big, brown muster table book, which was the roll of the ship's complement. Next to the draftsman's name on the register he had written, "DD 17 April 1769 Georges Island S^th Seas"—"DD" meaning "Discharged Dead." Then, for the next entry, he had headed up the date "18 April," because on official shipboard documents the day's date changed at noon. Alexander Buchan's place needed to be filled to make up the required complement and keep the record straight, so he had written in the name "Nich^as Young," Nicholas Young being one of the boys who had been brought on board by the officers. They lived with the tradesmen of the ship (like the sailmaker), so they could learn a useful career at sea, and in times of war were useful as powder monkeys, lugging bags of gunpowder from the magazine to the guns. Now, having recently turned 12, Nick Young was old enough to become an official part of the crew.

That the muster book was so handy gave Cook an opportunity to take instant advantage of Tutaha's step toward reconciliation. Temporary additions to the crew (such as pilots in foreign ports) were noted here, too—and somehow, probably with the help of Tupaia (who had learned some English during negotiations with the *Dolphins*), Cook made Tutaha understand that he wanted to ship four Tahitians as "Supernumeraries for Victuals." This meant that in return for temporarily joining the crew, and getting a share of the ship's provisions, they would help him re-establish friendly relations with the locals.

And the men he wanted to ship were Tairoa, Nunahau, Tupura'a i Tamaita, and Tupaia.

James Cook. Engraving by H. B. Hall's Sons,
New York, after a painting by Nathaniel Dance.
(Courtesy of the Alexander Turnbull Library,
Wellington, A-217-001)

It must have taken a while to get the suspicious Tutaha to agree, but eventually Cook turned back to the muster book, and listed "Terrea," "Nunahoe," and "Tobia Tomita" (his approximations of Tairoa, Nunahau, and Tupura'a i Tamaita) below Nicholas Young's name. Then he bracketed them together as "Guides for the interior Parts of the Island & Pilots for the Coast & to assist in forming connections with the other Natives." On the next two lines he wrote, "Tupia, Native of Polinesia," and "Tarheto, his S^t."—Taiata being a boy about ten years old who was Tupaia's acolyte (not servant, as Cook assumed), and also a close family member, probably his nephew.

What these men with no heritage of written language thought of seeing their names recorded for the first time in Tahitian history (or if they even truly understood what was happening), is, of course, unknown. Tupaia, however, was as quick to understand what this foreigner wanted as he had been the day Wallis hailed Purea as the queen, and commenced to play his role with the same efficiency.

From that day onward the Tahitians brought so much fruit to market that Banks (who had been put in charge of the trading tent) was overwhelmed. As James Cook noted at noon next day, though hogs remained scarce, "as to Bread fruit Cocoa-nuts and Plaintains the Natives supply us with as much as we can distroy."

CHAPTER 8

❦

Recognizing Tupaia

Throughout this confused beginning, not one of the four old *Dolphins* pointed to Tupaia as a face from the past. This may have been because he was in the wrong setting. They had been accustomed to seeing him standing apart from the rest, with the woman they regarded as queen, and now Tupaia was just one of many, merging unnoticeably into the throng of chiefs. And, though Tupaia himself surely recognized old acquaintances, he was probably too proud to go up to an ex-*Dolphin* and remind him of his identity, because of the great change in his status.

Buchan being dead, Sydney Parkinson had been given the extra job of drawing people from life, and so he sketched the heads of several Tahitians. They were not identified, so it is impossible to tell if he drew Tupaia. He painted out in the open (though under a mosquito net, because the flies enjoyed eating the paint), and always had a crowd of enraptured onlookers. They called him "Patini," their adaptation of his name, and he returned their affection, describing them in general terms as a "merry, facetious, hospitable people," with lively black eyes, and black hair that was often frizzy—which was probably a word-picture of Tupaia, too. Only the shaven chin of a priest would have set him apart from the rest of the tall, muscular, white-robed men, who sported short, square, Egyptian-style beards (though they all plucked off their "mustachios," as Parkinson called moustaches).

The *Dolphins* had also known Tupaia as one of the most powerful men in the land. Now, though he still had the dress and bearing of a noble, his place in Tahitian society was precarious. A few days after joining the complement of the *Endeavour*, he was eating dinner with Banks and his retinue in Banks's big marquee when someone noticed he did not like the dish of the day, pork pie. Remembering that a cuttlefish had just been delivered, one of the party sent for it, knowing it was a Tahitian delicacy. According to Parkinson, no sooner had the squid arrived on the table than Tupura'a i Tamaita strolled up and calmly appropriated it. He ate almost all of the cuttlefish, then had the leftovers packed into coconut shells, and sent to his house. For Tupaia, who sat silent and hungry, it was a humiliation that certainly would not have happened two years before.

The most likely reason the *Dolphins* did not recognize him, though, was that they were too busy to pay attention. The same day Tupaia's name was added to the crew list, Frank Wilkinson recorded, "Most of the People Emp[d] on shore." Gore, when he was not in charge of the deck, had his old job of taking out wooding parties, where he bought trees from their owners just as he had in his *Dolphin* days. Molineux was in charge of breaking out equipment and stores and sending them on shore. Wilkinson and Pickersgill, when not at work on the ship, were busy at the encampment, which Cook called Fort Venus. The ground had to be cleared and the tents pitched, then a breastwork built, with old barrels as a foundation. After that, pickets were cut for fences, and the ship's swivel guns were hauled on shore, and mounted on the corners of the surrounding wall. The oven was boated across the lagoon, while at the same time the scientifics' furniture was moved to the tents, along with crates of astronomical instruments.

There were other distractions. "Individuals form Freindships with Individuals & every man has his Tayo (or Friend)," wrote Robert Molineux on April 22, adding thoughtfully, "this might be productive of good Consequences but the women begin to have a share in our Friendship which is by no means Platonick." He was just as susceptible as his fellow officers, Solander gossiping later that Molineux's mistress (whose real name was Tiare) was nicknamed "Mrs. Boba" by the islanders, after his first name, Robert. John Gore's woman was "Mrs. Toaro," as it was impossible for the Tahitians to pronounce the letters J and G. Likewise, Tuarua, the favorite of the astronomer, Charles Green, was "Mrs. Eteree," while Charles Clerke's mistress was "Mrs. Tate," the letter C being problematical, too. The seamen found their own mistresses, Frank Wilkinson writing on April 25 that "we find the women of this Island to be very Kind in all Respects as Usal when we were here in the Dolphin."

Considering that the *Dolphins* had been so wrong about the abundant hogs, it must have been a relief that their stories of affectionate girls proved to be true. The queen, however, was still invisible. On April 23 (when Banks was on an excursion into the foothills with Solander, Green, Tupura'a, and also, most probably, Tupaia), Molineux, seeing "A great Concourse" of islanders at the gate of the fort, "look'd out diligently for some of my old

Acquaintance," but he could see only three: "an Elderly man with his Son whom we had dress'd & christen'd Jack," and a girl about nineteen. "With these I was very Happy," he wrote, "but still I could hear no news of the Queen."

Purea was not far away. After she, Amo, and their son, Teri'irere, had escaped from the ravages of the Paparan war, they had traveled through the mountains to take refuge with Amo's cousin, an *ari'i* of nearby Haapape district. Though she must have been watching events with intense interest, she had not come forward, the great change in her status having made her uncharacteristically shy. This time, too, she did not have her wise advisor to guide her. She made amends for this—once it became apparent that her ex-lover was the *taio* of this new set of foreigners, she sought him out and made friends with him again. So, when Molineux finally found his queen, she was with Tupaia, just as she had been in the past.

It was April 28, the first day the master had had a chance for a leisurely walk. There was a crowd inside the scientists' marquee, so he went inside to see what was happening—and there, at last, was the queen. Molineux was overjoyed to see her, and when she remembered him, Purea was equally happy. "Before I landed," he wrote, "the Gentleman seeing her a Principal woman by her dress attendance & other marks of Distinction had solicited her strongly to go on board," but even though Tupaia was there, Purea had diffidently declined. Having one of the Europeans hail her as the queen made all the difference—just like old times, she "Express'd a desire of going on Board."

Molineux was delighted to comply. "Gladly Conducted Her with one man only whom she call'd Tobia," he wrote, so at last he learned Tupaia's name. The officer of the watch was Gore, who recognized her at once, and "who Tobia knew Immediately." Wilkinson, who was working on board, saw her, too, and was pleased to report that she "Remembered Several of our faces that was here before."

Molineux and Gore ushered the visitors to the Great Cabin, where Cook enchanted Purea with a gift of a doll. The next two hours were spent touring the ship—"as she had formerly done the Dolphin," wrote Molineux. The many differences from the bigger, more ornate frigate must have surprised Purea, and set off quite a conversation with Tupaia as they progressed from one end to the other. The forecastle deck was furnished with a novel windlass ornamented with two large, carved heads, and the Great Cabin was not the grand place she remembered. The gunroom had no guns, and the much smaller quarterdeck did not even have an awning.

Molineux was to have a surprise of his own when he escorted Tupaia and the queen on shore. The queen, blithely assumed by the *Dolphins* to be a widow, "was receiv'd by her Husband & Attendants." For the first time,

Molineux found out her name, writing, "I now learn'd that her name was Oborea & that of her Husband Owaamoo." When Cook asked, Tupaia gestured at the queen and said, "*O Purea*"—"This is Purea"—which the Europeans heard as Oborea.

Though Cook was as intrigued as anyone by the sudden reappearance of "the Woman called by the Dolphin the Queen of this Island," her arrival was a complication, as he much preferred to deal with a single native monarch. The class system on Tahiti seemed to suggest that such a person existed: as the surgeon, William Munkhouse, meditated, "We have no doubt of its being of a feudal nature." This suited the British, who came from a highly stratified society themselves, and in the absence of the *Dolphins'* queen they had decided that the paramount chief—the *ari'i rahi*—was Tutaha. Not only was he the most distinguished, powerful, and mighty of all the *ari'i* they had met, but he had been observed collecting tribute from the others. "All these circumstances therefore inclined us," wrote Munkhouse, "to adopt the notion that he was King of Kings of this Isle."

So, should Cook be dealing with Purea instead? Certainly not, Tupaia communicated, at the same time managing to convey quite a lot of information, as a testament to his rapidly improving English. As Molineux recorded, since the departure of the *Dolphin*, "there has been an Invasion on this Part of the Island by which means Owaamoo & Oborea have been disposses'd of part of their Lands." The result, Cook concluded, was that "she is head or Chief of her own Family or Tribe but to all appearance hath no authority over the rest of the Inhabitants whatever she might have had when the Dolphin was here."

So, as far as the *Endeavours* were concerned, Tutaha was still the islanders' monarch. Purea had not lost her sense of theater, though. She led the way to her canoe to collect a hog and several bunches of plantains, which were paraded to the fort by a procession of attendants, with herself and Cook bringing up the rear. Naturally, Tutaha was not at all pleased, and particularly envied Purea that interesting doll: "but I soon put him into a good humor by takeing him on board and making him some presents," wrote Cook.

Given his own doll, the battle-seasoned warrior went away happy.

Having finally remembered Tupaia, the old *Dolphins* identified him as the queen's lover, or "Obereah's favourite," as Sydney Parkinson phrased it. They were quickly proved to be wrong in that, as well. The very next day Joseph Banks, fascinated by the sudden reappearance of the fabled queen, decided to "pay a visit to her majesty *Oborea*" at her double canoe. He was told she was asleep under the awning, but when he stepped inside he discovered her *in flagrante* "with a hansome lusty young man of about 25 whose name was *Obadée*." Purea was not at all embarrassed, simply rising naked as Venus "to put on her breeches," at the same time indicating that her companion (whose real name was Pati) was her latest gallant.

This interesting development meant that Tupaia's status was more enigmatic than ever. Even though the Englishmen had no idea that it had been Tutaha (with Vehiatua) who had violently dispossessed Purea and her husband, it must have seemed strange that Tupaia, who had been Purea's chief minister, was now a member of Tutaha's court, though still recognized as the high priest of the island. There was little time to think about it, however, as another crisis developed. At nine in the morning of May 2, Cook and Green went to the fort to set up the quadrant for celestial observations—and found the box empty. Some nimble-fingered Tahitian had managed to make off with the heavy instrument even though an armed sentinel had been standing less than fifteen feet away. It was a triumph of legerdemain for the thief, and a disaster for Cook and his astronomer.

Cook immediately issued orders that all the large canoes in the bay were to be confiscated, and the principal chiefs held hostage until the quadrant was returned. Purea was the only principal chief within reach, however, so Cook rescinded the second order before he went to meet Banks and Green, who had gone to fetch the missing instrument, retrieved by the ever-helpful Tupura'a, who had managed to collect a few other missing items at the same time, such as Banks's reading glasses. They arrived back in a group, to find that Tutaha had been taken captive despite the amended instructions. The quick-tempered Gore had exceeded Cook's orders by sending the boatswain to seize some canoes going along the shore, and Tutaha had been on board of one of them.

Lieutenant Hicks had confined the chief in a tent, and the whole bay was in a ferment of distress. As Banks testified, they could hear the general wailing two miles away. "The Scene between Tobia tomita and Tootaha, when the former came into the Fort and found the latter in custody, was realy moveing," wrote Cook; "they wept over each other for some time." Tutaha was released, and stalked off "sulky enough," as Banks described, "tho at his departure he presented us with a pig."

Over the next few days the fort was shunned by all the islanders except a few staunch friends. Even Tupaia was suspicious enough to check his old mistress's canoe for malicious damage: "*Tubia* (Oberea's right hand man who was with her in the Dolphins time) came and overhauld every part of her canoe," wrote Banks. Conscious of his responsibilities as an official intermediary, though, Tupaia remained loyal to the *Endeavour*s, Banks writing that "Tupia stayd with us all day and at night slept in Oboreas Canoe." He did not sleep alone. Banks, perhaps enviously (his flame with the sparkling eyes being among the missing), noted that Tupaia was "not without a bedfellow tho the gentleman cannot be less than 45." Tupaia's "dolly," as Daniel Solander called her, was a young woman by the name of Apupu.

Tutaha, meantime, had sent one of his servants with a demand for an ax and a shirt, evidently in exchange for the pig he had presented after being released. Cook refused, maintaining the old chief should come for them himself, with the result that it became impossible to get provisions. No fruit was delivered, and when a boat was sent along the shore to find trade there, Dr. Munkhouse recorded that "the people would not part with any Hogs, but said they belonged to Tootaha." By May 4, the situation was desperate, and Banks was forced to go to Tupura'a i Tamaita to beg for some breadfruit. Tutaha sent again for the ax and shirt, and Cook gave in, promising to deliver them personally in the morning.

Early next day, Tutaha sent attendants to remind him, and Cook boarded the pinnace with Solander and Banks. It must have taken some courage, as the few islanders they had met over the past three days had complained bitterly of the ill-usage of their chief, and no one had any idea of what kind of reception awaited. At Pare Arue they found a horde waiting at the landing place. The moment they set foot ashore they were closely surrounded, the crowd all shouting, "*Taio Tutaha!*"—"Tutaha is your friend!" Lacking Purea's gift for silencing a multitude with an imperious wave, Tutaha sent a policeman in a large turban, who beat the crowd back with a long white stick, and the three *Endeavours* gradually made their way to where Tutaha was sitting under a tree within a circle of old men.

Inspired by either Tupaia's advice, or reading Wallis's journal, Cook presented Tutaha with a blue mantle—"an upper garment made of Broad Cloth after their fashion"—as well as the shirt and the ax. Mollified, Tutaha invited the party to a display of "Publick Wrestling," and Purea materialized to lead them there. The arena proved to be a large courtyard, railed around with a bamboo fence, with a longhouse at one end that was open at the front. The gladiators came out one by one, to challenge the spectators by slapping their left arms. The response was to step forward and wag the elbows, at which combat commenced, both men grappling each other and straining. A single fall decided the victory, and led to another quest for an opponent.

At the end of two hours of this repetitive spectacle, Cook was given to understand that they were to follow Tutaha, who would treat them to a good dinner. The hungry Englishmen obeyed with alacrity, but, mystifyingly, the chief led them to their own boat. Then a small pig arrived, hot and savory from the earth oven. The *Endeavours* thought this was very civil, as it meant they could eat in privacy instead of within an overpowering crowd, but just as they were sharpening their knives Tutaha informed them he was coming with them to the ship, and they would eat the pig there.

Though Cook and Banks did not know it, this was a deliberate act of discourtesy, and a demonstration by Tutaha to his people of his power over the foreigners. The *Endeavours*, denied traditional hospitality, were forced to wait for their dinner, Banks commenting sourly that it was not pleasant to row "4 miles with the pig growing cold under our noses." Once on board, too, they had to watch a great deal of the succulent meat disappear into Tutaha's mouth, as "his majesty eat very heartily with us."

It worked out well in the end, however. When they went back to shore, it was to find that the sight of Tutaha "reconcild to us acted like a charm upon the people and before night bread fruit and cocoa nuts were brought to sell in tolerable plenty." For the moment, the Tahitians and the *Endeavours* were at peace.

On May 9, there was yet more evidence that Tupaia and Purea were back on friendly terms. Banks recorded that "Oborea," her swain "Obadee," and Tupaia arrived soon after breakfast with a hog and some breadfruit, plus the announcement that they were sailing off in her double canoe for three days. At dawn on the 12th Tupaia returned as promised, to take up his usual role as Banks' go-between at the trading tent—which was very fortunate for the scientist, as a double canoe arrived with two men and several women the *Endeavours* had never seen before, and an unfamiliar ritual commenced.

The first man stepped forward with a small bunch of feathers and six leafy branches, which he presented to Banks one by one—"*Tupia* who stood by me acted as my deputy in receiving them and laying them down." Presumably Tupaia was not as surprised as Banks at what happened next. The second man, who was holding nine pieces of tapa, laid down three of them, and a woman stepped onto these, lifted her garments to expose her lower half, and turned slowly around, giving the openmouthed young man "a most convenient opportunity" of admiring her naked buttocks. She stepped back and dropped her *pareu*, and three more pieces were laid, allowing her to repeat the ceremony—"the other three were then laid which made a treble covering of the ground between her and me, she then once more displayd her naked beauties," as Banks went on to relate. Deliberately, she stepped right up to him. The man followed her, picking up the cloth and folding the pieces, and the woman indicated that Banks was to accept the package of fabric as a present.

Joseph Banks. Engraving by J. R. Smith,
after a painting by Benjamin West.
(Courtesy of the Alexander Turnbull
Library, Wellington, C-017-01)

Presumably Banks handed the tapa over to Tupaia, as his mind was on
other things. Highly aroused, he took the young woman by the hand and
led her to his tent, followed by one of her female friends, "but could not
prevail on them to stay more than an hour." What happened during that
hour was left to his reader's imagination.

Purea, who had become tired of Pati, had her own eye on the handsome
and lusty young scientist. As Banks wrote, "I am if I please to supply his
place." He turned down this gracious offer, but Purea had better luck during
a chaotic episode a couple of weeks later.

This was on May 28, when a large party, including Tupaia, accompanied
Banks, Cook, and Solander on an overland trek to pay a call on Tutaha, who
had moved his residence some miles away, to Atehuru. They arrived in the evening, to find the old chief holding court under a tree, and night fell before the
civilities were over, forcing them "to look out for lodgings," as Banks put it.
Tutaha, as uncivil as ever, was not forthcoming with hospitality, so Purea
promptly offered Banks a bed in the awning of her double canoe, which he as
promptly accepted, after stripping himself, "as the night was hot."

Purea promised that his clothes would be well looked after, but when Banks woke in the middle of the night and groped around, it was to find he had lost his waistcoat and jacket, the latter being a fancy white one with silver frogs, surely the strangest of garments to wear on a hike about a tropical isle. Worse still, the pistols that had been in the pockets were gone, too, along with their powder and shot. "I wakd Oborea," he wrote. She got up and roused Tutaha, who was sleeping in the next canoe, and both chiefs went off, theoretically in search of the missing articles. Tupaia arrived, disturbed by the hubbub, so Banks gave him his musket, which, unlike his pistols, powder, and shot, had not been stolen. Then, just as Banks was taking refuge under the tapa sheet again, music started up nearby, accompanied by lights. It sounded like a party, so Banks pulled on his breeches and went to investigate, and blundered into Cook, who was hunting for his own stolen items of clothing.

James Cook was both mystified and furious. "I had my stockings taken from under my head and yet I am certain that I was not a Sleep the whole time," he complained. He was convinced that Purea and Tutaha were up to mischief, especially as the party was being staged in the hut where he and three others were trying to get some sleep—"Tootaha came to the Hutt where I and those with me lay and entertain'd us with a consort of Musick, consisting of three Drums four Flutes and singing," he penned. Ninety minutes of rhythm, piping, and song later, the musicians finally packed up and went, and still the missing articles had not been returned.

Purea rose at daybreak, as was the Tahitian custom, so Banks got up too. "Tupia was the first man I saw," he wrote, "standing with my Musquet and the remainder of my cloaths, his faith had often been tried, and on this occasion it shone very much." Purea gave Banks a *tiputa* in lieu of the lost jacket, "so that I made a motley appearance, my dress being half English and half Indian." The only *Endeavour* who escaped with his possessions intact was Dr. Solander, who had slept with a friendly family about a mile away, so Banks, like Cook, harbored dark suspicions of their hosts. Had Purea distracted him with her voluptuous hospitality while the coat and waistcoat were filched? It seemed very likely, the pistols alone being a valuable prize.

Cook and Banks spent the morning endeavoring to persuade Tutaha and Purea to organize a more serious search for the lost goods, but were forced to give up and go home, "dissatisfied enough with our expedition," as Banks grumbled. The only bright spot in the day was the sight of islanders cavorting in a wicked surf, pushing the stern of an old canoe out beyond the breakers, and then riding it like daredevils back to the beach.

Though Cook, Solander, and Banks did not know it, they were the first westerners to watch the sport of surfing.

On June 3 the persistently rainy weather cleared, just in time for their observation of the transit of Venus, which was part of an international scientific effort to find the distance between the sun and the Earth. To get a wide range of figures, Captain Cook ordered a number of telescopes set up in different areas. Banks, with Gore, Munkhouse, and Banks's clerk, Herman Spöring, took the ship's longboat to the offshore island of Moorea to make observations there, accompanied by a number of chiefs in double canoes.

Within an hour the "king" of the island arrived, with his sister. Banks stepped forward to receive them, and ushered them to the comfortable spot he had cleared under a tree. As a hospitable gesture, he unwound the length of tapa he wore as a turban, spread it on the ground, and beckoned to them to take their ease. What they thought about being invited to sit on something so closely connected with his sacred head is unknown, but surely they were very surprised. They were polite enough not to betray it, however, presenting him with a hog, a dog, and a quantity of fruit. Banks gave them an adze, a shirt, and some beads, and then, like Robertson, he showed them the sun through the telescope, but without playing any cruel tricks.

His gallantry was rewarded in the most delightful way possible. Soon after he arrived at his tent, he found to his pleasure that three pretty girls who had admired him from the midst of the king's crowd of attendants had followed. All three were easily persuaded to stay the night, "a proof of confidence which I have not before met with upon so short an acquaintance."

The next day, June 4, was the birthday of King George III, but as the scientists and officers were still straggling in from the various observation posts, the celebration was put off for twenty-four hours. Then they did it in style—"several of the Indians din'd with us," wrote Banks, "and drank his majesties health." Old *Dolphin* Molineux, who had certainly never seen the staid (and sick) Captain Wallis stage anything like this, was most impressed—"the Captain gave an Entertainment to all the officers & Gentlemen on Board in one of the Ships Tents fitted for that purpose," he wrote. The guest list included "many of the Principal Inhabitants," who "drank all the Royal Healths & behav'd as well as the most civiliz'd People could do."

What the Tahitian chiefs made of this toasting in wine was unrecorded—except for Tupaia's enthusiasm. To show his loyalty, as his friend Banks put it, he "got most enormously drunk." Whether Tupaia was pretending to be intoxicated in imitation of what he saw around him, or whether he felt dreadful the next day is unknown, but he was never recorded drinking alcohol again. Banks noted later that those natives who became drunk "seemd far from pleasd with their intoxication," and shunned wine and liquor from then on.

Cook was too preoccupied to make much note of the birthday celebrations, as information had been trickling in about two European ships that had dropped anchor on the east coast of the island the previous year. The commander, he was told, was called *Toottera* by the natives; the brother of chief Reti had gone away with them, and—most importantly—it may have been these ships that brought "the Venerial distemper" to the island. This was of great concern to Cook, not just because so many of the *Endeavour* seamen had caught some form of VD, but because it augured so badly for the Pacific peoples. In time, as he said, it would spread all over the islands, "to the eternal reproach of those who had first brought it among them."

So who were the culprits, the *Dolphins* or seamen from the two unknown European ships? Wallis had sworn that none of his sailors were infected when the *Dolphin* arrived at the island, and James Cook thought he could say the same about the *Endeavour*, writing, "I had taken the greatest pains to discover if any of the Ships Company had the disorder upon him for above a month before our arrival here." To this end, he had instructed the surgeon to check every man, and certify him free of the disease before landing. What he, Dr. Munkhouse, and Wallis did not realize was that venereal disease, syphilis in particular, was infectious long after the symptoms had disappeared and the patient had been pronounced cured. The muster roll of the *Dolphin* reveals, for instance, that Francis Pinkney, the man who ran the gauntlet, was treated for venereal disease early in the voyage. Ignorant of this, and ready to believe Wallis's vow, Cook was happy to lay the blame on the unknown ships.

But what ships were they? Banks and Cook showed Tupura'a i Tamaita a colored print of the flags of all nations, and when they finally made him understand they wanted to know which flag the ships at Hitia'a had been flying, "he at once pitched on the Spanish Flag," and was positive about it. The French and Spanish flags were both based on a white ground, but were not at all alike, the French flag being as white as a tablecloth, with no device at all, while the Spanish had a large escutcheon in the middle, emblazoned with the arms of the Bourbon-Anjou dynasty.

So all this proved was that Tupura'a had not visited Hitia'a when Bougainville was there, and was merely trying to be his usual helpful self, but many months passed before the two Englishmen learned the truth.

Tupura'a was too busy to put serious thought to the identification of the two mysterious vessels. A noblewoman related to his wife had died, and he had a position of responsibility in the mourning rituals. The body was placed on a shaded platform, surrounded by portions of food so that the spirits would have something to feed on other than the departed, and the women held a wake in which they struck their heads with shark-tooth-tipped instruments until they bled, then staunched the blood with pieces of tapa, which were thrown as offerings under the bier. Tupura'a's job, as chief mourner, was to carry out a spirit-scaring rite. Banks had begged to take part in this, and Tupura'a had given his consent, for the very good reason that having a European with them would allow the chief mourner's procession to pass by the fort.

For his role, Banks had to strip naked, bind his loins with a *maro* to package his private parts, and smear himself liberally with black candlenut grease. Tupura'a himself donned a "most Fantastical costume," metamorphosing into a tall, anonymous, tapa-swathed figure with a big pearl-shell mask, a round pearl-shell headdress, and a canoe-shaped breastplate of glaring pearl-shell "eyes." The apron hanging from the breastplate glittered with thousands of pearl-shell pendants that swished back and forth, and his shining round headdress shimmered with a halo of long, thin, quivering feathers. Light bounced off him from every direction. In one hand, Tupura'a carried a pair of pearl-shell clappers, and in the other a spear edged with sharks' teeth.

Because Banks was so fascinated with this exotic figure, Tupaia sketched the chief mourner's costume for him, a drawing that Banks "annexd" to his later description of the mourning ritual. Though primitive, it is not naïve—the work conveys a huge amount of information, suggesting that Tupaia drew it to demonstrate the different parts. It is also compelling—the viewer gets such a vivid impression of the strength of the man wearing the costume that it is unsurprising that the creator, when anonymous, was known as "The Artist of the Chief Mourner." That it is painted in color is interesting, too, as watercolors were so expensive and scarce that Banks had given instructions they should only be used for natural history paintings, which means that Tupaia either had privileged access to art materials, or painted it with tapa dyes. It is also noteworthy that Tupaia drew the figure on the far right-hand side of his piece of paper, as it is a strong hint he was left-handed, as right-handed people start naturally on the left, to save smudging their work.

Tupura'a set the ceremony into motion by praying near the corpse. Then he led his grotesque procession of imp-like attendants, including Banks, to the fort, "to the surprize of our friends and affright of the Indians who were there, for they every where fly before the *Heiva* like sheep before a wolf." Having chased them away, they darted to another group, dispersing them likewise. The next dozen houses they passed had been hurriedly vacated, so

Heiva **dancer and costume of the chief mourner. Watercolor by Tupaia. (© The British Library Board, 15508/9)**

the chief mourner declared the ceremony over, and Banks spent the next hour or more in the river, trying to scrub off the grease.

Because of his close friendship with Tupura'a and Tupaia, the attractiveness of his large frame and handsome face, and the dash and flamboyance of his nature, Banks was helping in no small measure to cement a strong relationship between the *Endeavours* and the Tahitians. With Tupaia as his friend and counselor, he was able to step aside from the formality of Tutaha's court, and meet ordinary people in everyday settings. Once, he wangled an invitation to a concert, where the band consisted of two flutes and three drummers who sang as they rattled out the beat. The songs were in praise of the *Endeavours*—or so Banks was told. In response, he and some shipmates sang an English song, which received rapturous applause, "so much so that one of the musicians became desirous of going to England to learn to sing."

Apparently for fun, Tupaia drew the musicians (though he included only two of the drummers). Though much sketchier than the mourner's costume, the drawing is so energetic the music can almost be heard. In the frozen instant of action Tupaia captured, the eyes of the musicians are turned to him, so that an impression of emotion is caught, too. They seem nervous, as

Tahitian musicians. Watercolor by Tupaia. (© The British Library Board, 15508/11)

if they wonder why the high priest—a man who could easily be terri-fying—is drawing their picture, and what he intends to do with it. For them, perhaps, the sketch did not seem as casual as intended.

Though apparently idle, this drawing is a gift to posterity, providing a rare glimpse of daily life in ancient Tahiti. Making informal pictures of people had been the job of Alexander Buchan, whose surviving paintings of Tierra del Fuego, at the southern tip of South America, have an appealing sponta-neity. After Buchan died, young Parkinson was expected to draw this kind of scene, as well as produce the hundreds of natural history paintings he had been hired to create. It was not his style, however; his training had not prepared him for it. Apart from a charming sketch of Taiata playing the nose-flute, he drew nothing to show men and women going about ordinary activities. Instead, his portraits are stiffly posed, and his group scenes formal enough to feature in a carved frieze. This meant there was no one to create trivial (yet historically important) sketches of ordinary people at their daily activities—until Tupaia picked up a pencil at a concert.

CHAPTER 9

❦

Tupaia's Mythology

No te rahu a Ta'aroa i riro ai te iho o te fenua ei fenua
Riro atu ra Havai'i ei fenua no te rahu o Ta'aroa
A oriori Ta'aroa i te iho o te fenua
Uene iho ra o Ta'aroa i te fenua, a aita i 'aueue a'e.
It was the incantations of Ta'aroa that made the substance of the land
Hawaiki became land by Ta'aroa's incantations
Then Ta'aroa moulded the substance of the land
And Ta'aroa shook the land, and it yielded not.
— *Tahitian Creation Chant*

On June 14, there was yet another disruption—a native stole an oven rake, and Captain Cook lost his temper. The response was far out of proportion to the crime. Wrote Molineux, "the Captain order'd all the largest Sailing Canoes to be seiz'd & Haul'd up the River behind the Fort & there detain'd till Restitution was made." By noon, the rake was back, but that was not good enough. James Cook was resolved to keep the canoes until such time as "the Marine Musquet," plus "a pair of pistols belonging to Mr. Banks, a sword belonging to one of the Petty officers and a water cask" were retrieved, because he was still convinced Tutaha and Purea were behind the thefts.

There was also the matter of redress for "the insolent treatment Mr. Monkhouse met with," as Parkinson phrased it. The previous day, Munkhouse had been attacked for the sacrilege of picking a flower from a tree overhanging a *marae*. One man had struck him from behind, and when the surgeon tried to defend himself, two more natives had grappled him by his long gray hair. As Munkhouse himself observed, they were "Mannahoona of Oparre"—men from Pare Arue, so were subjects of Tutaha. The chief had promised that they would be "tiparahi'd"—beaten—but there had been no sign of any punishment being carried out, so Tutaha was guilty on that count, too.

By day's end, none of the other items had turned up, so Cook refused to return the canoes. Tutaha, swearing that Purea was the one responsible and the thieving was nothing to do with him, flew into a rage of his own—"Tootahau was much displeased," as Parkinson put it; "and would not suffer any of the natives to supply us with bread-fruit, cocoa-nuts, or apples"—so again the *Endeavour*s were short of supplies. They knew from past experience that no matter how far they searched for hogs, the people would not sell them without Tutaha's permission, but Cook remained adamant.

Purea tried to bribe her way back into favor, arriving with plantains, breadfruit, and a hog (but none of the stolen articles). Pati was the one behind the thefts, she declared; she had beaten him and sent him away. No one believed her. She wanted very badly to sleep in Banks's marquee, but was spurned. Banks did allow Dr. Munkhouse and one of the lieutenants to use his tent to dally with a couple of her attendant girls, but then he and the surgeon fell out over who should spend the night there—"had very high words," wrote Parkinson, and for a while it looked as if it would end in a duel. When the spat was over, Banks decided to forgive Purea, and after giving Munkhouse the use of the tent, spent the night in her canoe.

The crisis was by no means at an end, Molineux noting that "Seizing the Canoes has frighted the Natives & we are strictly on our Guard for fear of a Surprise." Apart from Purea's attempts to inveigle herself back into their good books, their only visitors were their "most Intimate Friends." This, of course, included Tupaia, who proved particularly helpful a week later, when Purea arrived with another load of provisions, this time including "a very fat dog," which Banks studied very thoughtfully.

Ever since the *Endeavour* had been here, there had been a shortage of fresh meat, partly through Tutaha's contrariness, and partly because of the ravages of the recent war. Some islanders had sold their catches of fish, which provided meals for the officers and the sick, but the men, ordered by Cook to bargain for their own provisions, had been reduced to eating rats. They did not appear to mind, Molineux writing that "shooting of rats is not only a pleasant but a profitable amusement as they are also good eating & it is easy to kill 1000 a day as the ground swarms & the Inhabitants never disturb them." The Tahitians "abhor them as food," he added, with not a notion of the reason—that the rats were the islanders' toilet attendants. Any native who felt the need to relieve himself or herself retreated to the trees, leaving the rats to clean up the result. Little wonder the ground was swarming with rats—and little wonder, too, that the Tahitians preferred to eat fish, fowl, hog, and dog.

Being aware already that dogs "were eat by the Indians and esteemed more delicate food than Pork," Banks saw an opportunity of trying out the dish. The problem of killing it and preparing it for cooking was easily solved—the dog was handed over to Tupaia. While the *Endeavour*s watched with interest, he stifled it to death by muffling its nose in the folds of the pit of its stomach and holding its jaws shut. Then he dressed the carcass in much the same way as a pig was prepared. An earth oven had been dug, and a fire lit to heat the cooking stones. Tupaia singed off the hair over this, then scraped the skin clean with a shell. "He then opend him with the same instrument and taking out his entrails pluck &c. sent them to the sea where they were most carefully washd, and then put into Cocoa nut shells with what blood he had found in him." The carcass was wrapped with taro leaves after a few hot stones had been dropped into the stomach cavity, placed in the oven on top of the bed of red-hot stones, together with the shells of entrails and blood, and nicely covered with banana fronds. Then the oven was watered and closed in with heaped dirt, and the dog left to steam in its own juices.

Two hours later, the oven was dug open, and the meal served. "A most excellent dish he made," wrote Banks, while Cook, with unusual enthusiasm, declared, "Never eat sweeter meat." Perhaps soothed by the meal, or maybe because he had come to an understanding that because Tahitians were so different in culture and customs they could not be treated like the rough Englishmen of his crew, he added, "I now gave over all thought of recovering any of the things that natives had stolen from us and therefore intend to give them up their Canoes when ever they apply for them."

Not only had he lost hope of getting back the pistols, musket, and water cask, but, like Wallis earlier, he realized it was time to take his men away. The *Endeavour*s were fast outstaying their welcome, Parkinson noting there was a scarcity of breadfruit, and that to keep the ship supplied the islanders were forced to eat native chestnuts, roasted. Wise in the rhythms of their land, the Tahitians knew that worse was to come, for the season of abundance would not return until the seven stars of *Matari'i* (the Pleiades) reappeared on the horizon at dusk, late in the month the westerners knew as November. Meantime, supplying the demands of the *Endeavour* was going to become impossible.

Before departure, however, Cook wanted to make a proper scientific survey of the island. He had been given the same instructions as Wallis, and was determined to make a much more thorough and efficient job than his

predecessor. Sending John Gore off on a twenty-four-hour trek might have
been good enough for Samuel Wallis, but for James Cook nothing less than
a complete circumnavigation of the island would do.

While he and Banks were getting ready for this, Purea staged yet another
dramatic distraction. Since the day Cook had given her the doll, she had
been an informal presence, strolling in and out of the fort as casually as any
other noble. On June 21, however, she led the chiefs in a ritual greeting of
Amo Tevahitua, their son, Teri'irere (now about seven years old), and a spir-
ited young woman no one had ever seen before. And, because of that ritual
greeting, the *Endeavours'* carefully constructed ideas about Tahitian society
fell into disorder again.

The surgeon, William Brougham Munkhouse, a thirty-seven-year-old native
of Penrith, Cumberland, speculated often about the ranking system in
Tahiti. A small, narrow-shouldered man with a long nose and bright blue
eyes, he was an eccentric who adopted Tahitian dress, which would have
looked odd enough on his frail frame, and quite hilarious if he had worn
the customary surgeon's wig. Despite his unusual appearance, a blatant lack
of interest in the medical health of the men, and a weakness for women (he
was the only *Endeavour* to witness an erotic *arioi* festival), he was intelligent
and analytical. Indeed, he was the perfect tourist, fascinated by everything
he saw.

Munkhouse had ample time for this, since his job was a curiously lonely
one. While he had been rated as a naval surgeon since February 2, 1758,
and had spent many years of sea-time on the North America station (lately
on HMS *Niger*, where he treated Joseph Banks after the naturalist fell ill in
Newfoundland), he was just a warrant officer. This meant he had no right to
stand on the quarterdeck unless summoned by the captain, though he did
eat his meals in the gunroom. His wife had been convicted for the theft of a
cloak and transported to America, which would not have helped his social
position, either. He was equally isolated from the other warrant officers and
the seamen, as he shared no duties with them, and did not keep watches.
The *Endeavours* scarcely mentioned him in their journals—when they wrote
affectionately about "the Doctor," they were talking about the popular botanist, Daniel Solander, not the ship's surgeon.

Over the previous weeks, Dr. Munkhouse had come to the conclusion
that there were four classes of Tahitian people. At the top of the social heap
was the "Aree de hi" (*ari'i rahi*), or paramount chief, while at the bottom
were the "Toutou" (*teuteu*), who carried out menial work and owned nothing, except perhaps the humble huts and fishing canoes they built. Below

the paramount chief came the nobility, which he called "the arees" (ari'i), and between them and the menials were intermediate people called "Manna-hoona" (manahune).

Originally, it had been hard for him to work out who was noble and who was not, because of the islanders' impish sense of humor. As the surgeon went on, "The moment they found us set upon informing ourselves who were Arees; and that all such were particularly distinguish'd; our list increas'd very rapidly—In short every Man and Woman who had a tolerable house over their head, or possess'd of a double Canoe, became an Aree." He finally came to the conclusion that what distinguished a chief from the lower classes was whether he or she owned land: the "arees" were the "Lords of manors," who possessed estates, and loaned them out to the next class down, the "Mannahoona," who lived and worked on their properties in return for seasonal tribute.

Tupaia informed him he was mistaken. "Tobia now tells me that the Man-ahoonas have land," the surgeon wrote, though they were obliged to "supply the Arees with whatever provisions they demand." Also, this land ownership was only on sufferance: "It would seem then that the Mannahoona has no property but at the will of his Lord." Usually, the chiefs' demands were for such things as fish and hogs, but the surgeon had also seen Tutaha send his attendants around to collect the gifts the *Endeavour* people had handed out. Strangely, one of the men who had been forced to give up the clothes, nails, and trinkets Banks had given him was Tupura'a, who was a chief—or so everyone had assumed. But, as Tupaia told Dr. Munkhouse (perhaps with satisfaction, considering the purloined cuttlefish), "Toobora tomite" was, in fact, "a Mannahoona of Oparre." The fact that Tupura'a was also an *ari'i* of Fa'aa district went unmentioned: Tupaia was exercising his own sense of humor.

Tutaha's true status was even harder for the surgeon to pin down. Everything Dr. Munkhouse had observed—the collection of tribute, Tutaha's domination of the sale of hogs, the great estates he appeared to control—had confirmed his first impression that the muscular old chief was the *ari'i rahi*. The others agreed with him, Solander reckoning that Tutaha was the "Eari or grand chief of Otaheite." Over the weeks, Tupaia had also hinted that Tutaha might have been behind the defeat and dispossession of Purea and her husband—"Tobia has told me of one Aree taking anothers land from him," the surgeon wrote, which seemed to confirm that Tutaha was indeed the "Aree de Hi," by right of conquest, if not by birth.

But then Purea's husband came to the fort with Teri'irere and the young woman, bringing Tutaha's place in society into question again.

The first intimation that particularly important visitors were about to arrive was when Purea bared her upper half by dropping her draperies from her shoulders to her waist, a strange act that was immediately copied by all the Tahitians within the fort. With Tupaia, similarly stripped, at her side, Purea then led a procession to the gate. The officers and scientists, understanding that the unveiling was a "mark of obeisance," as Parkinson put it, tagged along, to behold Amo, the boy, and the young woman coming their way, attended by the usual host of courtiers and servants.

Purea carried out introductions, for the benefit of those who had not met Amo the day she had first arrived at the encampment. "This man Oboreah called her husband, and Toobaiah his brother," wrote Parkinson, adding condescendingly (for he knew perfectly well that Tupaia had been her lover, not her brother-in-law), "but there is little regard to be paid to what they say." Dr. Munkhouse wrote down Amo's name as *Oamo aree no Papalla* (Amo, chief of Papara), heavily underlining the words to stress that Amo was obviously important. Cook also thought Amo "must be some extraordinary person," but was puzzled because very little notice was taken of him once everyone had pulled their clothes up again.

The girl who had come with them, who looked about sixteen years old, would have liked to enter the fort, but though the *Endeavour*s did their best to persuade her to step through the gate, the Tahitians prevented her from doing it—"at some times almost using force," wrote Banks. Even more mystifyingly, much of the time the little boy was carried on a man's shoulders—"although he was as able to walk as the Man who carried him," marveled Cook, who did not know that it was because the ground Teri'irere walked on immediately became sacred. When the visitors had first arrived, Solander had taken the lad by the hand and led him into the fort, but the scandalized chiefs had at once sent him outside, where his father had made him jump onto the man's back.

Amo had come to persuade Captain Cook to return the canoes, not knowing it was unnecessary, as Cook was trying to give them back to anyone who could prove that he or she was the rightful owner. The next day, he and Purea came again. After a long conversation in which, as Banks recorded, Amo asked (through Tupaia) "many shrewd questions" about the manners and customs of the people of England, four canoes "were set at liberty," so the Paparan chief went away pleased with what he thought he had accomplished.

"Our friends all went to the westward," wrote Banks on the evening of June 24. Then, a couple of mornings later, he and Cook left on their circumnavigation of the island, so they did not see them again until after they had returned.

Amo had not gone far. He called at the fort several times while Banks and Cook were away, giving Munkhouse a chance to study the ritual of dropping their robes, which the *Endeavours* called "ahou," their version of the Tahitian word for cloak, *ahu*. It proved to be as mysterious as the system of social stratification. Sometimes people stripped when the Paparan chief arrived, but at other times did not. "We don't know to whom this Compliment or homage is paid," the surgeon admitted, as it seemed to depend on the company Amo kept.

Amo arrived alone one day, and no homage was paid. The following day he brought the boy and the young woman, and everyone stripped—"She lands at the Fort, everybody strips, the boy is not observed: By and by Oamo observes the boy running about and orders him to mount upon a mans back." When the young woman left, Amo ordered the boy to follow her—"the moment he is gone Oamo pulls his Ahou over his Shoulders; the people follow his example. At another time," Munkhouse continued, "Oamo brings the boy only—the people strip."

This seemed to confirm Purea's claim that her son was the future king of Tahiti—"We are told this boy is Oamo's son by Oborea and that he is aree de hi of Otahite, also Aree of Papalla." Over the following days the surgeon learned not just the boy's proper name, Teri'irere, which he heard as "Tareiderra," but also that Teri'irere had a cousin, "who is the only Aree de Hi of Oborianoo"—Papeno'o, the name of a district, which the Europeans wrongly thought was another name for Tahiti Nui, the larger bulge of the island. This cousin was Tutaha's ward, Tu (spelled "Otoo" by Munkhouse), the son of Tutaha's nephew, and—though Munkhouse did not know it—the young woman was probably his sister. Young Tu had kept his distance throughout the visit, but if he had put in an appearance, the people most certainly would have stripped. So why was "Supreme homage" paid to two heirs at the same time? And why did no one strip for Tutaha?

Munkhouse asked Tupaia, who was still at the fort, being far too cautious to accompany Cook and Banks to Tahiti Iti, where Vehiatua ruled supreme: while Tupaia might have made a pact with Tutaha, he had not made his peace with Vehiatua, the other chief who had defeated Amo and Purea. "I applied therefore to Tobia," wrote the surgeon, and learned "that there is but one Aree de Hi of Oboreanoo—that Otoo is that person—that this boys Father & Grandfather are living—& that Tootaha is only an Aree." Not only was Tutaha a mere chief, but he was the servant of Tu, since "the moment the Heir to an Aree de Hi is born, the infant becomes Aree."

So there was the answer to the puzzle of why Teri'irere was awarded the supreme homage, but his father, Amo, was not, and why the people would strip for Tu, but not for Tutaha. Both Tutaha and Amo had lost their high rank when their wards were born, and were simply acting as regents. During the minority of his charge Tutaha wielded great power, but he did not have the status to match. "Here then we find the matter explained," wrote the surgeon with great satisfaction.

And Tupaia, his job of interpreter of Tahitian customs over for the moment, made preparations for a journey south. He planned to meet Cook and Banks as they crossed the isthmus from Tahiti Iti, and then escort them to Papara, to show off his greatest achievement.

"At 3 O'clock this morn Captn Cooke and myself set out to the eastward in the pinnace," Banks recorded, back on June 26. They rowed for five hours, then went ashore to eat breakfast with a friendly chief, "Tituboaro" (Tetupuaro), who served as their guide as they trekked to Hitia'a, "the place where the Spanyards were said to lay," with the boat keeping pace. Reti received them kindly, showing them where the foreigners had pitched their tents. After the civilities were over, and the two Englishmen had asked all the questions about the "Spaniards" they could manage, lacking an interpreter, they took to the boat again.

Tetupuaro had warned them they were leaving Tutaha's territory, and were in grave danger of being attacked and killed. Instead, when dark fell, they came across a small fleet of double canoes belonging to people they knew, apparently travelers like themselves. To Joseph Banks's delight, one was none other than "Ourattooa" (Urutua), the lady who had exposed her lower half three times during the tapa-presentation ritual. Naturally, he spent the night in her double canoe.

Laboriously, on foot as well as by boat, the two Englishmen circled Tahiti Iti, at one stage meeting the dread figure of Vehiatua, who turned out to be a thin, white-bearded, old man. There was much of interest to see, including double canoes that seemed to be built to a different design, with very high, ornamented sterns, and awnings supported by carved pillars. On every point of land was a *marae*, "on the pavements of which I saw several vertebrae and sculls of men laying about as if no care was taken to bury them," wrote Banks. There were many other hints of the past war. They saw an English goose and a turkey cock that had been sent to Purea by Wallis, and also, more gruesomely, the mandibles of fifteen men, hanging from a board, and seemingly quite fresh, "not one at all damagd even by the Loss of a tooth." Naturally, Banks was curious, and asked a lot of questions, to which he got no answers.

It was almost equally impossible to obtain provisions. They were either unavailable, or very expensive. Banks was forced to go without sexual solace, too. As he confided to his journal, he usually "stuck close to the women" wherever they were stopping for the night, "hoping to get a snug lodging by that means." Instead, though the girls readily flirted, "they dropd off one by one and at last left me jilted," obliging him to find his own bed. It was a relief to leave Tahiti Iti, pass the southern mouth of the isthmus, and land at Vaiari, where they found Tupaia waiting.

Tupaia first took them to the local *marae*, a neat affair with a five-foot pyramid. On the cobbled pavement beneath the altar table lay 26 animal skulls, with three human skulls propped in a row nearby. "From hence we proceeded farther and met with a very extraordinary curiosity call'd Mahuwe," wrote Cook. An effigy over seven feet high, it was made of basketwork and covered with black and white feathers—"white for the ground," Cook continued, and "black imitating hair and the Marks of tattou." The head had four knobs, "resembling stumps of horns," and the loins, covered with a *maro*, had more knobs, in imitation of male genitals.

Cook jumped to the conclusion that this figure was used in "publick entertainments, probably as punch is in a Puppet Show." Tupaia corrected him—this, he said, was a representation of the famous demi-god Maui. One of the second rank of the gods who inhabited the Earth before the creation of man, Maui was "an immense giant" with seven heads, of "immense strength and abilities." There were "many Absurd stories told of his feats by Tupia"—such as the tale of Maui and the clouds, which Tupaia proceeded to relate, while Cook jotted notes.

When Maui was born, the clouds were not hung in their proper positions in the sky as they are now, but sat on the tops of the mountains. Many heroes and demi-gods had tried to lift them, but had been crushed to death by their weight. Maui, stronger than any before, heaved them up and hung them in the heavens so securely they have floated there ever since—and that was not the greatest of his many feats. When Maui was born, the Earth was made up of just one piece of land. Maui took hold of this, and shook it hard, breaking it into islands big and small. Because of Maui, the world is the way men know it now.

As the missionaries were to find out later, Tahitians were usually reluctant to speak of the adventures of their gods, high priests in particular. Perhaps because storytelling came naturally to Tupaia, or maybe because he simply wanted to share his lore with these foreign friends, he then launched himself into the most fundamental of Polynesian myths—the creation of the world, and its peopling.

Tahitumu, in the beginning, he related as Cook scribbled, there was just the great god Ta'aroa, also known as *Te tumu*. Ta'aroa existed before everything—he had no father or mother, but existed alone in the void. There was no sky, or sea, or land—"Except a rock" called *Te papa*. Ta'aroa embraced the rock, and begat a daughter, Aone, and after that, "he begat the earth the sea fresh water sun moon stars &c." Then he created the demi-gods, *atua*, and finally men.

The first man was the son of Te tumu and Aone, also called by Tupaia "Aonewhenarua" (*Onefenua*), which means earth heaped up. As Tupaia went on, this first child was born in the shape of a ball, which his father fashioned to form a man. And when he had done that, as Tupaia further related, his father called him *E oti* (spelled "Eothe" by Cook), which means finished. E oti's true name was *Ti'i*—Ti'i the propagator. Lying with his mother and then his daughters, Ti'i fathered a succession of incarnations of the goddess Hina, such as Hina-goddess-of-tattooing, Hina-who-beats-tapa-in the-moon, and *Hina-ta-a-uta*, who was the mother of the great war-god Oro. Three sons were also born—and, as Tupaia said, "from these three men & the women sprung all mankind."

Ti'i lived on an island named Hawaiki, which lay to the northward of Tahiti, and from which "come Hogs Dogs Fowles &c.," as Cook noted. The year was "the child of the sun & moon, she produced the months, who in their turn intermarrying with each other produced the days." And the stars? "The stars are the children of the sun & occupy the heavens as men do the earth." Some stars were *ari'i*, some were *arioi*—"others are married & have children."

This was a very brief reply—Tupaia was either tired, or becoming uncomfortable about revealing so much. Though more questions were undoubtedly asked, the rest of that page of Cook's notes is blank.

Did Cook and Banks understand that this was a historic moment—that they were the first Europeans to be so trusted? Not only was this the first time any Polynesian myth had been written down on paper, but it was the first time, too, that westerners had heard the name of the fabled island, Hawaiki.

Cook, it seems, dismissed the legends as incomprehensible. The rough notes he made as Tupaia talked were never transcribed into his journal. Instead, as he confessed in his account of the South Sea islands, he understood so little of their religion that "I hardly dare touch upon it." All he could say was that Tahitians believed in one supreme god (though he could not remember his name), and that "from him sprung a number of inferior Deities <u>Eatuas</u> as they call them these 'they think preside over them and intermeddle in their affairs."

Banks, in his own report, remarked that even though "the most stupid" peoples must wonder about the origin of the universe, Tahitian priests preached instead about "two original beings one of whom they call *Ettoomoo* and the other which they say is a rock *Tepapa*," and from them came everything—the plants, the stars, even the divisions of time. They also begat the first man—"*Eothe* which signifies finishd," he wrote. Less inhibited than Cook, he then enlarged on the incest involved in producing several generations of daughters—until at last a man was born, "who by the assistance of his many Sisters peopled this world and is the ancestor of us all."

Both Cook and Banks found it impossible to take Tupaia's storytelling seriously. It was a dismissive attitude that was to have consequences for the priest later on.

Tupaia, with Cook and Banks, spent the night at Amo's house, where they were hosted by Purea's father, as Amo and Purea were still at Matavai Bay. Next morning, Tupaia led the two Europeans along a promontory, to show off what Cook called "a wonderfull piece of Indian Architecture," and what Banks described as "a most enormous pile, certainly the masterpiece of Indian architecture in this Island."

This was Tupaia's supreme achievement, the great *marae* at Mahaiatea. It was on the same general design as the other *marae* they had seen, but very much more massive; it was so vast, in fact, that the ground was groaning and cracking beneath its weight. Marveled Banks, "It is almost beyond belief that Indians could raise so large a structure without the assistance of Iron tools to shape their stone or mortar to join them."

Tupaia explained the functions of the different parts of the *marae*, sketching perspectives to illustrate what he was saying—artwork that might demonstrate little idea of the diminishing effect of distance, but which provides more evocative evidence of a longlost way of life. The *ahu*, like some huge Aztec pyramid, rears up at the far end of the paved open area where religious rituals were carried out; the offering tables—*fata*—stand in the foreground, while two braided coconut-leaf effigies of priests guard the middle area with its sacred thatched house, *fare atua*, where the feathered gods and *marae* drums were stored.

After describing the different parts of the complex, Tupaia retreated to an upright stone, knelt on one knee, and cried out a prayer to the heavens, ending with a series of eerie whistles to attract the gods' attention. It was

Ahu at Mahaiatea. Pen and pencil drawing by Tupaia. (© The British Library Board, 15508/16)

obvious to the Europeans, though, that the gods had failed Tupaia's people in the past, Cook writing, "Near to this Morie were Several small ones all going to decay, and on the beach between them and the Sea lay great quantitys of Human bones."

The bones were beyond counting, a great field of death. When they finally turned away and walked back to Purea's house, ribs and vertebrae crunched under their feet. Tupaia was besieged with questions about the grim sight. While he was careful to avoid naming Tutaha, he readily informed them, as Banks recorded, "that in the month calld by them *Owiráhew* last, which answers to our December 1768," Vehiatua's warriors of Tahiti Iti descended on Papara, and slaughtered great multitudes of people. Amo and Purea had fled, while the victors carried off the turkey and goose as loot, and jawbones as trophies, "in the same manner," Banks concluded judiciously, "as the North Americans do scalps."

Cook was anxious to return to Matavai Bay and get the ship under sail. There was still the matter of returning the rest of the confiscated canoes to their proper owners, but after that it was time to weigh anchor—which meant it was also time for Tupaia to come to a decision. Ever since April 18, when he had signed onto the muster roll of the *Endeavour*, he had been trying to make up his mind whether to stay with the ship when she departed, comparing the dangers with the likely rewards.

The chance to navigate the *Endeavour* to his native island of Raiatea was attractive. For the past eight years he had lived on his wits as a refugee, flourishing only because of the patronage of the once-powerful Purea, which made returning home in style on a square-rigged ship very tempting. The complicated political situation in Tahiti was another factor. Tutaha had supposedly forgiven him for urging his assassination, but memories were long, and the warrior chief had a trigger temper. Once the *Endeavour* with its novelties and distractions had gone, old rivalries would stir again.

Tupaia must have recognized that he had passed the climax of his career, and it was very unlikely he would ever wield the same power he had held when the *Dolphin* arrived. Going to London could solve that problem, as he was bound to be an object of curiosity, respect, and wonder when he returned. There were no personal ties to keep him in Tahiti— though he had friends here, there was no family to mourn his departure. His acolyte and foster son, Taiata, would sail with him, which was another advantage. Overriding all was the seductive vision of procuring arms. Tupaia still held a grudge against the Bora Borans for their invasion of Raiatea, and undoubtedly hoped he could come back with English guns, like the great New Zealand war-chief Hongi Hika, half a century later.

Despite all this, Tupaia inevitably felt some qualms. He was certainly unafraid to voyage, and still young enough to relish the challenge of adventure, but he had no idea what life would be like in England. The thought of feeling his way through unknown customs and taboos must have been a daunting one. There was also the more mundane problem of food and lodging after the ship arrived. When Banks first approached James Cook with the proposition that Tupaia should sail with them, Cook objected, for the excellent reason that he had no way of looking after him in England. The

Cook family lived in a narrow house in East London, Cook had no personal fortune, and the government would certainly not take over the responsibility. Samuel Wallis had been reluctant to carry an islander home for exactly the same reason: he worried (quite properly, as it turned out) about his prospects after the *Dolphin* arrived, and the Cornish hamlet where he lived was no place to take a Tahitian.

Louis de Bougainville had not had the same problem. A man of means, and with connections in Paris, he was able to take Ahutoru into his house, and give him enough pocket money to seduce all the novelty-seeking Frenchwomen he liked—which is exactly what Ahutoru did, becoming quite a lion in certain levels of society. Banks, being a very rich young man, had the same resources as Bougainville, so he countered Cook's doubts by offering to take on the responsibility. He even had a berth suitable for a noble Tahitian in one of the gentlemen's cabins—the berth once occupied by Alexander Buchan. It was still empty. Twelve-year-old Nicholas Young might be on the muster roll now, but the lad was just a cabin boy, so certainly did not merit a stateroom.

Banks did not stop to consider the social problems involved in giving one of the favored berths to a native Polynesian. The officers of the *Endeavour*, already displaced, could well have resented it, and the ordinary seamen, conservative and snobbish by nature, would certainly not understand an "Indian" being given a place in the upper crust afterquarters. Tupaia himself would have thought it only proper. In future years, Polynesian nobles often cadged inter-island passages on European and American ships, and though they might sleep on the floor by preference, they invariably chose to camp in the stern cabins, recognizing that this was where the nobility of the ship lived.

As for Banks, according to his reasoning, he had bought the gentlemen's cabins for his retinue, and if Tupaia sailed, it would be as one of that number—as a prized specimen, in fact. "I do not know why I may not keep him as a curiosity, as well as some of my neighbours do lions and tigers at a larger expence than he will probably ever put me to," he blithely penned, without a word to acknowledge how lucky they would be if Tupaia did agree to come on those strange terms. As Cook admitted, his presence would be a big asset. "This man had been with us most part of the time we had been upon the Island which gave us an oppertunity to know some thing of him," he wrote: "we found him to be a very intelligent person and to know more of the Geography of the Islands situated in these seas, their produce and the religion laws and customs of the inhabitants than any one we had met with."

Tupaia himself was perfectly aware that he had a great deal to contribute to the expedition. He was an experienced star-navigator, able to name directional stars and constellations, and orientate himself according to their rising and setting. His knowledge of the tropical Pacific encompassed myriads of islands in a great tract of sea that was still mostly empty in European charts. As proof of this, he had recited the names of fifty-seven of these islands to Robert Molineux, which the sailing master copied down in careful phonetics, adding short descriptions, such as the number of days it took to sail there—names like "Molekaa" (described by Tupaia as a large, low, uninhabited island, ten days' sail from Tahiti), "Oawaow" (a large, high, fertile island to the northwest of Tahiti), and "Woahaowroa" and "Aowroopou" (large islands to the northeast and east, inhabited by unusually tall people).

"Towbia has seen many of these Islands & has a number more on Tradition that are not here mention'd," concluded Molineux, before going on to note a vocabulary of Tahitian words, "according to Tobia."

Robert Molineux had already been told stories about these islands, recording in his journal as far back as May 9 that, though the *Dolphin* was the first European ship to drop anchor at Tahiti, it was not the first time the Tahitians had seen Europeans, "a Ship being Stranded some years agoe upon a Reef belonging to a small Island adjacent." The crew had bravely defended themselves, but "were at last overpower'd & Kill'd every man of them." Not long after the murders, a canoe had arrived at Tahiti with two of the corpses "& some Iron Bolts from the Wreck"—which indicates that this is the story of the Dutch explorer *African Galley*, which was lost in the Tuamotus in 1722, and pulled apart for its nails.

Five of the *Galley's* seamen had escaped the wreck in the ship's longboat, and were never seen again, so presumably were the murdered men. But why were they killed? They may have been attacked at first sight, but it is more likely they had broken important taboos. If, instead, they had been fortunate enough to find an intelligent intermediary to interpret and intercede, they could have been saved from paying the price of their ignorance.

It was yet another incentive for Tupaia to sail. If he was there during first encounters, his European friends would have a much better chance of dealing amicably with Polynesia. With Tupaia as an intermediary, they were less likely to blunder onto sacred ground.

Indeed, his presence could mean the difference between life and death.

CHAPTER 10

❧

Return to Raiatea

A last-minute crisis was only to be expected, considering what had gone on before. On July 9, Parkinson reported that, "two of our marines being enamoured with a girl," had run off to the western part of the island. As Cook testified, the men were Clement Webb and Samuel Gibson. They had found it easy to get away from the fort, because it was in a state of disorder, the fences chopped up for firewood, and the guns being hoisted back to the ship—"as it was known to every body that all hands were to go on board on the Monday morning & that the ship would sail in a day or 2," the captain added, "there was reason to think that these 2 Men intended to stay behind." Cook was willing to give them the benefit of the doubt, however, and wait a day to see if they returned of their own accord.

The next morning dawned with no sign of the marines. The islanders readily informed Cook that the men had taken their native wives into the mountains, but were very vague with details of exactly which mountains and where. Knowing that adopting two Europeans with their specialized skills would be quite a prize for the locals, Cook promptly decided to "seize upon as many of the Chiefs as we could." Purea and Tupura'a i Tamaita, with seven other nobles, were already in the fort, so were easily confined, but Cook was determined to capture Tutaha as well. Not only was Tutaha apparently the most powerful chief on the island, but he had already made one attempt to snatch one of the seamen, a Portuguese, back on June 23. Accordingly, Cook sent off Lieutenant Hicks with the pinnace to collect the old warrior, and bring him on board the ship.

As Cook dryly remarked, no sooner were all the chiefs in custody, "than they became as desireous of having the men brought back as they were before of keeping them." Their only stipulation was that a sailor or two should accompany the party they sent out to retrieve the two marines. Cook cooperatively supplied a midshipman (Jonathan Munkhouse, the surgeon's young brother, known to the natives as "Matte," because he had been the one who killed the man who stole the musket), and a corporal, John Truslove, and off they went.

Only one man came back—Clement Webb, one of the original fugitives. Munkhouse and Truslove had been ambushed and disarmed, he said, and their captors had sent the message they would not be released until Tutaha was freed. Cook furiously informed Tutaha that he and the other chiefs would remain hostage until his two officers were returned, and "if any harm came to these men, they, the Chiefs, would suffer for it." Tutaha, equally angry but scared that Cook would carry out his threat, agreed to send a party with Hicks to the place where the missing men were kept. As Banks concluded, "a boat armd went immediately in search of the people." Tupaia went with them as negotiator.

By seven in the morning Tupaia was back, mission accomplished. The rescued captives were with him, so the hostages were released, to be received with great joy by the multitude on the beach. Banks met them at the landing, "but no sign of forgiveness could I see in their faces, they lookd sulky and affronted." In the afterquarters of the *Endeavour*, by contrast, there was general relief. All the men on the muster roll were present and accounted for, and preparations for departure could resume.

"None of the Indians came near us till the next day," wrote Parkinson, "except Toobaiah, who is a sort of high-priest of Otaheite; and he designed to sail with us." Banks was delighted. "This morn Tupia came on board," he wrote; "he had renewd his resolve of going with us to England, a circumstance which gives me much satisfaction. He is certainly a most proper man, well born, chief *Tahowa* or preist of this Island, consequently skilld in the mysteries of their religion; but what makes him more than any thing else desireable is his experience in the navigation of these people and knowledge of the Islands in these seas; he has told us the names of above 70, the most of which he has himself been at."

Having delivered his final decision, Tupaia went on shore again, taking a miniature portrait of Banks to show to the circle of friends he was farewelling, and an assortment of knickknacks to hand out as parting gifts. Banks saw him again when he went ashore to make a plan of Tutaha's *marae*, Tarahoi. Not having the time or opportunity to go to Mahaiatea, Tupaia had chosen the serenity of the dappled shade of the scattered trees that grew among the time-worn stones to meditate on his journey, and the cobbled apron before the ancient *ahu*, which lifted its much-eroded stoops to the mountains and the sky, as the place to commune with the gods.

Banks found Purea and the other chiefs at Tutaha's house, and "a perfect reconciliation ensued." The imminence of the ship's departure had mellowed the general mood, and the surly resentment of the previous day had vanished. The chiefs who had been such unwilling and frightened captives now "promisd to visit us tomorrow morning to take their leave of us, as we told them that we should sail before noon." At that moment arrived Tupaia, "who most willingly returnd in the boat with us aboard the ship where he took up his lodgins for the first time."

"About 10 this morn saild From Otahite leaving our friends Some of them at least I realy believe personaly sorry for our departure," wrote Banks next day. About a dozen nobles crowded the afterdeck, tapa robes fluttering in the damp wind as they watched the unfamiliar activity on the foredeck, where eight men heaved down on the handles of the windlass to the accompaniment of hearty cries. In response to the cranking, the chain holding the ship to her one remaining anchor rumbled upward. Almost imperceptibly, the bark *Endeavour* inched forward, until the last of the anchor-chain was straight up-and-down, immediately under her bowsprit.

A lookout on the forecastle cried out a warning: "Anchor a-peak!" Officers shouted orders, and the rigging thrummed as men scurried aloft and sidled along the yards, while other men stayed on deck to grab hold of ropes, and haul on them in unison. Broad sails dropped in a long-drawn-out rattling and snapping as the bark unfolded her wings in pyramids of rippling white. Then she was set to fly, held back only by the taut, straight chain.

It was time for the chiefs to say goodbye, "tenderly enough," wrote Banks, and "not without plenty of tears," then drop down into the canoes where the paddlers were lamenting in their usual style. "On our leaving the shore, the people in the canoes set up their woeful cry," wrote Parkinson—"*Aue, aue,*" they wailed. Tupaia wept too, according to Banks: "Tupia who after all his struggles stood firm at last in his resolution of accompanying us parted with a few heartfelt tears." He was English enough already to make a manly effort to hide them, though, and after his one-time mistress and his many friends had left the ship, was steady enough to accompany his patron to the topmast head.

Gripping tarry ropes, he and Banks swayed together, 150 feet above the glittering sea. All about them a bewildering web of rigging stretched from massive horizontal yards to upright masts. It was not at all like the showy leave-taking of a Tahitian *pahi*, with pennants snapping and conches blowing, the tall matting sails taut and singing with wind. Here, everything seemed deliberate and laborious, with packs of men working in unison, in accordance with long-learned drills.

More lines were hauled, and with a squeal the uppermost yard on the fore-mast came round until its sail was blown backwards, counter to all the rest, turning the ship's bow to face the sea. Another shout from the deck, another heave on the handles of the windlass—and at long last the *Endeavour* sailed. Up the anchor surged, dripping black sand. Water chuckled along freshly scrubbed strakes as the little ship straightened her sails and gathered way.

The shimmering water was alive with canoes, their muscular crews ululat-ing as they paddled, while people massed the beaches to watch the depar-ture of the visitors who had become so familiar over the past three months. On the masthead, Tupaia waved vigorously until the last of the canoes were left behind. Then, after gazing a final reflective moment at the mountains, beaches, and forests that had been his refuge for the past eight years, he descended to the sloping deck, and, as Joseph Banks recorded, "show'd no farther signs of seriousness or concern."

It was July 13, 1769.

Tupaia's initiation to the strange rituals of a British navy ship at sea was not long in coming. Precisely at six next morning, the boatswain, John Guthrey, and his mate, John Reading, strode to their stations at the aft and forward hatchways, little silver pipes named "calls" lifted to their lips. After shrilling a summons on these, they shouted repeatedly, "D'ye hear there! All hands aft to witness punishment!" Marines clattered up ladders from below, led by Sergeant John Edgcombe, all of them sweating in their tightly buttoned red coats, muskets and bayonets at the ready. Bare-footed sailors in loose frock shirts and wide-legged breeches mustered, mostly on deck but some forced to perch in the rigging, because the ship was so small.

Captain Cook, in full uniform of dark blue with blue satin lapels, marched onto the quarterdeck, accompanied by a knot of officers and trailed by the surgeon, who had been summoned to make sure the culprits were fit to stand the lash. The boatswain's mate stood on the main deck, his instrument of punishment—the notorious naval cat-o'-nine-tails—held loosely in his hands. The nine tails of the whip hung down from the two-foot handle, which was made of stiffened rope for maximum flexibility.

The two offenders were prodded forward. They were Gibson and Webb, the two marines who had eloped with their native mistresses at Tahiti, and whose capture had been negotiated by Tupaia.

Silence. Everyone waited. It was a fine, clear day, and the early sun shone down. On the starboard beam the stone spire and great hunched shoulders of the island of Moorea crouched in outline against the sky, and the silhouette of the northern coast of Tahiti—like a great, buttressed cathedral that had collapsed about a central steeple—filled the horizon astern. Above the men's heads buntlines pattered on the bellying sails as the breeze gusted, and the ship leaned a little in response, with a series of faint creaks. Iridescent water rippled slowly down the sides of the hull, then gathered and gradually spread in green and white to form a straggling wake.

They all listened numbly as the captain described the crime, recited the Articles of War that covered the offense, and determined the punishment: two dozen lashes. Though Tupaia had no way of knowing it, this was in defiance of the rules, as according to the regulations a captain could not order a man to be given more than twelve lashes without consultation with his commander-in-chief. However, the Admiralty was far, far away, the rules were broken by most captains at sea, and Cook was a fair master as well as a strict one. It could have been much worse—if Britain had been at war, desertion would have been punished (after a proper court-martial) by a flogging round the fleet, which meant an excruciatingly painful, long-drawn-out, very public death.

Because one blow from the cat was enough to knock down even the strongest sailor, the man being punished had to be tied to something first. Normally on navy ships this was the capstan, but on the little *Endeavour* the space about the capstan was too cramped to swing the lash, so Gibson was triced up to a hatch grating that was secured to the rigging. His shirt was pulled down over his widespread legs, exposing his naked back, and his outstretched arms were tied high. When the ship rolled on the glassy sea, he was forced to dance on the tips of his toes to keep his full weight from painfully jerking his wrists.

Captain Cook said to John Reading, "Do your duty."

The boatswain's mate braced himself, readied the lash, and said, "Sir."

All the officers removed their hats. Reading swung a muscular arm, the cat whistled down, and the punishment began. Back in November, Reading had been flogged himself, as a punishment for not flogging hard enough, and so he used his full strength. There is no record of whether Samuel Gibson screamed, but probably he did not. The pain was bad enough, but the shame would be worse.

After Gibson had withstood his twenty-four blows, he was cut down from the rigging, and it was Clement Webb's turn. The lashes came at twenty-second metronome-like intervals, counted off by the boatswain, so the whole unpleasant process took less than thirty minutes, from summons to dismissal. Both men were sent below for inspection of their blackened, bruised, and bleeding backs by the surgeon, and then they were dismissed to their duties. As Cook noted in his logbook, "Punished the two Marines, who attempted to desert from us at Georges Island, with 2 Doz^n lashes and then released them from confinement." The miscreants had been disciplined, and as far as he and the crew were concerned, the matter was forgotten.

The scientists may have felt uneasy about their Polynesian witness, however. On April 29, Henry Jeffs, the ship's butcher, had been flogged for threatening Tomio, wife of Tupura'a i Tamaita. With the idea of allowing the offended couple to see for themselves the severity and impartiality of English justice, Captain Cook had invited them on board to watch the punishment. As Banks recorded, Tupura'a and his wife stood quietly as the butcher was stripped of his shirt and tied up in the rigging, "but as soon as the first blow was given interfered with many tears," begging Cook to stop the punishment.

So evidently the islanders were a soft-hearted people. As Dr. Munkhouse had found after he had been attacked for picking a flower off a sacred tree, Tutaha had sworn that offenders were "tiparahi'd," or beaten, but no one had seen any evidence of this. "We never saw any punishment inflicted," he wrote. So how did Tupaia feel about what he had just witnessed?

It was possible to point out to him that the sailor was much better off than his brothers back in Britain, where a man—or woman—could be hanged for any of almost two hundred offenses, including minor theft. The gibbet, the whipping post, and the stocks were all public affairs, so the assembling of the crew to witness the punishment was nothing unusual. Whatever protests were made and excuses given, however, Tupaia had no trouble setting their minds at rest. Beating and execution were common in Tahiti, too, he declared; theft, for instance, was a capital crime, and, as Banks noted afterward, there was a range of punishments for "smaller crimes in proportion."

Any parallel to British justice that might have been drawn by his listeners was immediately called into question, however, as Tupaia went on to inform them that a husband who caught his wife and another man in the act of adultery had every right to kill them both. Even more foreign to his listeners was his next revelation, that rank played a significant part. As Tupaia related, it was easier for the offended husband to execute the couple if he was superior to the man who had committed the crime. If the offended husband and the man who had cuckolded him were of equal rank the situation was more complicated, so much so that the husband usually found it easier to forget all about it, unless he could find a highborn chief who was willing to sponsor the killing, and send attendants to assist.

So Tupaia found the flogging quite intelligible. It was revenge for running away from the ship, and Cook was able to order his attendants to carry out the punishment because he was nobly born, and Gibson and Wells were not.

It would not take him long to learn he had jumped to the wrong conclusion.

Indeed, many of the assumptions drawn from earlier observations proved to be unfounded. An immediate mystery was the style of the Great Cabin. Though the Great Cabin of the *Endeavour* was the most important room in the ship, just as it was on the *Dolphin*, it was not nearly as large. Nor was it as formal—instead of resembling a grand drawing room, the Great Cabin of the *Endeavour* was more like a gentleman's den. In the place of great, multi-paned windows, there were four square sternlights, and instead of a chart table set against the forward partition, there was a desk with library shelves above, reserved for the use of Mr. Banks. In the middle was a long table that was often cluttered with books and specimens, which belonged to Joseph Banks, too.

This—the way the cabin was used—was the most puzzling of all. When Tupaia and Purea had arrived on board the *Dolphin* in July 1767, the Great Cabin had been easily recognized as Captain Wallis's palace, the *sanctum* from where he ruled the ship. Beyond doubt, it was the captain's sole do-main, for the door was guarded by a sentinel, so no one could enter with-out an invitation. Captain Wallis had laid out his charts here, and eaten his meals on his own long table, usually alone, but occasionally with invited officers and guests from shore, including Tupaia himself. He slept there, too, in a stateroom that ran off the side, and he had two glassed quarter galleries, one for his private toilet, and the other for observations. Forward was the officers' dining room—the gunroom—but there were no cabins to either side of this, so at night, unless the midshipmen and master's mates slung their hammocks there, Captain Wallis had the whole afterdeck to himself.

On the *Endeavour*, by contrast, Captain Cook shared the Great Cabin with Joseph Banks and his scientists. It was true that he slept in a stateroom that led off this room, just as Captain Wallis had on the *Dolphin*, but Mr. Banks slept off the Great Cabin, too, having a slightly smaller cabin on the star-board beam. In fact, because the door to the afterquarters head (the toilet used by the captain, scientists, and officers) led through Banks's room, he preferred to sling his swinging cot in the Great Cabin itself. Not even at night did Captain Cook have his private space.

As it was so obvious Banks had owner's rights here, Tupaia had no hesitation in settling into the Great Cabin on the afternoon of that first day at sea. The four stern windows could be opened, and as the ship drew away from Tahiti he knelt on the wide windowsill, his tapa robes fluttering in the draft as he studied the ship's wake and the horizon beyond. Though he might have looked at idle ease, he had slipped into his old role of navigator, and was watching the profile of Tahiti intently, making sure from his view of their departure island that the *Endeavour* was steering in the right direction—navigating by backsight, in the traditional way.

The breeze became light and frisky, and so he took on the mantle of priest, to pray for better winds. "*O Tane, ara mai matai, ara mai matai,*" he intoned—"O Tane, bestir thyself, and send me a wind." The guardian spirit's response was disappointing, as the light airs were ahead, coming from the direction in which their destination lay. So, according to Parkinson, Tupaia became angry. "*Ua riri au,*" he exclaimed—"I am exasperated with you," and sure enough, the wind turned fair.

Banks wrote with retrospective condescending amusement, "Our Indian often prayd to *Tane* for a wind and as often boasted to me of the success of his prayers, which I plainly saw he never began till he saw a breeze so near the ship that it generally reached her before his prayer was finishd." It was actually a good demonstration of Tupaia's skill and experience in detecting a wind before it arrived and knowing if it would be favorable, but Banks did not see it that way. For him, it was hocus-pocus. Instead of impressing his patron, Tupaia was undermining his credibility.

The first island they neared was Tetioroa, the only coral isle in this group of mountainous islands. Like any typical atoll, the circular island had a lagoon in the center, which was rich with fish and pearl oysters, and its beaches were dense with palms, where monstrous coconut crabs climbed. Tupaia told Cook it was a good fishing ground, and served as a temporary refuge for chiefs in times of trouble, but that it was not a good place for the round-bottomed ship to find an anchorage. So they kept on to Huahine.

At eight the next morning they were close to the northwestern shore, wafted there by a sou'southeast breeze that was dampened by a few showers. After some hesitation, a few canoes approached the ship. The Huahine people were a cautious lot, because of frequent incursions of Bora Boran war parties. They were also reluctant to make the *Endeavour* welcome, as they had heard about the extortionate demands for food at Tahiti, and that a man had been shot dead for stealing a musket. Sighting Tupaia on the deck made all the difference. Reassured as well as very surprised, they came aboard to find out what he was doing on the square-sailed canoe without an outrigger.

With them was a high chief, Ori. One of Banks's two footmen, James Roberts, was most admiring, describing Ori as a statuesque figure, well over six feet tall, with "the finest hair I Ever saw." Cook, who thought Ori was the king of the island, wrote, "he had not been long on board before he and I exchang'd Names and we afterwards address'd each other accordingly." The high chief took advantage of this instant brotherhood to ask a favor. The stories of the havoc the *Dolphin's* cannon had wreaked were legion in the islands, and Ori very much wished "Tute" to do the same damage to the Bora Borans. As Roberts said, he "Express'd great desire of our going to Kill the Bollo Bollo Men who come Every Month taking away their things from them & Killing those who Oppose them." Tupaia added his own arguments to the translation, but Cook had no intention of getting involved in tribal politics.

A boat was sent out to sound the bottom before anchoring, while a quartermaster wielded a lead-line from the fore-chains. Tupaia thought this a risky way of doing things, as the lead was liable to miss a lurking coral head and give a false reading, and it was obvious that the deep-bottomed *Endeavour* needed more water underneath her than even the largest *pahi*. He called out to a man in a canoe, who cheerfully dived overboard, swam the length of the ship's bottom, and then reported back. With the assistance of this human sounding device, Tupaia piloted the *Endeavour* to a safe anchorage off a village called Fare, which was the residence of the chief.

After ushering Cook, Banks, Solander, and Munkhouse on shore, Tupaia led the way to a longhouse, where the local nobles were waiting to receive them. Then he commenced ceremonies by dropping his robes off his shoulders, and gesturing to the surgeon to follow suit. "The Moment we landed Tobia striped him self as low as his waist and desired Mr. Munkhouse to do the same," wrote Cook. Baring the torso was almost impossible for a man wearing shirt, stock, and waistcoat, topped by the tightly fitting, skirted coat fashionable at the time, so the flamboyant surgeon must have been still wearing Tahitian tapa.

Tupaia then recited a prayer—certainly involving a formal identification of his companions and their mission—which was answered at intervals by Ori and another chief. According to Cook, this lasted fifteen minutes, a long time for men who were standing out in the sweaty heat, but it was a proud moment for the refugee priest. To honor the *marae* gods, Tupaia presented two handkerchiefs, a black silk neckcloth, some beads, and two little bunches of sacred feathers, receiving other feathers in return, along with a hog—"for our God," wrote Cook that night, adding with dry humor that the *Endeavours* were about to commit blasphemy, as the hog "hath already received sentence of death and is to be dissected tomorrow."

Then Tupaia disappeared, much to Banks's irritation, as he had to make do with Taiata as his guide, and the boy was a lot less forthcoming with information than his master. Tupaia, Banks resentfully muttered, was "too much engagd with his friends." The noble priest was busy, visiting local *marae*, being welcomed at his Huahine estates, and playing his part in rituals of feasting and gift exchange. It was safe to leave the *Endeavours* to their own devices, as his careful introduction had brought an acceptance of their presence that would have been impossible if they had blundered on shore without an intermediary. Banks, however, was unhappy. The local people were "stupid and lazy." He wanted to go up in the hills botanizing, but they refused to lead him there, for "fear of being killd by the fatigue," he imagined.

Two days later, after much trading of hatchets for pigs, hogs, and coconuts, Cook carried out his own rite. Chief Ori had come on board with his retinue, having heard that the ship was on the verge of departure, and Cook presented him with some medals, coins, and a metal plate engraved with the words, "*His Britannick Maj. Ship Endeavour, Lieu^t Cook Commander 16th July 1769.*" Ori received these courteously, Tupaia translating his promise that they would be carefully preserved, and then made another appeal for an attack on the Bora Borans. As the English papers reported, after the *Endeavour* got home: "The name of a Bolobolo man is their greatest dread, and they repeatedly solicited us to destroy them with our guns."

Again, Cook ignored the request. After that, Tupaia stood with the scientists at the rail, watching the canoes return to the beach. It was another milestone in his action-packed life. Undoubtedly, he wondered what strange events would pass before he saw Huahine again.

A breeze attended with persistent rain carried them to Opoa, on the southeast coast of Raiatea. Not only had they arrived at the most sacred *marae* in eastern Polynesia, Taputapuatea, but they had reached the heart of the legend of Hawaiki. The ship dropped anchor at noon, to be boarded by the occupants of two canoes, including two women, who brought a pig as a present and seemed very afraid. They cheered up when given a spike nail each, but had bad news for Tupaia. Despite intermittent uprisings, the Bora Borans occupied the entire island; the Bora Boran chief, Puni, ruled from his house on Tahaa (an islet just to the north of Raiatea and within the same encircling reef), and Tupaia was a marked man.

Consequently, Tupaia warned Cook and Banks they would have to make haste—as Banks noted, "Tupia who has always expressd much fear of the men of *Bola Bola* says that they have conquerd this Island and will tomorrow come down and fight with us." Naturally, the priest was anxious to pray at the *marae* that was his *alma mater* before being interrupted by a Bora Boran force, so he urged Cook and Banks to get on shore as soon as possible.

"On landing Tupia repeated the ceremony of praying as at Huahine," wrote Banks, which meant that the Europeans stood numbly, rain running down their noses and gathering in the gutters of Captain Cook's cocked hat as Tupaia, stripped down to the waist, went through the long ritual of introducing himself and his companions, and presented gifts to honor the gods. The *marae* they contemplated as they blinked away raindrops was awe-inspiring in its ancient immensity, its once-towering *ahu* eroded to a height of just eight feet, the huge rectangle of its cobbled apron studded with tall stones and carved wooden boards, and shadowed with dripping, sacred trees. Nearby, a *fata*, or altar table, bore the latest sacrifice, a big roasted hog. Closer to the edge of the shore a small platform of rougher stones formed a navigators' *marae*—a chapel dedicated to seamen—which was studded with "a great many long boards set up, carved in various figures," as described by Parkinson. Beyond, the gray sea rippled rhythmically on the low shore.

Finally, the ceremony was over, and the party was free to move. To Tupaia's horror, Banks immediately strode up to one of the thatched god houses and thrust his hand inside. The naturalist felt, according to his own account, a "parsel about 5 feet long and one thick wrappd in matts." While Tupaia protested in vain, he tore with thick fingers at the coverings of the feathered god, until at last he came to a layer that resisted his fumbling, and gave up.

Why an intelligent scientist with the benefit of three months of intimate association with Tahitians (not to mention coaching by a high priest) should commit such blasphemy is hard to understand, unless he was influenced by continued irritation with Tupaia. Back on Tahiti, Dr. Munkhouse had been attacked for the relatively trivial crime of plucking a flower on sacred ground. Here, on the greatest *marae* in eastern Polynesia, the whole party would have been slaughtered if they had not been under Tupaia's protection. Undoubtedly Tupaia had to talk to the appalled local priests very fast indeed.

Banks moved on to a small, standing canoe, to make the gruesome discovery that it had eight fresh jawbones dangling down from it. Tupaia grimly told him they were the mandibles of Raiatean men killed in an uprising, presumably hung by the victors as a warning to the rest, though Banks speculated they were trophies won back from the Bora Borans. Intermittent warfare seemed to be a feature of life here—when Banks went for an evening walk along the shore with Tupaia, he found a god house, "the under part of which was lind with a row of Jaw bones." The next grisly question was whether any of the victims were still alive when these jaws were severed. After the ship arrived home the newspapers reported, "Whenever these villains take any prisoners, they always cut off their lower jaws, and leave the wretches to linger and die; and from such acts of singular barbarity they are a terror to the other islanders." According to Cook, this was an exaggeration, but Tupaia was happy to let them believe it, if it would help demonize the Bora Borans.

The Bora Borans, he disdainfully told his companions, were nothing better than a set of common felons. "Toobiah informed us," wrote Parkinson, "that, some years past, the chiefs of Otaheite, and the neighbouring islands, banished such of their criminals as well convicted of thefts, and other crimes which they thought did not deserve death, to an adjacent island called Bolobola, which, before the commencement of that law, was almost barren and uninhabited." As the convicts' numbers increased they began to organize themselves—"Being men of desperate fortunes, they made themselves canoes, turned pirates, and made prisoners such of the people of the islands near them as had the misfortune to fall in their way." A particularly audacious chief, "Opoone" (Puni), was adopted as their leader, and under his command they "adventured to make war" on the neighboring islands, conquering and then annexing them to their power. And, of these, Puni's greatest prize was Tupaia's homeland, Raiatea.

Meantime, in an echo of the ceremony carried out in Tahiti a little more than two years earlier by the second lieutenant of the *Dolphin*, Cook stuck a stake in the ground of Opoa, and hoisted the Union Jack, a ceremony accompanied by a stamp of boots and a salute of muskets that startled the birds from the trees. He then "took possession" of Raiatea, Huahine, and Bora Bora "for the use of his Britannick majesty" (as Joseph Banks put it), a lofty claim that certainly would have been questioned by the Bora Borans, if they had known.

Next day, Banks, Solander, and Tupaia went on shore to watch the local canoe-builders at work, while Cook and his officers surveyed the coast and charted the anchorage with small boats. Banks was fascinated by the "incredible cleverness" of the specialist shipwrights, who fashioned great canoes that were between thirty and sixty feet in length, not counting the steep upward curves at the ends, and were based on a dugout keel, which was built up with smoothly planed and sanded strakes, and finished at the top with hollowed longitudinal sections of tree-trunks, so that the bilge curved inward. All these parts were sewn together with sinnet (coconut fiber), the holes being bored with awls made of human arm bones, ground sharp and fixed to a wooden handle—"This work difficult as it would be to an European with his Iron tools they perform without Iron and with amazing dexterity."

The weather deteriorated even further, so that next day Banks and Solander botanized in the drenching rain, finding at the same time that the locals avoided them, and that any people they accosted were very cool in manner. Naturally, the Raiateans were distancing themselves from the dangerous

sacrilege Banks had committed, though the imperceptive Parkinson meditated, "We did not know the occasion of their reservedness, but conjectured
that the Bolabola people had been amongst them."

There was no sign of the Bora Borans themselves, except for jawbones
hanging from the lintels of houses, beached canoes, and the branches of trees,
as a reminder that the land was occupied by a hostile force. There was little
else to do or see—as Cook wrote, "this side of the Island is neither populous
nor rich in produce." He would have taken his departure gladly, but the wind
was foul, blowing onshore and trapping them in the anchorage.

On July 24, after three days of frustration, he attempted to go out by
another passage, with results that could have been disastrous. When the
ship made her first tack to windward she was still within the reef, and
close to it. The quartermaster was perched outside the hull, beneath the
forward bulwarks, holding himself in place with an elbow crooked about
the chains, the coil of the sounding line in his left hand and his other fist
gripping the end of the twenty-fathom rope. For those watching from the
quarterdeck, he was a black shape in the forward channels, silhouetted
against the pewter-colored water and the wavering purple and indigo shadows of underwater coral. Powerfully, he swung the line back and forth in
widening arcs, the ten-pound lead weight a black blob at the end, as everyone watched anxiously—Tupaia in particular, for, as Banks related, he
"never sufferd her to go in less than 5 fathom water without being much
alarmed."

The rope whirled three times in the air, whistling audibly, and then was
dropped dead ahead. A moment while the ship sailed up to it, then up it
came, threading through the sailor's hands. In a shout that was harsh with
fright, he bawled, "Two fathoms!"

Two fathoms—six feet, when the ship drew at least fourteen. It was
impossible; the Endeavour should have been a wreck. Instead, she glided forward, while every man on deck held his breath. As Banks observed, "either
the man was mistaken," or the ship, by great good fortune, was sailing along
the edge of the reef, which was as steep and flat as a wall. Shocked by the
close shave with disaster, Captain Cook ordered the anchor dropped.

Banks went ashore again, but saw nothing more interesting than a small
marae. Gruesomely, it was "ornamented with 2 sticks about 5 feet long, each
hung with Jaw bones as thick as possible and one having a skull stuck on
its top."

With fair breezes and kind currents, the history of the Endeavour might have
been very different. But the offended gods were not listening to Tupaia's
prayers, and Cook became less than enamoured with bucketing about

Polynesian isles in the teeth of foul winds and against contrary currents. To
get out to the open sea, he was forced to beat against the onshore wind, a
slow and arduous process in a square-sailed ship of the time. Fetching
Tupaia's recommended anchorage, Haamanino, on the northwest coast of
Raiatea—or a similar haven on Bora Bora—or on Raiatea's sister island,
Tahaa—or on any island *at all*, so desperate did Cook become—was an even
more taxing, nerve-wracking, and long-drawn-out affair.

Again and again the ship was tacked, only to get no farther, or lose the
small ground she did gain by falling off to leeward. Infuriatingly, Cook could
see the passage into the northwest end of Raiatea, where "Tupia says there a
chan[1] into a very good harbour," but he was getting nowhere near. The next
day, he tried another approach, laying down a course for the strait between
Tahaa and Bora Bora. They did discover a small, low islet, "4 or 5 Leagues
from Bolabola," as Cook recorded. Tupaia told him it was called "Tubai,"
and that "only three Families live upon it, but that the people from these
Islands resort thither to catch fish." The winds blew all about the compass,
and the ship could make no headway in that direction, either.

To add irritation to exasperation, Banks, Solander, and Molineux commandeered a boat and landed on Tahaa, and Cook was forced to lay off and
on—make short tacks to keep in the same place—while he waited for them
to return. They came back with hogs and fowls, and as many plantains and
yams as the boat would hold, plus the strange news that the Tahaa people
dropped their robes to the waist on seeing them—"they paid us the same
Compliment they are used to pay to their own Kings," wrote Banks. Nonetheless, Cook was annoyed that he had to order two guns fired to summon
them back to the ship, and that it was dark before they arrived.

They set sail again, and were this time pushed toward Bora Bora's dramatic double-peaked silhouette, like the shadow of a supine giant, leering at
the sky. It took several tacks before they could weather the southern end of
the island, and sail close to the inhospitable-looking shore. As Banks noted,
it seemed quite infertile: "Tupia tells us that between the shore and moun-
tain is a large salt lagoon, a certain sign of barrenness in this climate." There
were very few people to be seen on the beach, as all the rest were in Raiatea-
or so Tupaia told them. He was anxious for them to land and claim the
island for the British king, so assured them that there were plenty of hogs
and fowls for trade, if only they would sail to the other side. Instead, they
bore away, the wind still blowing in their teeth, forced away from Bora Bora
by a heavy swell from the south.

The sixth night since leaving Opoa was spent like those before, laboriously working to windward, while Cook worried about running onto coral
outcrops and unseen reef islands called *motu*. It was not until the next

afternoon that the wind moderated, allowing them to enter Haamanino harbor. They had to warp the ship inside the reef, and struggle with an anchor that became stuck in the coral, but at last the glad moment came when the tide turned and allowed the ship to sail over the stuck anchor, and release it.

It was the evening of August 1. After six days of exasperation they were finally at anchor.

Considering that Tupaia was a recognized enemy of the Bora Boran occupation, his fellow *Endeavours* must have felt surprised that he was so willing to pilot the ship into the anchorage, and go ashore. Haamanino, for him, was a place of great regret, because here he had been rich with property. Wrote Banks during their stay in this harbor, "We had often heard Tupia speak of Lands belonging to him which had been taken away by the Bola-Bola men; these he tells us now are situate in the very bay where the ship lies." Perhaps the scientist thought Tupaia was exaggerating, or putting on airs, because he questioned the locals about it, but they "confirmd What he had told us," he wrote, "and shewd us several different *whennuas* which they all acknowledged belong of right to him."

Meantime, Tupaia had been informed by friends that revisiting this scene of past violence and long-held grudges was not nearly as risky as he had originally thought. Puni was just as scared of him as he was of Puni—or so men on Cook's second expedition learned. According to James Burney, second lieutenant of the *Adventure*, the old bandit was so worried Tupaia would persuade his powerful English friends "to take his part" and attack the Bora Borans, he had ordered his people to pay the utmost respect (the reason the Tahaans had so humbly and mysteriously lowered their robes), and had kept a low profile himself. So Tupaia felt perfectly free to go wherever he liked.

On August 3, the second day after anchoring, he, Banks, and Cook were exploring the adjacent country when they were distracted by the fast pulse and rattle of drums in the distance. Tracking down the sound, they discovered a company of strolling players—"*Heiva*," wrote Banks; "who detained us 2 hours and during all that time entertaind us highly indeed." The troupe was made up of three drummers, two women dancers, and six men—"these Tupia tells us go round the Island as we have seen the little *Heivas* do at Otahite."

Cook was unusually impressed, writing with approval that the female dancers were costumed with decency, "such as we had not seen before." Their heads were crowned with wreaths of plaited human hair and sweetly scented gardenias, and though their shoulders and arms were bare, their breasts were modestly covered with cloth decorated with two posies of black feathers. A great quantity of pleated tapa was bound about their hips, bunching up into a ruff above their waists, and forming a petticoat that fell as far as their feet.

"In this dress," wrote Banks, "they advanced sideways keeping excellent time to the drums which beat brisk and loud." Then they began to shake their hips, setting the folds of cloth into shimmering motion, while at the same time their hands and arms undulated, and their mouths twisted into strange grimaces. Fascinated, Banks hunted down the *heiva* twice more after that, each time finding the performance staged in a different place and further away—"Tupia tells us that it will in this manner move gradually round the Island."

The second time, Banks took Sydney Parkinson with him, "that he might scetch the dresses." Parkinson did not mention making his sketch; nor did anyone record that Tupaia made his own drawing, using up the blank half of the paper where he had already painted the costume of the chief mourner. The young Quaker was so beguiled with the dancers that he devoted his entire journal entry to describing them "putting their bodies into strange motions, writhing their mouths, and shaking their tails, which made the numerous plaits that hung about them flutter like a peacock's train." The drums pulsed, while the dancers kept perfect time, and an old man roared out the movements.

In the interval a cast of Bora Boran men acted out a farce—one that Tupaia must have watched grimly, as it was the story of their subjugation of the island, "in which they exhibited the various stratagems used in the conquest, and were very vociferous, performing all in time to the drum. In the last scene," Parkinson concluded primly, "the actions of the men were very lascivious."

CHAPTER 11

༄

Tupaia's Map

By Tuesday, August 8, Cook was ready to leave Raiatea. The ship was fully provisioned, and the ship carpenters had fixed an annoying leak in the gunpowder room, so he could sail "as soon as ever the wind will permit us to get out of the harbour." The weather cooperated. At eleven next morning, after a night of heavy rain, a breeze sprang up and carried them out to sea.

Banks wrote blithely in his journal, "Launched out into the Ocean in search of what chance and Tupia might direct us to." He was quite mistaken, for Cook—not Tupaia—had decided on the next course of the voyage: "to the Southward, the way I now intend to steer." Even Parkinson knew better, writing, "On the 9th of August we weighed anchor, and proceeded from this bay to the southward, to see what discoveries we could make there, pursuant to the directions of the admiralty."

When James Cook left London, he was carrying two sets of orders. The first set concerned the voyage to Tahiti, the cultivation of "a Friendship with the Natives" despite their "rather treacherous" nature, and the observation of "the passage of the Planet Venus over the disk of the sun on the 3rd of June 1769." Once the observation was made and the ship was ready to go back to sea, he was to follow "Additional and Secret Instructions"—which were to make an important and most remarkable discovery. The intelligentsia in London were convinced that a temperate, fertile, and mineral-rich "continent, or land of great extent"—the fabled *Terra Australis Incognita,* or Great Southern Continent—lay in the south Pacific, to help counterbalance the weight of Europe, Asia, and Russia in the north; and James Cook was advised to search for this rich prize south "of the Tract lately made by Capt[n]

Wallis" until he arrived at latitude forty. Then—and only if the *Endeavour* had not discovered the Great Southern Continent—he was to turn his attention to the less glamorous task of looking for the east coast of New Zealand.

When Samuel Wallis had set out in the *Dolphin* in August 1766, he had been given very similar instructions. Prefacing his document with the remark that it was essential for "the dignity of the Crown of Great Britain," that a British ship should get to the fabled *Terra Australis Incognita* first, their Lordships of the Admiralty had directed him to search the huge tract of ocean "between Cape Horn and New Zealand" with diligence and care. After leaving Tahiti, however, Wallis had not even tried to follow orders and go south. Instead, he had steered for the East Indies, the Cape of Good Hope, and home.

He had no excuse, apart from his own bad health. His ship was sound: the *Dolphin*'s hull had been sheathed with thin sheets of copper against wood-boring teredo worms before her first discovery voyage, in 1764, and careening her in Matavai Bay had found her bottom as clean as the day she left the shipyard. Because of Purea's generous patronage and Tupaia's good management, she was lavishly provisioned, and after five weeks of eating well, all his men were scurvy-free. Unfortunately, as their Lordships were to learn to their displeasure, Wallis lacked the true explorer's zeal to drive his ship and his men into unimaginable dangers. Instead, his one and only ambition had been to get back to England.

James Cook was made of much sterner stuff. It is a testament to Tupaia's persuasive powers that instead of immediately following his directions "to proceed to the southward" as soon as he put back to sea, he had sailed northwest to "discover" Huahine, Raiatea, and their sister islands. Tupaia had assured him there were plenty of hogs available at Huahine and Raiatea, which gave Cook a good excuse. Additionally, he had reasoned that a few weeks of gentle cruising would give his men a chance to recover from their excesses, "the too free use of women" having left them in "a worse state of hilth" than when they had arrived at Tahiti.

But now it was time to follow orders.

Perhaps in a gesture of apology to Tupaia, who had piloted them so conscientiously over the past four weeks, Cook consented to have a cannon fired as they left Raiatea. As Gunner Stephen Forwood noted, they "fired a 4 Pounder Shotted to satisfy the couriousaty of the Indian on board." So, most satisfyingly for the dispossessed exile, they made their departure from Raiatea in a cloud of sulfurous smoke, with the echoes of the explosion ringing about the hills.

Banks did not notice their southward course for at least two days, for as soon as the ship had her offing in a choppy sea he was seasick, confined miserably to his swinging cot. Tupaia must have detected it at once, but still he anticipated discoveries and rediscoveries, James Roberts writing, "Tobiah says there is 3 Larg Islans near us which his fathar was at and seem'd to be the Southonmost land he is acquainted with." They passed one of these, which Tupaia called "Manua," without seeing it, though Tupaia pointed out its whereabouts. "He says however," wrote Banks on August 12, the day he recovered his equilibrium, "that tomorrow or next day we shall see another which he calls *Oheter—a.*"

This island was, in fact, Rurutu, one of a group now known as the Australs, which includes Rimatara, Tubuai, Raivavae, Rapa Iti, Marotiri, and four tiny atolls within the Nororotu reef. Tupaia seemed sure of its identity, however, telling Parkinson that this island was "one of a cluster of nine," all of which "bore the title of Oheite added to them." When Banks noted that he was informed by Tupaia "that there were many other Islands from south to south west of us most of their names beginning with *Ohete*," he added dubiously, "none however were in sight."

At dawn, the cliffs of Rurutu loomed ahead. By nine the ship was running near, and the pinnace was lowered so Gore, Banks, Solander, and Tupaia could go on shore—"and likewise to see if there was Anchorage in a Bay which appear'd to our veiw," wrote Cook, concluding tersely, "not that I intended to anchor or make any stay here." As it happened, landing was impossible. Tupaia's name should have been familiar to the older inhabitants—"Tobiah was here about 23 Years ago since which they have had no Intercourse with the Northern Islands," wrote Roberts—but the natives proved to be difficult.

Initially, everything seemed to go well. A canoe came alongside the pinnace in response to Banks's friendly shouts, and the paddlers eagerly snatched the nails offered to them. Then three strong men sprang on board, and there was a struggle for possession of the boat. Gore's musket jammed, but two more muskets were fired into the air, scaring the natives into diving for their canoe: "one of our people however inconsiderately leveld a 3rd," wrote Banks. A swimmer was hit in the forehead, and though he seemed relatively unharmed, a large and angry crowd had gathered on the beach by the time the canoe returned.

As the pinnace followed, a challenge was roared by a prancing stalwart, "which we understood from Tupia was a defiance sent from the people." Another combative figure, wearing a tall feathered headdress and stiff tapa dyed yellow, red, and brown (earning him the nickname Harlequin), executed his own war dance. These two were joined by an older, more sober man, who held a long conversation with Tupaia, asking him where they had come from. Evidently tales of the *Dolphin's* broadside had reached this

distant place, because Tupaia told Parkinson later that the old man "begged
that our people would not kill them." Tupaia having assured him of their
peaceful intentions, he launched into prayer. "Tupia made his responses,"
wrote Banks, "but continued to tell us that they were not our freinds."

Despite this warning, Banks, through Tupaia, tried to negotiate a pact, so
they could come on shore and conduct a little trading, along with the botanizing that was so dear to his heart. Leave was finally given, but only on the
condition they left their muskets in the boat, so the idea was abandoned.
Some natives waded out to barter some interesting cloth that appeared to be
varnished, plus a few fearsome spears and war clubs, but otherwise it was
an unrewarding visit. "After leaving these unhospitable people," Banks concluded, "we Stood to the Southward as usual and had in the evening a great
dew which wetted everything."

As Cook noted that same afternoon, ever since they had left Raiatea, "Tupia
hath been very disireous for us to steer to the westward." He was not prepared
to listen—going west was pointless, he thought, despite Tupaia's assurance
that they would find "plenty of Islands, the most of them he himself hath
been at." This was because Cook had decided the islands Tupaia was talking
about were "those discover'd by Captain Wallice and by him call'd Boscawen
and Kepple," which lay no less than "400 leagues to the westward."

Boscawen and its tiny sister islet, Keppel (Tafahi and Niuatobutabu, in
the Tongan archipelago), were insignificant volcanic outcrops, and four
hundred leagues was approximately twelve hundred miles, a long distance
for the *Endeavour*, which was averaging about sixty miles a day at that
time. Tupaia assured him (perhaps smugly) that a fast voyaging *pahi* could
get there in ten days—"that is," wrote Cook with a hint of sourness, "their
large Proes sail much faster than this ship." Tupaia did do his best to be
scrupulously honest, adding that the return journey to Raiatea could take
thirty days or more—though he did also mention the advantages of waiting for "the Months of November, December and Jan[ry]," when the winds
were constant from the west, and the passage would be much quicker.
Cook was willing to credit that "they know very well how to take the
Advantage of these winds in their Navigations," but would not have been
happy with the implied criticism of the *Endeavour*. Like any good captain,
he was fiercely proud of his unlovely ship, reporting to the Admiralty after
his return home that she was a reliable sailer under a topgallant gale—"-
with the wind a point or two abaft the beam she will then run 7 or 8
Knots," he loyally wrote.

This irritation would have been added to uneasiness about Tupaia's position on board. On Huahine and Raiatea more respect had been paid to

Tupaia than to Captain Cook himself, so that it was possible to harbor a suspicion the islanders considered the star navigator the "admiral." The Chinese have a saying that a ship with two masters is a "two-headed dragon," and Captain Cook, acutely aware that a ship can have only one commander, would have emphatically agreed with this. Another factor was that Cook was both ambitious and conscientious. Acutely aware that Wallis had ruined his career by not obeying his strict instructions "to discover and obtain a complete knowledge of the Land or Island supposed to be situated in the Southern Hemisphere," Cook was determined not to make the same mistake. If they came across the islands Tupaia had described, well and good.

Otherwise, as he wrote, "I shall spend no more time searching for them being now fully resolved to Stand directly to the Southward in search of the Continent."

It is impossible not to wonder what the story of James Cook in the Pacific would have been like if he had paid more attention to his Polynesian navigator. Because Cook was not listening properly, he did not realize that Tupaia was not nattering on about mere tips of submerged mountains like Tafahi and Niuatobutabu, but trying to describe major islands like Upolu, Tutuila, Tongatapu, and Savai'i—the last of which he called "the father of all the islands," referring to its mythic status as the cradle of Polynesian civilization. If Cook had pursued Tupaia's course, he would have explored the far reaches of Tonga, Samoa, the Cooks, and Fiji—but he was not to realize that until he made another voyage, and "discovered" many of Tupaia's islands, without the benefit of having the prestigious linguist and intermediary on board.

Cook also missed a golden opportunity to learn how a Polynesian master navigator found his way. How, for instance, did Tupaia keep an accurate course? How did he carry out the dead reckoning necessary to keep a running fix of his position? By what signs did he know that islands were there, when they were beyond the horizon? Cook was a fine navigator himself, and should have been interested. But instead of listening to Tupaia's lyrical descriptions of what awaited in the west, and *asking* questions about how he would make his course there, he and Banks put Tupaia to work *answering* questions—for the reports they were writing about the manners and customs of the Tahitian people.

Banks had made a start on loose sheets of paper already, and had given this draft to Cook, who cribbed from it freely as he composed his "Description of King Georges Island," which he had started on July 13, the day they had left Tahiti. Plagiarism was commonplace on the *Endeavour*, as it was on all His Majesty's ships, not excluding the *Dolphin*. The master's mates and midshipmen had to keep journals to prove they had served at sea when they applied for their certificates (at Trinity House, in the case of the mates, and at Whitehall, where the midshipmen sat for their lieutenants' examinations), and in order to keep them up to date—often days or weeks after the actual events—they copied from each other. Captain Wallis had certainly consulted with George Robertson when he wrote his own report, as just about the only Tahitians he had dealt with at length were Tupaia and Purea, and the only Tahitian whose manners and customs he had observed in detail was the young man they had named Jonathan. Robertson had been mostly involved with charting the lagoon and having romantic flings, however, so Wallis's report had been most unsatisfactory, mostly a self-justification for hammering the Tahitians with his broadside. James Cook was determined to do better, and if cribbing from his scientific passenger would help, he would do it.

On the night they left Rurutu, Banks began a fair copy of his own report in his journal, heading it, "Manners & customs of S. Sea Islands," and starting a new book for the rest of his diary. Tupaia readily provided information when asked, because it made him feel as if he was still playing an important role on board, particularly as he made a humiliating mistake the following day. In the morning, as Banks related, they were told that land was in sight—at least, everyone assumed it was land, including Tupaia, who was so sure of it he "gave it a name." But it turned out to be just a cloud.

Tupaia was not as sunny tempered as before, though, being so brutally frank when describing the practice of infanticide that Cook was shocked. He also managed to offend every Englishman within hearing distance by criticizing King George III for having so many offspring (six legitimate sons and daughters at that point of time). His basic argument—that his people did not produce hosts of idle and expensive young nobility—was logical, but the loyal Britishers did not see it that way.

It was another reason for them to undervalue Tupaia's contribution to the voyage. Yet, though his relationship with Cook and Banks might not have been as good, the information he provided for their reports was—and is—an invaluable record of Tahitian society at the time. Knowing the fighting strength of the various districts well, he was able to give the precise number of warriors each could raise, which meant Cook and Banks could make a good guess at the total population of the island. He also listed the duties and responsibilities of a priest, withstood jibes from Banks about priestly profiteering and his people's inflexibility in clinging to ancient customs, tried unsuccessfully to teach them the archaic language of litany, revealed secrets of successful fishing, talked about canoe-building, and described methods of waging war at sea—producing a riveting picture of three war canoes to illustrate what he was saying.

War canoes at Tahiti. Watercolor by Tupaia. (© The British Library Board, 15508/14)

Hastily created, this sketch runs across the bottom of a tattoo-like drawing of trees and a longhouse, ruining the balance of the original work, but at the same time vividly depicting the sequence of action. Two of the craft are fighting canoes, equipped with what Cook described as "an oblong platform about 10 or 12 feet in length and 6 or 8 in breadth," where little figures stand "to graple one another and fight it out with Clubs" to the death, while other warriors wait to take over after these have fallen. The third canoe, a supply vessel with sails, hovers nearby to pass over more weapons as needed.

Though the sketch was obviously intended as an aid for communication and not art for art's sake, it is vibrant with energy, a vivid contrast to the static style of the original drawing. The rapidly scribbled figures are like little war-gods, their short legs braced, their shoulders squared, their backs hollowed with effort. John Marra, a seaman who joined the *Endeavour* late in the voyage, at Batavia in Java, wrote that Tupaia's shipmates told him "Toobia" was a real genius, "a priest of the first order, and an excellent artist." In maritime parlance of the time, an "artist" was a "sea artist," or navigator, not a creator of artwork (who was called a draftsman). But, with this sketch of war canoes, Tupaia earned his rating as an artist in the modern sense, too.

It is not surprising the seamen recognized that Tupaia was "an excellent artist," meaning navigator. They had watched him spend many hours on deck with Taiata, pointing out key constellations and stars at night, and by day counting and judging the swells as they ran under the hull, and narrowly studying the silhouettes of islands as they moved past the ship. As they told interested listeners later, so precise was Tupaia's dead reckoning, and so retentive his memory, that at any moment, day or night, he was able to point accurately to the position of Tahiti. Now, Taiata was learning to do the same. Not only did Tupaia have a bounden duty to pass on his knowledge to his apprentice, but keeping a precise mental log was a crucial part of the wayfinder's craft.

If it was so commonly known by the seamen that Tupaia was a brilliant navigator, why did Cook not seem to notice? Tupaia was willing to share information that was normally kept a deadly secret, not just because he was dispossessed and an exile, but because he wanted to share the joys of discovery—like Cook himself, he had the soul of an explorer. He had not personally traveled the full extent of the old trade routes, as since his grandfather's time the arc of Raiatean voyaging had greatly narrowed, so he was excited by the prospect.

This also counted against him. James Cook, noting that Tupaia had told him he had visited just thirteen islands, most just short voyages from Raiatea, implied this was a good reason for not following his advice to steer west, as presumably he would find it hard to navigate to places he had never visited before. Tupaia, however, had complete confidence in his mental library of seaways. Even if he was put off course by bad weather, and the stars, sun, and moon were hidden by clouds, he could fix his position by casting around for lines of reefs and swells that arrowed to the desired destination. Also, he would not have contemplated a single long passage, but a series of dog-legs. Most islands were much less than three hundred miles from their nearest neighbor, so far-off destinations were reached by island-hopping from one target to another. On most of these there would be resident star navigators, to confirm the onward course.

Cook did listen well enough to experience a brief moment of insight. Musing that when Tupaia's people sailed west, they voyaged "from Island to Island for several hundred Leagues, the Sun serving them for a compass by day and the Moon and Stars by night," he speculated that this was how the Pacific had been peopled. If the Raiateans island-hopped to destinations up to a thousand miles westward of them, he wrote, "it cannot be doubted but that the inhabitants of those western Islands may have been at others as far to the westward of them, and so we may trace them from Island to Island quite to the East Indies." Yet, despite drawing this conclusion that Tupaia's people had a long history of finding their way to the edges of the Pacific, he did not ask him how they did it, being satisfied with his vague notion of the sun, moon, and stars "serving them for a compass."

Cook had equal reservations about the island names Tupaia had shared with him, Banks, and Molineux in an attempt to demonstrate his knowledge of the Pacific. Though Molineux had written them down in his journal, Cook (like Banks) had not, saying that while Tupaia had given him "an account of upwards of seventy," because the information was "so vague and uncertain" he would defer copying them down until Tupaia had described "the situation of each Island with a little more certainty." The job of writing down the list was shelved until the end of March 1770, and by that time Cook had lost whatever notes he might have made, because he explained at the end that there should have been many more names, but he was confined to the ones on Tupaia's map: "The above list was taken from a chart of the Islands Drawn by Tupia's own hands," he wrote; "he at one time gave us an Account of near 130 Islands but in his Chart he laid down only 74."

This is Cook's one and only allusion to the map Tupaia now drew in a further attempt to convince the Europeans to steer west. Yet the chart is a remarkable testament to Polynesian knowledge of the Pacific, and Tupaia's grasp of it. Covering a great ribbon of ocean that encompasses the southern tropics from Rotuma to the Marquesas, it extends about twenty-five hundred miles in an east-west direction, and contains a myriad of islands the Europeans had never heard of before. Surely Cook, the great European cartographer, should have been curious about the vast fund of three-dimensional knowledge laid onto this piece of paper—but he was not. The others were even less receptive, for Cook's journal is the only one that even *mentions* the chart. The seamen knew about Tupaia's islands, telling Marra that he "laid down a plan of more than 100 of his own knowledge, most of them within the Tropics." If Cook's crew found his chart noteworthy, why did he find it so easy to dismiss it? Banks was no more perceptive: he noted that "the clever ones" among Tupaia's people could predict the rising and setting of the stars, and that he had been told "they make very long voyages, often remaining out from home several months, visiting in that time many different Islands," but he made no note at all of the chart, let alone how, when, where, or why it was made.

Because of this, it is only possible to imagine Tupaia dotting down islands as he tried to explain how a navigator worked his course, saying such things as, *this* is my departure point, *this* is my destination, and *this* is my reference island; then prodding the nib of his pen on another group, saying again, the canoe leaves from *this* island, the target is *that* island, and *there* is my reference island for this particular passage, which will take a certain number of days. Because no one described this, it is impossible to know for sure if Polynesians *did* use passing islands as reference points—islands that might lie invisibly over the horizon, but were detected by the skilled navigator

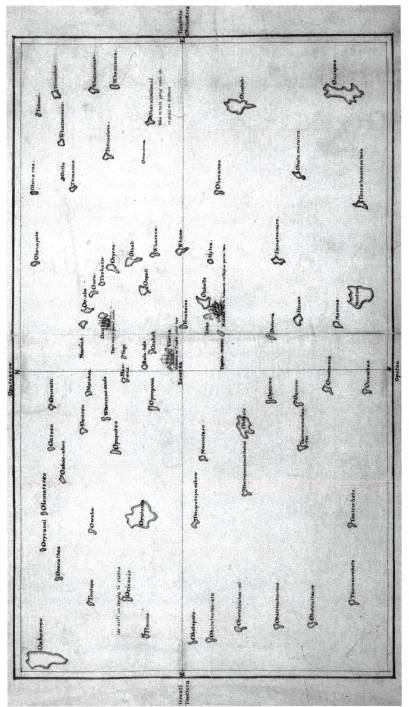

Tupaia's map. (© The British Library Board, 21593c)

because of the disturbances in the winds, swells, and currents they create. What is certain is that Tupaia drew the map in an effort to share his knowledge, but exactly what he was trying to communicate is unknown, because none of the *Endeavour*s bothered to write down what he said.

Naturally, the European officers thought they had good reasons for their lack of interest. In their eyes, Tupaia's chart should never have been called a map at all! The words "chart" and "map" were (and are) large concepts for westerners, embracing compass directions, latitude and longitude, land drawn to scale, and accurate estimates of distances. Tupaia's sketch had none of these elements—his idea of distance was how far a *pahi* could sail in a day; miles and leagues meant nothing to him. According to western tradition, a chart should be a guide for planning and executing a voyage—but no mortal man could take that piece of paper and use it to find his way about the Pacific!

Tupaia made history yet again when he drew his map, for it was the first attempt by any Polynesian to make a chart of the ocean on paper. Raiatean master navigators taught their apprentices directional stars with the help of little stones set out on the ground, and Tupaia *may* have had an equivalent of what the Marshall Islanders call *mattang*, sticks tied in grids and curves to show patterns of swells. Even this was not the equivalent of a European map, as it was used for demonstration on shore, and never taken on voyage. Tupaia could have watched the master of the *Dolphin* work on his charts of Matavai Bay, and certainly was interested in Molineux's drafting, but the concepts that Europeans attached to maps were not part of his tradition. Indeed, the idea that a canoe could be sitting on invisible lines called "latitude" and "longitude" would have seemed as mad to him as the notion of navigating by disturbances in the swells would have seemed to Molineux, Pickersgill, and Cook.

Oddly, none of the *Endeavour*s seemed to notice that Tupaia's chart also documented some Polynesian history, written down in five small captions that he dictated, and Cook (theoretically) copied in tiny print. One caption, over the island named "Orevavie" (Raivavae, in the Austral Islands, pictured northwest of Tahiti instead of in its true southwest position), reads "toe miti no terara te rietea" (*toi maitai no tera ara i te Raiatea*), meaning "fine adzes come over that sea-way to Raiatea." Another, "Maa te tata pahei rahie ete te pahei no Brittane" (*Maa te taata, pahi rahi, iti te pahi no Brittane*), is placed under "Ohevatoutouai" (Tahuata, in the Marquesas Islands), and can be translated as: "men eat men, canoes large, small are the ships of Britain," meaning that English ships were small in comparison; it most probably referred to the cannibal Marquesans, who built huge sea-going double canoes.

The other three captions accompany Tupaia's tiny sketches of square-rigged ships. These are not copies of the *Endeavour*, as would be expected, but drawings of ships of a much older style, with beakheads, and old-fashioned rigging. How did Tupaia know what they looked like? His learned lore must have been detailed indeed. These little drawings appear to describe past visits of European ships. "Tuboona no Tupia pahei tayo" (*Tupuna no Tupaia pahi taio*), reads the script by the island of "Ulietea" (Raiatea), a shorthand way of saying that in the time of Tupaia's grandfather a friendly ship had come to a mooring there, to trade peacefully with the people. The small print under the ship drawn below the island of "Otaheite" tells a very different story. "Medua no te tuboona no Tupia pahei toa" (*Metua no te tupuna no Tupaia pahi toa*), it reads, meaning "The father of the grandfather of Tupaia saw a hostile ship."

The third ship-sketch is next to the atoll of "Oanna" (Anaa) in the Tuamotu Islands. "Tupia tata no pahei matte" (*Tupia taata no pahi mate*), reads the caption—"Tupaia [says] the people of the ship were killed." This very possibly refers to the *African Galley*, which would mean that the men who were murdered were the same ones described to Robert Molineux in Tahiti. But who was the friendly visitor to Raiatea? It may have been a wandering galleon, or even a pirate ship. Only guesses can be made—for the *Endeavours*, it seems, did not bother to ask.

Something else Cook, Banks, and the others failed to mention was that copies of Tupaia's chart were made, presumably for their curiosity value. According to Johann Forster, a scientist who sailed with Cook on the second expedition, and who used an etching of the chart to illustrate the book he wrote about his adventures, there were three versions. First was the one drawn by Tupaia, with island names dictated by him and written (presumably) by Cook; a second was a copy (apparently) made by Cook but owned by Banks; and a third was made by Richard Pickersgill. This last was loaned to Forster for his book, and afterward lost, perhaps in the printer's office.

Whether these differed one from another is impossible to tell, as only one copy exists. It is generally believed that this survivor is not the original, because an anonymous note in the right-hand bottom corner, "Drawn by Lieut James Cook 1769," infers it is the copy made by Cook, and taken over by Banks. If it were not for this note, it would be obvious that the existing chart is the one made by Tupaia's "own hands," as it is drawn on exactly the same kind of paper as his artwork. This was high quality watercolor paper manufactured in England by James Whatman the elder, a man who was so proud of his best heavy stock that he included the initials of the famous Dutch papermaker, Lubertus van Gerrevink, in his watermark—"LVG" with a fleur-de-lis, in a shield with a crown above. Evidently, Banks gave some of this very expensive paper to Tupaia, though it is equally possible the navigator-priest found it in one of the lockers of the cabin he took over, because it is exactly the same paper used by the deceased painter, Alexander Buchan.

Until 1778, Tupaia's chart was forgotten, and then the etching appeared in Forster's book. The map itself was buried in the vast collection of Banks's papers endowed to the British Museum, and was not identified until 1955, so for a long time geographers and scientists were limited to the book illustration for their studies. One of the first of these (if not *the* first) was Horatio Hale, the brilliant young ethnologist with the United States Exploring Expedition, which in August 1838 departed from Norfolk, Virginia, with the aim of improving scientific understanding of the Pacific and its peoples. There was an excellent library on board the flagship, *Vincennes*, and the puzzle of Tupaia's map caught Hale's interest when he picked up Forster's book.

Meditating that "when Tupaia's map was drawn more than half the islands contained were unknown to Europeans," Horatio Hale went on to wonder whether it was printed the wrong way up. His clue was the word "*opatau*" at the bottom of the map, which does not mean "south," as "those for whom Tupaia drew it" assumed, but the direction toward which the south wind blows—meaning *north*. This upside-down theory solved puzzles like the placement of Rarotonga ("*Orarothoa*") in the northwest, when Tupaia must have known it was southwest of Tahiti, but inverting the chart led to other problems. Islands that had been approximately right before became misplaced—Huahine, for instance, was now southeast of Tahiti. Hale explained this away by claiming that the gentlemen who "overlooked Tupaia while he was drawing" (Cook, Banks, and Pickersgill), forced him with their "superior knowledge" to shift the islands whose positions they already knew, while leaving those they did not know (like Rarotonga) alone.

That they could coerce Tupaia seems unlikely, though. He was certain of his facts, and had such a strong, obstinate personality that it is hard to believe he was so easily dominated. Unsurprisingly, a host of alternative theories have been proposed since. The map has not just been turned this way and that, but has been divided into quadrants, which have been individually flipped. A recent study, based on the traditional method of drawing lines in the sand and placing pebbles in patterns, plausibly speculates that Tupaia's map is not a primitive attempt to imitate the European visualization of the world as a flat piece of paper, but instead is a sophisticated mosaic of sailing directions.

Undoubtedly, the debate will continue. No matter how persuasive an argument or compelling an idea, nobody can be absolutely sure that it is the correct one—because the right questions were never asked by Cook et al., and Tupaia's valiant attempts to explain were never written down.

Considering that Cook and Tupaia were both master navigators within their own societies, James Cook should have felt comfortable with the idea of consulting with the noble, highly educated Polynesian, but it seems it was impossible for him to credit that a man who worked with a mental library could be the equal of a European who was armed with sextant, almanac, and compass. And, because of Cook's decision not to steer west, Tupaia was not given the chance to prove he knew exactly what he was talking about. Where there might have been a language barrier (because Tupaia, while fluent, was still refining his command of English, and Cook's Tahitian was very rudimentary), a demonstration would have made all the difference.

Instead, the ship continued south. Cook and Banks finished their reports, set them aside, and returned to the routine that had been established on the voyage to Tahiti. And Tupaia, now with no function on board, was left to his own devices.

CHAPTER 12

❧

Latitude Forty South

The weather became unpleasant as they left the tropics behind, with almost constant icy rain. A heavy swell made the ship roll sickeningly. Loose gear slid from one side to the other, while the rigging thrummed, and the hull groaned. The pad of seamen's bare feet was replaced by the clatter of boots and shoes, and the hogs on deck huddled together for warmth, shivering and squealing, skidding in their muck and tumbling comically as the ship rolled back and forth.

Tupaia and Taiata, resistant to seasickness but not to cold, changed from loose, comfortable tapa robes into European clothes. Taiata could now be mistaken for just one of the boys, having adapted to ship life very easily. The cold meant little to a lad who could chase friends about the decks, and skylark in the rigging. He was also popular with the seamen, who told Marra later that he was "the darling of the ship's company from the highest to the lowest."

Tupaia, by contrast, was both lonely and alone. He went below to the crowded berth deck, to strike up conversations with old *Dolphin*s Richard Pickersgill and Frank Wilkinson, and talk with madcap midshipmen like the American James Magra (who wrote the gist of Tupaia's story down), but would not have been made welcome. The sailors, contrary by nature, accepted that as a highborn "man of real genius," Tupaia should be respected, but at the same time they resented it. As Marra was told just over a year later, Tupaia was "by no means beloved by the *Endeavour*'s crew, being looked upon as proud and austere, extorting homage, which the sailors who thought themselves degraded by bending to an Indian, were very unwilling to pay." And when they were disrespectful, Tupaia complained to the officers, which did not help matters at all.

It was such a foreign world, and the routine was so very strange. Time, which had been measured by the sun, stars, and tides, was now marked by bells and watches, so that an officer who asked the time of day would be answered with something like, "Two bells in the morning watch, sir!" At dawn—five A.M., two bells in the morning watch—the men on duty broke out buckets, and washed and scrubbed the decks. This was not incomprehensible, as in Tahiti the people rose at dawn, and went to the nearest pool to wash—but there was nowhere for personal washing on the *Endeavour*, so Tupaia became as unpleasantly smelly as his companions. Breakfast was eaten at eight bells, eight in the morning, which was familiar enough, being close to the time Tahitians broke their fast with a few leftovers from the day before. The noontime dinner, however, was almost as alien as the first issue of a pint of grog that followed, because in Tahiti noon was the hottest part of the day, not the time for heavy meals. The sailors' early supper hour of four in the afternoon was more acceptable for a man who was accustomed to eating in the shadowy late afternoon, but the scientific gentlemen who shared the afterquarters with Tupaia thought it quite bizarre that the seamen should have their second main meal of the day when the first was scarcely digested, and opted to have their supper much later, at eight in the evening, or even nine.

This meant that the Great Cabin had its own schedule—imposed not by the man who was supposed to be in charge, Captain Cook, but by his passenger, Joseph Banks. Indeed, Tupaia must have wondered whether Cook was really the *ari'i rahi* here. At eight in the morning, after the breakfast of wheat porridge was cleared away, Banks and his assistant botanist, Daniel Solander, spread their specimens and their books on the big table, and settled to work. According to a reminiscent letter Banks wrote in November 1784, the pleasurable activity of identifying and classifying "lasted from approximately 8 o'clock in the morning until 2 o'clock in the afternoon." Then everything was put aside so the steward could lay the table for the scientists' dinner. About four o'clock, "when the smell of cooking had vanished," Sydney Parkinson was summoned, and Banks and Solander brought out their specimens, and "showed him the manner in which the drawing should be done." When it became too dark to work, the table was cleared again, and the scientists' supper was laid.

Obviously, this affected everyone who lived and worked in the afterquarters of the ship. The table in the Great Cabin should have been where Captain Cook laid out his charts, but his only opportunity for this was before breakfast. Once Banks and Solander had taken over, he had to use the little desk in his stateroom, or cope as best he could on the open deck. A workingman all his life, Cook was accustomed to eating his dinner at noon, not the gentleman's hour of two-thirty in the afternoon, so it is probable he sat with the officers in the gunroom when he had his midday meal. Whether Tupaia joined him is unknown but unlikely; Tupaia was not accustomed to eating in the middle of the day, and he did not like European shipboard food—something which became a major factor in his voyage.

Sydney Parkinson—almost always referred to by Banks as "the draughtsman," instead of by his name—was another one affected by this routine. When he was not being instructed in sketching techniques at the big table in the Great Cabin, the only place he had to draw was the little desk in his cabin. Yet, despite the cramped, difficult circumstances, he managed to produce hundreds of beautiful paintings of botanical specimens, and dozens of sketches of posed Polynesians and their artifacts. Called "Patini" by the Tahitians, he was a quiet, gentle young man who liked children—he was the only *Endeavour* to write about Tahitian boys and girls, commenting that they were "remarkably kind to one another," for they shared the gifts he gave them. Judging by his journal, he liked to talk with Tupaia, mentioning conversations often, but otherwise he kept to himself. Dr. Solander laughed at him, calling him "Shyboots Parkinson."

The gossipy Daniel Solander, a thirty-six-year-old native of Sweden, was a disciple of Linnaeus, the genius who had been banned by the Vatican for inventing a system of plant classification based on sex organs. Solander had traveled to England about 1762, to teach the Linnaeus method, and had charmed everyone on sight. His English quickly became perfect: according to Banks's reminiscent letter, it was taught to him by "two of the most beautiful and wittiest women in England"—the wife and daughter of the Chancellor of England, Lord Northington. Within weeks he was given a well-paid job at the British Museum, and was elected a Fellow of the Royal Society, meantime entrancing society with his charming manners and lively conversation. As Banks went on, because "his company was so informative, so merry, and so agreeable," he was sought out "by all learned people." These included Benjamin Franklin and George III—both valuable contacts, for though they did not know it, the personable Daniel Solander was leading a double life, as a spy for the Swedish government.

Solander met Joseph Banks in 1764. At first sight, they did not have much in common. There was a difference of a decade in their ages, and Daniel Solander came from an academic background. Though expensively schooled at Harrow and Eton, Banks had emerged only half-educated—he could dance, but he could not draw, and his written Greek was better than his written English. When Banks was fourteen, however, a chance encounter with some countrywomen collecting herbs for a local apothecary had opened his eyes to the wonderful world of plants, and he had been obsessed with botany ever since. Drawn together by this mutual passion, Banks and Solander became lifelong friends.

When Banks had told him about the upcoming adventure, Solander had demanded to come too, and now he was one of the happiest people on board, having easily adapted to the life of a discoverer. Liked by all the officers, he was equally popular with the seamen, who collected fish and seaweed for him, Solander writing to a friend they "soon became such good philosophers" that they knew which specimens would please him.

In Tahiti, instead of keeping a mistress, Solander had enjoyed observing the exploits of others, one unlikely candidate being Parkinson, who had pretended to despise the sexual free-for-all that Tahiti offered. As Solander gossiped later, the truth came out when Banks picked up a girl and went home with her—to find "Shyboots Parkinson" in bed with the girl's sister! This woman was nearly thirty years old, but according to Banks, Parkinson had "chosen her as more discreet than a young one." This was more of a love match than Banks and Solander made it sound, as it seems that the girl was fond enough of her young Quaker lover to keep his baby—a young man named Patini, who could easily have been Parkinson's great-grandson, was shipped at Tahiti in 1864 by the captain of the American whaleship *Ocean*, and liked the cruise so well that he joined another whaler, the *Benjamin Cummings*, on September 27, 1866.

Considering the teasing, and the way Banks had betrayed him, it is not surprising that Parkinson made no attempt to draw pictures of any of his companions in the afterquarters, including his employer.

Another subject of gossip was another quiet, honest character—James Cook himself. According to Solander, the general opinion in the afterquarters was that John Gore, the junior lieutenant, should have been in command of the *Endeavour*! Gore, he said, was considered by those in the know to be "the best practical seaman now in the navy." Gore had the benefit of experience, being an old *Dolphin* who had circumnavigated the world two times before joining the *Endeavour*—as Solander wrote to his patron, Linnaeus, "Mr. Gore has done it twice, which is more than anyone now living can say." James Cook was "jealous of him," he said, because Gore was more experienced "in naval affairs," and had more dash and "determined courage," too. There was a kind of running feud between the two men—or so Solander reported to friends in London—as Gore (the first Briton in history to fire a musket at a Tahitian with intent to injure!) was of the strong opinion that Cook treated the natives too harshly.

Snobbery must have been part of it, a prejudice that the highly ranked Tupaia would have shared, once he knew Cook's origins. Cook was humbly born, the son of a farm laborer—if he had been Tahitian, he would have belonged to the lowest level of society. Social mobility not being part of his tradition, Tupaia would have found it difficult to understand the combination of intelligence, cartographic brilliance, and sheer good luck that had given the command of the *Endeavour* to a man who had been born in a mud-and-thatch hovel, and had little formal education. Banks appears to have had the same bias, for he behaved as if he considered Cook merely a talented sailing master working for the Royal Society (which meant Banks himself)—when the ship was becalmed he commandeered a boat to go shooting for seabirds, and the seamen collected specimens according to his whim. Not having enough understanding to realize that Cook was ruled by the winds, the weather, and good commonsense, Banks also became extremely irritated when they did not stay long enough at promising islands and bays for him to do all the botanizing he wanted, and he let everyone (especially Cook) know it.

There was one man in the afterquarters who would not have subscribed to the opinion that Gore should have been in command. Indeed, he would have found the idea quite comical. This was the astronomer Charles Green, a man with democratic leanings leavened by a sense of humor. In October 1763, when he was sailing to Barbados on the *Princess Louisa* with the astronomer Nevil Maskelyne to test Maskelyne's lunar tables, he noted that one of the seamen had been flogged for mutiny: "this Insolence & Mutiny consisted of saying Mr. Graham a mate was Drunk," which was nothing but the truth, as the mate "realy was so." He was a resourceful man in a crisis, too. On the 1764 return voyage from Barbados, on the *New Elizabeth*, the captain's brother fell overboard, and Green, assisted by William Harrison (son of John "Longitude" Harrison, inventor of the chronometer), calmly fished him up with a rope dropped out of the captain's toilet window. He also enjoyed partying. "After dinner we had a general game at Romps," he wrote on the same ship; the cabin passengers and officers chased each other about the deck with buckets of water ("except the Captain who was kept Prisoner in the Fore Top"), until everyone was thoroughly drenched. As James Cook dourly inferred much later in the voyage, Charles Green was rather too fond of the bottle.

While Green appeared to respect Cook, he had a very low opinion of the navigational abilities of his officers and petty officers. Back in 1767, Wallis had airily revealed that the *Dolphin's* purser was the only man on board who could find the ship's longitude, and on the *Endeavour* just about the same applied, for when they left England Green found to his disgust that he and Cook were the only ones who understood the system of "working lunars" to locate their position. Obviously, none of the old *Dolphin*s had bothered to make up for their ignorance, which was remiss of Gore, and inexcusable in the master, Molineux, and his mates, Pickersgill and Wilkinson, who were supposed to be in charge of navigation. Green took on the task of teaching the mysterious process, making himself thoroughly unpopular in the process. "P, C, and S" were not cooperative or helpful, he complained bitterly once, "P" and "C" being Pickersgill and his fellow master's mate, Clerke, and "S" being Midshipman Saunders.

Green must have enjoyed the dusty pursuit of school teaching, because he also took pains to coach Tupaia and Taiata in the elements of English grammar, greatly improving their fluency, according to Parkinson. He did not try to compare Tupaia's astronomy with his own, though, perhaps because he considered it based on superstition. On August 29, when Green reported a comet in the sky, Tupaia informed him it was a sign of a massacre back on Raiatea—as Banks noted, he prophesied "the people of Bola bola would upon the sight of it kill the people" who had not flown to the mountains. Astronomy and astrology were closer cousins then, but it is likely that Green dismissed this ominous prediction as hokum.

The *Endeavour* trudged south with not a sign of the Great Southern Continent. The seamen passed the dreary time away more or less constantly drunk, Banks complaining that those who had invested in barrels of wine at Madeira found them sucked almost dry with straws. On August 28 he recorded that bo'sun's mate John Reading was found "so drunk that he had scarce any signs of life and in about an hour he expird." Other men were sick. Some were starting to develop scurvy, some had colds, and some were being poisoned daily by Dr. William Munkhouse, who was half-killing them with mercury in the current belief it was a cure for syphilis. As Banks's servant, James Roberts, gloomily noted, not only was the weather ghastly, with "Strong gales and Excessive hard Squalles of hail and a great swell," but because so many were sick, the ship was "Weakly Man'd."

At this dismal time Tupaia may have kept up his custom of kneeling at the stern windows of the Great Cabin and praying for favorable winds, but it is improbable, as Banks and Solander were a team of two who disliked being interrupted. Tupaia could have sheltered in his cabin, a cramped space just six feet square, half-filled with a bank of lockers, which was topped with a mattress where he was supposed to sleep (though he may have preferred a mat on the floor). Here, Buchan had kept his personal possessions, as well as his pens, pencils, brushes, and Whatman paper, and it was here that Tupaia found stowage room for his tapa cloth, his pillow-stool, his flywhisk, and his priest's sacred robes, including a deeply fringed cape, and a braided scarf.

Despite the awful conditions, it is much more probable he was out on deck, counting the waves and watching the moon and stars as he kept mental track of their course. For it was there that Solander found him, when he was collecting words for his Tahitian dictionary.

Like others, Solander had compiled a vocabulary at Tahiti, including terms Europeans considered excitingly earthy (though Tahitians did not), such as the words for sexual intercourse ("*Taimorhadi, Tamo, lo-hiahia, tatue, a-a-i, ti-a-a*"). More unusually, he kept the list going on board, recording in phonetics the terms Tupaia gave him for the motions and parts of the ship. "The ship rolls," observed Tupaia, and Solander rendered the Tahitian as, "*Ehithori de Pahi*." Tacking ship became "*Epehi de mau*." The "spray of the sea" was "*Huatai*," (*ua tai*—"sea rain"), while Tupaia's version of "the sail is full" was given as "*Onie te Aea*," and the word for "sail" as "*Eiee*."

As they forged south, the words Tupaia supplied became more ominous. Evidently concerned about how little Tupaia ate, the botanist asked him if he had enough, because Tupaia said, "*a'paya*," which Solander translated as "satisfied of eating." It is likely this was noted about August 27, because Parkinson recorded that on that day "we killed a dog, and dressed him." Though the Polynesian dog had apparently not eaten anything since leaving Raiatea, "he was excessively fat," so he had probably foraged with the hogs, vegetables being his usual food. Whether he was killed because someone was concerned about Tupaia's lack of appetite for the shipboard food was not noted, but the following day, Banks wrote, "Tupia not well today, he complains of a pain in his stomach; his distemper probably proceeds from cold." Presumably at the same time, Solander added more words to his list—"sick—*Matte*" on one line, and "of bellyache—*Matte dehabu*" on the next. It seems likely that Tupaia had overeaten in his enthusiasm for the familiar dish, and his half-starved digestive system had rebelled.

Banks and Cook had expected that Tupaia, being a seasoned voyager on canoes that lacked store-carrying holds, was accustomed to a sparse seafaring diet, and would enjoy the generous quantities of rough food served on English navy ships. Food did indeed have to be carefully rationed on Polynesian voyaging canoes, but it was good to eat, filling, and nutritious. When the canoes set out, they were stocked with coconuts, fresh water in sealed nodes of giant bamboo, cooked and pounded breadfruit, taro, and banana packed in banana leaves and gourds, and a back-up store of fermented breadfruit. According to Captain Cook, this last had a "sour and disagreeable taste," but Tahitians liked it so much it was a staple on land as well as at sea. Fish was available on a voyage, too. As the huge double canoes were unwieldy in coastal waters, a small fishing canoe was often lashed to the platform, to be lowered when a meal was needed. The fish was either eaten raw, or the catch was cooked in a special bowl over a fire of coconut husks.

A diet of fatty, gristly salt meat, and porridge made of oats, wheat, or peas, often with strange additives, was a most unenticing alternative, particularly when it was eked out with ship's bread—large, round, thick crackers baked to tooth-breaking hardness on shore, and stored on board in barrels. These crackers teemed with vermin, Banks writing, "I have often seen hundreds nay thousands shaken out of a single bisket." Within days of leaving Raiatea, the vastly more attractive fresh fruit and vegetables had vanished from the menu. Banks first noted that the taro had gone rotten; then that the livestock had finished off the plantains. Two days after that, the hogs and fowls began to die, because they would not eat the food that kept English-bred animals alive, being dependent on fresh fruit and vegetables. Tupaia was in much the same fix.

Another complication was Cook's dedication to adding strange concoctions to the regimen, in a campaign to stave off scurvy. This was a legacy from Wallis, who may not have been a discoverer at heart, but was unusually successful at keeping his men alive. Over the stormy six-week passage from Tahiti to Tinian in 1767, the *Dolphin* had lost only one man, from a fatal tumble from the mainyard. The sickbay was full of patients who had gone down with scurvy, though, so as soon as the anchor was dropped Wallis sent hands on shore to collect coconuts and oranges, and pitch tents to house the invalids. They stayed there for a month, with Surgeon John Hutchinson in command of the makeshift hospital, and John Gore stalking the island with his gun, to keep them supplied with fresh meat.

In October 1767, the ship set sail with everyone fit. A man was lost on the next part of the passage, but again the death was accidental—a marine "taylor" fell overboard drunk. At the beginning of December the *Dolphin* sailed into Dutch-held Batavia (modern Jakarta), firing a salute of thirteen guns. After one horrified look at the fetid, mosquito-infested canals meandering through the town, Wallis issued orders that no one was allowed on shore, except on essential business. The *Dolphin* sailed just six days later—"All the people in good health." Five days after that, men began to fall ill: despite the short time in port, dysentery had arrived on board. By New Year's Day forty were down with fevers and fluxes, and three had been buried (though one died of injuries, not disease), so Wallis made alterations to his ship.

Healthy sailors were shifted to the half-deck—the area aft of the mainmast—and the berth deck was turned into a hospital. This was hung with painted canvas, washed with vinegar twice a day, and fumigated by a man walking around with a shovel of burning sulphur. Drinking water was sterilized by plunging "a dagger made red hot" into it, and instead of grog, the patients were given wine from the captain's own stores. "They have saloup every morning for Breakfast or sagoe (the Surgeon having laid in a great quantity)," Wallis wrote, "saloup" being a gruel made from the roots of an orchid. On February 6, 1768, the *Dolphin* sailed into Cape Town—to find smallpox raging in the port. So Wallis found a secluded field where hospital tents could be pitched, and there they stayed until the start of March, when the ship sailed for England, with everyone fit and well again. Incredibly, since New Year's Day Captain Wallis and his hardworking surgeon had not lost a single man.

Their Lordships of the Admiralty, understandably impressed, asked Dr. Hutchinson to write an account of his precautions. He put it all down in a letter addressed to his captain—which was handed on to Captain Cook. As well as recommending saloup mixed with wine and honey, Hutchinson was a strong advocate of collecting herbs at every coast, and adding this "sellery" or "scurvy grass" to porridge, advice that Cook followed religiously whenever possible. Cook was also a staunch believer in fermented cabbage. As he reminisced in his journal the day before arriving at Tahiti, he tricked his men into eating sauerkraut by having some "dress'd every day for the Cabbin Table," and pretending he did not care if the seamen ate it or not: "such are the Tempers and disposissions of the Seamen in general," he went on, that he had to ration the sauerkraut they had formerly refused to eat, as "the Moment they see their Superiors set a Value upon it, it becomes the finest stuff in the World."

Unfortunately, he could not trick Tupaia, who ate (or declined to eat) at the cabin table—and because Tupaia would not eat these exotics, not only did Cook become frustrated and irritable, but he claimed it was Tupaia's own fault when he developed scurvy.

The weather became even more appalling, with strong gales and sleet to add to the discomfort of the heavy swell. "The sea ran mountain-high, and tossed the ship upon the waves," wrote Parkinson; "she rolled so much, that we could get no rest, or scarcely lie in bed." On September 2 Cook noted they had reached latitude 40° south, "having not the least Visiable signs of Land." For the first time he betrayed a hint of regret that he had not followed Tupaia's advice, musing that steering north might be a good idea, to spare the battered rigging and sails.

It was a particularly miserable time for Tupaia, who was not suffering from just malnutrition. He gave Solander another word for his vocabulary—"*Pooenooanoo*," which Solander rendered as "shiver with cold." Later, the missionaries wrote down another version, "*panoonoo*," meaning to shake with apprehension and anxiety. Perhaps memories of Banks's mishandling of the feathered god at Taputapuatea had returned to haunt him, augmenting the bad omens of the comet, the storm, and the cold.

Another word Tupaia told Solander was "*Heama,*" which he translated as "shame." Today, the word used by anthropologists is the Maori version, "*whakama.*" It means more than simply being embarrassed by something one has done, as understood by Europeans; it is a mixed state of grief, humiliation, and anger, triggered by an insult—by a sense of undeserved guilt—by being made to feel unworthy of respect.

By being made to feel inferior in an alien setting.

One of the early symptoms of scurvy is deep depression. It does seem likely, though, that Tupaia felt used and then rejected by Banks, whom he had once considered his friend, and insulted by Cook's rejection of his navigational knowledge.

The weather gradually improved as Cook sailed west along latitude 38° south, steering for New Zealand in obedience to the second part of his instructions. On September 29, 1769, the wind diminished to a smart breeze, and it was a fine, bright day, though still very cold. The ship was surrounded by a cacophony of birds. Tupaia was not asked to identify them, Gore being considered the expert—according to Banks, "Mr Gore" identified a crowlike gull as a "Port Egmont hen," a kind of skua found in the Falkland Islands. The water had changed color, and there was seaweed floating on the surface, so Cook ordered a sounding line dropped. The quartermaster found no bottom at 120 fathoms, but nevertheless Cook decided they were near land, and promised a gallon of rum to the man who sighted it first.

On the ship crept, with Cook cautiously ordering sail taken in at night, in case they ran onto an unknown shore in the dark. There was a dead calm on the morning of October 3, and Banks commandeered a boat so he could shoot Cape Pigeons, prions, and storm petrels as they danced daintily over the surface. Many of the birds were purloined by the officers' cook to stew for their dinner, Molineux confessing that they were hungry for anything new, but Banks also scooped up some seaweed and driftwood rich with clinging organisms, so had a gratifyingly large bag of specimens to lay out on the table of the Great Cabin.

"Now do I wish that our friends in England could by the assistance of some magical spying glass take a peep at our situation," Banks wrote in his journal, and went on to put that situation in words: Solander was sitting at the table "describing" specimens, while he was at his desk, "journalizing." On the table lay a bunch of seaweed, and a barnacle-studded piece of driftwood.

Despite the proximity of land, the two botanists still reigned in the Great Cabin that should have been Captain Cook's realm.

CHAPTER 13

❧

Young Nick's Head

Though those on board had no way of knowing it, the *Endeavour* was sailing in the wake of the first Polynesian settlement canoes, which, five or six centuries earlier, had most probably hauled up on the same beaches where they were headed. It was a planned settlement, not an accidental arrival. Each canoe was carrying everything necessary to establish a community in this far-off land—not only did the voyagers have the tools and animals and plants that had been part of their traditional way of life in eastern Polynesia, but they carried traditional knowledge, too. On board were specialist priests and builders and shipwrights and gardeners, all of them rich with knowledge and skills.

Some of the cargo was lost almost right away. The pigs and chickens either did not survive the voyage, or died soon after landing, and bananas, breadfruit, and coconuts failed to thrive. But there were still the dogs and rats—though the rats might have been stowaways, it was possible for the most fastidious to eat them, if hungry enough. Carefully nurtured sprouts of taro, yams, gourds, kumara, and paper mulberry (tapa) acclimatized after a fashion, along with the Pacific *ti* cabbage tree with its sugary root.

The land itself posed problems. People who were accustomed to small tropical islands had to get used to lakes, rivers, immense forests, cold winters, and a short growing season for their gardens. It was a shaky land, too, prone to earthquakes and volcanic eruptions that occasionally devastated local districts. As if in compensation for this, the new arrivals found the seas and beaches rich in seafood, and the forests abundant with birdlife. Despite the difficulties, they flourished and kept their traditional ways. And that was how it was for perhaps two hundred years.

Then disaster struck. Sometime in the fifteenth century, New Zealand was hit by a mega-tsunami, or a cluster of tsunamis. It is impossible to tell exactly what caused this unbelievably violent event (or series of close events). According to Chinese lore, a comet plunged into the sea just south of New Zealand in June 1430. Alternatively, there may have been a massive underwater volcanic eruption; perhaps part of the ocean floor collapsed. Whatever the source of the disaster, from archaeological evidence the horrifying results are clear. An immense wall of water struck the east coast of the North Island, broke with a tremendous roar, and surged inland, carrying a whirling flotsam of houses, animals, people, plants, and double canoes.

The immediate catastrophe was bad enough, but it had consequences beyond imagination. Because the gardens, forests, and fishing beds were destroyed, thousands who had survived the deluge starved to death. Ancient artifacts were lost, and tools and weapons had to be reinvented. The old people, with their restrictive prohibitions and traditional knowledge of how things were supposed to be, were all gone, not having the strength to survive privation. Many of the women and children, at home when the tsunami struck, had drowned or died of injuries, so mostly young men were left— men who had been on hunting or fishing expeditions, who returned to their homes to find them destroyed. Fighting over the scant food resources and surviving young women may have been the path that led to tribal warfare.

The men of great *mana,* who had lived in favored positions near the coast, were among the first victims. The craftsmen, the priests, the star navigators, and the shipwrights were annihilated, along with their specialist knowledge. Many family histories—*whakapapa*—were stalled, as the elders were not there to recite them anymore. Without the old shipbuilders, canoes had to be redesigned, and so the double canoe was replaced by the single-hulled canoe. Voyages back to Raiatea became impossible. *Ka kotia te taitapu ki Hawaiki*, the people mourned. The sacred seaway to Raiatea was cut, and the homeland was lost, remembered only in surviving ancient myths.

Three hundred years after the disaster, the *Endeavour* arrived.

It was two in the afternoon on October 6, 1769, when Banks was at last able to record, "a small boy who was at the mast head Calld out Land." This was Nicholas Young, who must have been spending playtime with his friends in the rigging, as normally he was below assisting the surgeon, his job being now that of loblolly-boy. Not only did the twelve-year-old get his gallon of rum, but the bluff he spied was duly christened Young Nick's Head. Banks, who was on deck at the time, was hugely entertained by the sight of men who materialized from nooks and crannies when the boy cried out, to point excitedly at land they swore they saw, though it was not yet possible to see anything, except from aloft. They had to wait, as the breeze was tantalizingly faint. By sunset they were very little closer, so Banks clambered to the masthead himself, to see "an Island or Islands," which seemed promisingly large.

At dawn the shape of the land dominated the horizon. About eleven in the morning a billow of smoke appeared in the sky, followed by several more, perhaps seasonal burning off of gardens, for the fires seemed deliberate. At sunset just about everyone was in the rigging, peering toward a vista of white cliffs and rolling hills, with tall mountains in the distance: "all hands seem to agree that this is certainly the Continent we are in search of," optimistically wrote Banks.

Cook was not quite so ebullient. He had the job of keeping the ship on short tacks all night, to keep near the land without running her ashore. His judgment was sound, for at dawn they were just four miles off a long beach. James Roberts could see "white Clifts" extending in a great curve north from the bluff Nick had sighted, and every sign of a rich, fertile land—"Every where cloath'd with Green trees." Rivers coiled down from the hills, and in and out of dense bush.

Slowly, casting a sounding line every few hundred feet, the ship found an anchorage. The *Endeavours* could see canoes, people running along the sand, houses with eaves almost to the ground—and smell smoke, too. While the land was otherwise unfenced, the top of one of the hills was enclosed with palings, which puzzled the Europeans. Some reckoned it was a deer park, while others conjectured that it was a field for oxen and sheep. No one asked Tupaia for his opinion.

As the shadows grew long, two boats were sent to a river mouth at the northern end of the beach. Cook, Banks, Solander, and Dr. Munkhouse went in one, and the other—the pinnace—carried a squad of marines. The marines were put ashore on the northeast side of the river, to line up and carry out their usual exercises on a broad swath of turf between the water and the trees, while the other boat—the yawl—set Cook, the surgeon, the two scientists, and Midshipman John Bootie on the opposite bank. The pinnace was sent to patrol the mouth of the river, and the yawl was left in charge of four boys.

Once Captain Cook and the men with him had mounted the slope and were out of sight, the marines finished their show of presenting arms, broke ranks with a final stamp of boots, and wandered off into the forest. As soon as they were gone, the four boys left the yawl to play on the beach. No one saw the four natives who had hidden themselves in the reeds.

When Cook and his companions arrived at the village, it was to find it deserted. They crawled through a low doorway into the dim interior of the largest house, and rummaged around for a while, finding a net and a mat-like cloak, both made out of some strong grass. There was a smell of old smoke, and a fireplace, recently used. John Bootie was impressed with the warmth, dryness, and cleanliness of the building, remarking that its roof was closely and neatly thatched, "after the manner of our houses in England." When the party came out again, they found a burnt stump with a piece of pumice roughly carved into a human figure on top. It had a religious significance—or so they conjectured as they turned it about in their hands and passed it from one to another. They were not able to consult Tupaia, because the high priest had not been invited to come.

Perhaps it belatedly occurred to them they were committing some sacrilege, because they hastily and carefully replaced it, "and ornamented it with some beads and nails," noted Munkhouse. Then they wandered in different directions. Solander and Banks collected botanical specimens while Munkhouse and the rest explored the grass, finding some well-made fish traps, temporary huts they called "wigwams," a midden with limpet and lobster shells, and "a ground oven in the Otaheite style." Then birds were set screaming by the abrupt report of a musket.

The men dashed for the river, hearing a second bang as they ran, then another musket shot. Arriving, they found the four boys sitting confused and red-faced in the yawl, and the pinnace rowing hurriedly up. The tale was quickly told—the coxswain of the pinnace, spying four natives making for the deserted yawl with spears in their hands, had fired a shot in the air to warn the boys, who had dived back into the boat, to find themselves menaced. The pinnace fired a musketoon to frighten away the natives, but to no effect, and so the coxswain had killed the native leader with one shot. The other three, he said, had dragged the body off for some distance, dropped it when they realized he was dead—"breathless," as Bootie put it—and then backed off into the trees.

Cook and the others crossed the river in the yawl and followed the trail of blood, to find the dead man lying about fifty paces up a forest path. Though they had no way of knowing it, his name was Te Maro, and he belonged, like his friends, to the local Teitanga-a-Hauiti tribe. He had been shot through the heart.

Dr. Munkhouse studied the body with interest, finding Te Maro to be a short but powerful man, with spirals tattooed on his right cheek and four arches etched deeply on the left side of his forehead—"this was an exceeding new and singular appearance," wrote the surgeon, accustomed to seeing Tahitians with untattooed faces; "and seem meant to give fierceness to the Visage." The man's coarse black hair was tied into a topknot—"his teeth were even and small but not white—his features were large but proportional—his nose well formed—ears bored—his beard short." His garment was intriguing, being a well-made cloak of finely woven fiber.

"The ball had passed from the sixth rib on the left side thro' the right shoulder blade," the surgeon concluded. "Some nails and beads were put upon the body, and we took our leave of the shore."

In the dark of the night the men on the *Endeavour* heard cries and shouts from shore. When dawn broke, it was to see a fifty-strong army marching to the southwest bank of the river and assembling there. Though the Europeans had no way of knowing this, either, it was a war party from a different tribe, the Rongowhakaata, that had come from their inland village on a more southern river, the Waipoua. Watching the *Endeavour* from a vantage point, they had first decided she must be a floating island, because of her cloud of white sails, but then when she anchored and the sails were furled, they had understood she was a bulky canoe. So they had come in force to seize her.

A wild surf crashed on the beach, to add to the drama of the scene. It must have taken courage for Cook to order the boats lowered, and to go ashore himself, but he was determined to make friends with these people. He was not stupid, however. The boats were heavily manned with both seamen and marines, and this time he took the precaution of including Tupaia in the party. All of them, including Tupaia, were carrying muskets. Cook was also cautious enough to land on the opposite side to the massed Maori warriors (close to where Te Maro's body still lay), but took only Banks and Solander with him, leaving Tupaia in the boat.

"We call'd to them in the Georges Island Language," he wrote, but the only response to this friendly but incomprehensible greeting was a yell of derision. Then the warriors executed a *haka*—"a war dance," as Munkhouse called it. Forming up into ranks, "each man jump'd with a swinging motion at the same instant of time to the right and left alternately," roaring out a chant that was also in perfect unison; "their lances were at the same time elevated a considerable height above their heads."

Cook and the two botanists beat a hasty retreat to their boat, and the marines were ordered on shore. The red-coated soldiers put on their finest show, in fitting response to the *haka*. They marched in order, bearing a flagstaff flying the Union Jack before them, their black-gaitered legs tick-tocking in time to the *rat-tat-tat* of the drum. With a stamp of boots they came to a halt, wheeled, marched to the edge of the river, presented arms as the sergeant snapped out orders, and stamped again. Then, as the marines stood to attention, Tupaia walked out and formally greeted the Maori multitude, introducing himself in his language.

To everyone's astonishment, including the Maori themselves (particularly as Tupaia was dressed in breeches, shoes, shirt, stock, and skirted coat), they understood him perfectly. Whether he was using the ancient language of liturgy to these people who had been disassociated from the heartland of eastern Polynesia for about five hundred years is unknown, though possible. What is important is that the Maori broke ranks to hold an animated conversation, shouted over the rippling river.

First, understandably, they wanted to know what a man like Tupaia was doing here. "*Ko wai koe; no hea koe?*" they asked—"Who are you, where do you come from?" And what was he doing on the fat canoe that carried its own cloud? What did he want? Surely Tupaia had not brought the fat canoe so far just to get firewood and water! Then, with equal good reason, they wanted to know how and why a Maori man—Te Moro—had been killed—from a distance, with an exploding stick.

Tupaia, who had not been present at the time, did his best to plead that it had been in self-defense. The exploding stick must have taken a lot of explaining, too—Munkhouse said it was a very long conversation—but he did his best to reassure them that the foreigners' intentions were friendly, and that if some spokesmen would come across the river and parley, it would be greatly to their advantage.

The problem with this, he gradually found, was that the Maori people had no idea of the value of nails. As Banks wrote that night, they had never come across iron, "the use of which they certainly were totally ignorant." What they really wanted was to get hold of the exploding sticks, and any other weapons the goblins might have about them. As Tupaia was rapidly coming to understand, this was a warlike race.

He must have felt some sympathy for their ambitions, for though he did not know the local politics, he was very familiar with tribal war. Meantime, he tried to persuade them to drop their own weapons, and come across the river. Finally one brave elder complied, but swam only as far as a rock in the middle of the river, known as *Toka-a-Taiau*. There he stuck, until Cook put down his own musket, and waded over to join him. The elder hesitated, and then, with a surge of courage, leaned forward and pressed noses with the foreign captain. It was the first instance of the *hongi* greeting experienced by westerners—and a signal for other Maori to come across too, after a celebratory *haka* had been performed. Some, however, did not put down their weapons, but held them underwater as they swam.

A chaotic situation rapidly followed, as the Europeans found out for themselves that the Maori men were not interested in trinkets and nails, but instead were eager to trade the weapons they had smuggled across for swords and exploding sticks. They proved agile negotiators, Munkhouse describing them "every moment jumping from one foot to the other; and their eyes and hands as quick as those of the most accomplished pickpocket," while Tupaia repeatedly warned the *Endeavour*s to take care. In the midst of the melee a man offered a beautifully wrought greenstone hand-weapon to the astronomer, Green, doing his best with gestures to persuade him to take it in exchange for the short military sword that hung in his belt. As Green turned away from his annoying persistence, the man snatched at the hanger, successfully snared it, and ran back to the river, whooping and waving it over his head.

Furiously, Green fired his musket. It jammed, so he triggered his pistol, but this was loaded with a cartridge of small shot, meant to sting rather than wound. Banks aimed his musket, but it was loaded with small shot, too. It was Munkhouse who brought down the thief with a musket ball.

Two Maori warriors who had retreated to the rock at the first explosion jumped into the water and plunged back to the body. Thinking they were about to grab the sword, Munkhouse rushed at them with his bayonet, but all they wanted was the prestigious greenstone *mere*. One ripped this away from the fallen man, while the other fended off the surgeon with his spear. Then they escaped to the other side of the river.

"Matters were now in great confusion," wrote Munkhouse later. All the natives were running away, while men (including Tupaia, who aimed at their legs) fired at their retreating forms. Several Maori were wounded before Cook's shouts put a stop to it. Silence descended, and then the Rongowhakaata warriors retired slowly from the scene, wailing as they went—"a most lamentable noise," wrote Munkhouse.

The name of the fallen man was Te Rakau. He was still alive. Tupaia spoke to him, but no one knows what was said. Munkhouse was busily noting a human tooth hanging from one of Te Rakau's ears, and that he was wearing "a girdle of Matting about four inches broad." Other Europeans were busy trying to wrest a "paddle" out of his convulsive grip—a *pouwhenua*, a double-handed weapon with a point for stabbing at one end, and a flared blade at the other.

Later accounts, as well as the fact that he had been carrying a *mere pounamu*—a weapon made of polished greenstone, and the most revered in the Maori armory—indicate that Te Rakau was an important chief. Establishing a truce with him would have been a great step forward. Instead, Te Rakau expired, his life lost for a common cutlass worth just eight shillings, for which he had been willing to exchange a possession beyond price.

As an exercise in public relations, it was a disaster. The idea had been to start trading relations by impressing the natives with a demonstration of strength, but instead it was Cook's British sailors who were impressed—by the tenacity and courage of the Maori warriors. According to Roberts, they thought the daring of the two men who retrieved the greenstone weapon quite remarkable, marveling that though the natives had never experienced the killing power of European arms before, they had refused to be intimidated.

Parkinson, watching from the ship, recorded that Cook then took possession of the country in the name of King George III, so presumably the flag was planted, and a salute of muskets fired, but it was hardly a celebratory occasion. Instead, the atmosphere was grim as everyone re-embarked in the boats. Cook now intended to make a circuit of the bay in search of a better watering place, the river being disappointingly brackish, but it was a doomed quest, because of the high surf. Then two fishing canoes sailed in from the open sea, and the situation became still worse.

Cook made up his mind to kidnap some of these unarmed fishermen, and take them on board the ship. It was a bizarre decision, made with the best of intentions—he wanted to demonstrate with kindness that the Europeans wished to be friends. Tupaia called out to the seven men in the nearest canoe "to come alongside and we would not hurt them," but instead, suspecting treachery, the fishermen paddled away. So Cook ordered a musket fired over their heads, justifying this later by saying he thought "this would either make them surrender, or jump overboard."

He had seriously underestimated the raw courage of these people. The fishermen immediately hurled everything that came to hand at the approaching boat—paddles, fish spears, bailers, their anchor stone, their fish—"this," wrote Cook, "obliged us to fire on them." The men who pulled the triggers were Banks, Solander, and Cook himself. Four fishermen were gravely wounded. Two fell overboard and drowned; two collapsed into the bottom of the canoe, and the unhurt three jumped into the water. They were only boys. The two youngest were captured relatively easily, but the oldest put up a struggle, swimming away with the speed and agility of a seal. Finally he was plucked out of the sea and hoisted on board, and the boats rowed for the *Endeavour*, leaving the canoe with its welter of blood and dead or dying men to drift into the surf.

It was a long pull for the ship, while the Europeans did their best to calm their captives. The three boys were unresponsive, cowering silently in the bottom of the boat, until Tupaia found that they expected to be killed—and, to his disbelief, eaten. Though they might have found it hard to believe Tupaia's reassurances, a snack of ship's biscuit and raw salt beef from the boat's provisions won them over, Munkhouse noting that it "produced a very singular change in their looks and behavior." They told Tupaia their names were Te Haurangi, Ikirangi, and Marukauiti. Te Haurangi, the champion swimmer, was about eighteen, while the second, his brother, was a handsome lad, perhaps fifteen, and the youngest, Marukauiti, was just ten.

It was six in the evening before the boats arrived at the ship, and fires were being lit in the long shadows on shore, while loud voices echoed over the water. The men on deck gathered curiously as the Maori boys clambered on board. Te Haurangi had his lips dyed blue, but otherwise all three had no tattoos at all, which Parkinson found surprising in people who looked so "much like the natives of Otaheite." They were loud and rude in speech, he said, making "frequent use" of the letters "G" (he meant the "ng" sound) and "K," which were not in the Tahitian language, though "Toobaiah understood them very well." And they were a lot less polished in manners than the Tahitians he had known, too.

The British seamen, never having had much to do with the polished Tahitian nobility, took the young Maori to their hearts. The boys were taken below to tour the berth deck, with Tupaia hovering protectively and translating the stream of questions and answers. Was their country large? Yes, very extensive. Did they keep animals? No, just dogs. So what did they eat? Fish and roots—and enemies. Everyone, according to Roberts, dismissed this last as a "Stratigin" to make sure they were delivered back to their own people. While Tupaia did not reveal his reaction, it is likely he was of the same opinion. The sailors, wrote John Bootie, "gave them sevl presents and cloathed them," one of the gifts being a red coat, presumably donated by a marine.

A meal was served, and the three lads put Tupaia's pickiness to shame. Cook would have watched wryly as they ate everything that was put in front of them. Not only did they have adolescent appetites, but, as Banks's footman, Roberts, remarked, poison was evidently unknown to their people. Salt pork went down very well, and they particularly liked the jaw-breaking ship's bread, Munkhouse recording that they asked if it was taro baked in a different way. Taro, they revealed, was one of the roots they ate, yams and sweet potatoes being others.

They talked to the officers about the habit of eating people, too, but tactfully attributed it to their neighbors. Tupaia, naturally, asked them about their *atua*, and they named three tribal gods—Te Rongomai, Te Kahukura, and (probably) Haere. When supper was over they danced for their hosts, in a portent of many similar exhibitions staged on European decks in future years. It was not a war dance, like the *haka* the warriors had performed on the riverbank, but a *haka waiata*. Naked except for loincloths, the youths stood back-to-back, lifted their arms to shoulder height, and quivered their extended fingers while their feet thumped out the beat, then bent from one side to the other, singing hoarsely as their arms and fingers undulated, all in perfect time.

Beds were made up for them on the lockers in the Great Cabin, and Banks said they "laid down to sleep with all seeming content." He did not sleep well himself, because of his tormented mind. "Thus ended the most disagreeable day My life has yet seen," he wrote; "black be the mark for it and heaven send that such may never return to embitter future reflection."

His troubled conscience still had him awake when one of the boys tossed and mourned aloud. Tupaia, who was not asleep, either, came in from his room. "Tupia who was always on the watch to comfort them got up and soon made them easy," wrote Banks, who listened to the murmuring of voices in the dark, and then the tune of a soft *waiata*, "like a Psalm." After that, they settled down again.

In the morning, as Banks remarked, "they were all very chearfull and eat an enormous quantity." They dressed in their European clothes and were given some Tahitian ornaments to wear, then a boat was lowered to take them ashore. Tupaia, Cook, Banks, Munkhouse, and Solander went with them. Two other boats were already down, carrying the marines and a wooding party to the river where the confrontations had taken place, and Cook's boat followed in their wake. The boys became agitated when they realized where they were going. Their home was at the southern end of the bay, they told Tupaia—if they were landed here, their enemies would kill and eat them. Cook was adamant, however. If the boys wanted to be landed farther south, they would have to wait. Meantime, they could stay with his party.

Tupaia told them this, but after the party had crossed the river to where the Rongowhakaata force had assembled the day before, the boys suddenly left them. Banks saw tears in their eyes as they turned away. Then they disappeared into the bushes.

Tupaia, with Cook and the others, trekked southwest along the edge of a marsh, the idea being to shoot ducks for a fresh meal for all hands. The sergeant of marines and four of his men patrolled the top of a bank, their silhouettes alert as they kept pace with the party, watching the country all around. An hour went by, and then a shout warned Cook to expect company. A marine came panting down the slope with the news that "a large body of Indians," as Banks put it, had been sighted coming this way from the interior. While Cook's party gathered hastily together, the three boys suddenly materialized from a bush. They had been trailing Tupaia and his friends, and now they wanted their protection.

The boys led the dash to the beach as the first spears bobbed into sight over the top of the bank. More warriors arrived as the party hurried along the shingle, and the spears became a thicket. Strangely, however, the natives moved slowly, so they made it safely to the river—but the pinnace was not there. Gore, who was in charge of the wooding party, had shot a bird, and sent the boat to retrieve it. Only the little yawl was available. It took three panicky trips to get everyone to the other side of the river, where the body of Te Rakau still lay.

No sooner had they arrived than the Maori warriors began to assemble on the other side. They came in twos and threes, but soon there was a multitude. Silently, they stood in ranks, staring at Cook's party. It was the same kind of stand-off as the day before—and, as the Europeans had found out the hard way, these were men who were not easily frightened by small arms. The ship was out of broadside range, so the only sane recourse was retreat. The pinnace and the third boat had at last turned up, and the *Endeavour*s were cautiously moving toward them when one of the boys suddenly called out.

According to Tupaia, he was telling the army that the foreigners wanted to be friends, and they had been treated kindly. There was a chorus of shouts in reply, and then Te Haurangi, evidently in response to an order, walked over to where Te Rakau lay, took off the red coat he had been given, and laid it over the corpse. Then he went back to his self-adopted role of intermediary.

"They told them of Tupia and that he was almost one of themselves," wrote Munkhouse, having heard Tupaia's translation. Instant babel followed, as Tupaia's name was "echoed incessantly." He stepped forward, to face a storm of questions and accusations. Obviously, the people were very angry, and Te Rakau's *mere pounamu* was produced with many shouts and gestures. Had Te Rakau been killed for the sake of his *mere*? He might have been a thief, but he had made no attempt to wound the man when he had stolen the cutlass. Unarmed fishermen had died—for what? For their *fish*? The goblins killed without reason, and without the ritual formality of a challenge—and yet they wanted to be *friends*?

The tense dialogue went on for a long time. The boys refused to go into the water, and no one on the other side was willing to come across. Finally, however, Tupaia persuaded an old man to make the plunge. He arrived carrying a green bough, which he presented to Tupaia as he came out of the water.

Paternal affection had spurred this brave decision, as he proved to be the father of the youngest boy, Marukauiti. He and the ten-year-old wept as they embraced. All three boys and Tupaia gave him presents, and then he and Tupaia hunkered down for a long conference. Tupaia never revealed what was said, but he was probably asking about the politics of the area, which were too complicated to explain to Europeans. The Teitanga-a-Hauiti, who controlled this northeastern end of the bay, were at war with the boys' tribe, the Rongowhakaata of the southwest. They had been temporarily driven away by the events of the day before, which was the reason Te Maro's body, further up the forest path, had not been retrieved, and the Rongowhakaata were free to come and go—in the meantime.

Finally, Tupaia stood up, but without coming to any agreement about wooding and watering. The Europeans presented the old man with nails, ribbons, and beads, which he accepted, but he refused to come on board the ship. They expected him to go away, taking the boys with him, but instead he walked to a bush, broke off a branch, and danced sideways to the corpse of Te Rakau. According to Munkhouse, he moved in the same fashion as a cock sidling up to an opponent, twisting and turning, and flicking his free foot back with each pace. When he arrived, he stripped off his cloak, so was naked when he threw the bough at the body.

Then he shrugged his cloak about his body again, and went back across the river—unaccompanied by the boys, because they insisted they were safer with Tupaia. Though the *Endeavours* were well aware that boys have their own reasons for what they do, usually very human ones, it was still very puzzling. Perhaps the young fishermen did not want to lose their finery to their elders. Having been made pets of by the seamen, and being young and adventurous, they may even have wanted to join the ship. It was very possible, too, that they were swayed by memories of delectable shipboard food, because it was almost time for dinner.

As the boats rowed away Munkhouse looked back, to see all the natives gathered about the old man, obviously engrossed in his story. After getting to the ship, he saw "a kind of raft" being launched. A ceremony was performed around the place where Te Rakau had fallen, and the body was carried over the river. Then, as he said, "the whole company retired inland."

The boys ate a huge dinner, which made them cheerful enough to make no objection when Cook announced he had ordered two midshipmen to put them on shore, his plan being "to sail in the morning." Indeed, as Banks noted, after saying goodbye to Tupaia and their other new friends, the boys "went most nimbly in the boat." Once at the riverside, however, they abruptly changed their minds and waded back, begging the midshipmen to return them to the ship, but "the orders were positive to leave them so they were left."

On the *Endeavour*, everyone watched uneasily to see what would happen next. They saw a number of Maori appear on the opposite bank, and then the raft launched to fetch the boys. The moment they were on the other side of the river, they were surrounded by a dense crowd, and there was no movement for a long time. Hopefully, the assemblage was riveted by the boys' stories—stories of bread, and salt meat—of sleeves, pockets, buttons, breeches, nails, beads, and blankets—of men who slept in hammocks and sat on chairs and ate at tables—and of good treatment and generous gifts. Optimism seemed justified, for when the sun was low and the shadows were long, the boys suddenly popped out of the crowd, ran to the beach, and jumped three times, waving their hands at the ship. Some did wonder if it might be a desperate signal, but the boys turned and walked in leisurely fashion back to their people. "We therefore hope that no harm would happen to them," wrote Banks; "especially as they had still the cloaths we gave them on."

"We now prepared to leave a place totally unfit for the purposes of wooding and watering, and too open and exposed for the safety of the Ship," recorded Munkhouse. The anchors were weighed at six the next morning, October 11, and the ship stood out of the bay, named Poverty Bay in Cook's dry style, since, as he said, "it afforded us no one thing we wanted."

According to him, nothing had gone right there. They had taken on a little firewood, but no fresh water or provisions. Banks was irritable and annoyed because he and Solander had so few specimens to add to his collection. At least four natives had been killed and an unknown number wounded, and Cook knew he would be criticized for this. The kidnapping could have been even more tragic, though. Because of Tupaia's kindness and his ability to communicate, the boys had made friends with the crew. Tupaia had also saved the situation not once, but twice, in tense confrontations at the riverside. Both times, he had managed to retrieve a precarious situation with fast talk and charisma. If Tupaia had not been there, undoubtedly Europeans would have lost their lives, too.

But, if Cook realized that, he made no note of it in his journal.

CHAPTER 14

❧

Becoming Legend

Cook's plan was to follow the coast south for a while, then turn back after reaching that magic latitude 40. The wind was very light, so the *Endeavour* coasted quietly, the men on deck watching the same rolling hills and white cliffs they had seen the day they arrived. The fortified hilltop village was in silhouette to the north, and this time, in an indication of his restored importance, Tupaia was asked for his opinion. As Munkhouse recorded, he suggested it was a *marae*, which the surgeon wrongly interpreted as a burial ground. It was, in fact, exactly what it looked like—a fort, or *pa*, which could be equipped to withstand a siege, just like a medieval castle. Tupaia was not completely wrong in clinging to this idea, however, as in Tahiti and Raiatea warriors assembled at *marae* when summoned for battle.

In the afternoon the ship lay becalmed just to the south of Young Nick's Head. After some hesitation, a few canoes came off from shore, and hovered within shouting distance, while Tupaia did his best to persuade them to come closer. Then another canoe sailed into sight, coming round the bluff from Poverty Bay. It came alongside without hesitation, and the four Rongowhakaata occupants clambered up the chains. One was recognized as the man who had pressed noses with Cook on the rock Toka-a-Taiau, so of course Tupaia inquired about the fate of "our poor boys" (as Banks put it), to be assured they were at home and unhurt. Indeed, as he relayed to Banks, the reason the Maori had boarded with such confidence "was the account they had given him of the usage they had met with among us."

The four men engaged Tupaia in deep conversation. Evidently Tupaia was telling them about his homeland and himself, including that he was *arioi*, because Munkhouse saw him pull down his breeches to favor them with a sight of his tattooed hips. Meanwhile, the rest of the people came alongside, emboldened by the example of the Poverty Bay men. More than twenty gathered on the decks, their tattooed faces and finely woven cloaks the objects of great curiosity for the scientists, and thirty more held onto the sides of the ship as they stood up in their equally interesting canoes to receive presents and barter with the crew. The seamen, quicker than their superiors to realize that nails were not the currency here that they had been in Tahiti, found that tapa was in great demand, one warrior even giving up his greenstone *mere* for a length of Tahitian cloth. Others sold their paddles, Cook remarking that they hardly left themselves "a sufficient number to paddle ashore." One set of men offered to sell their canoe!

This could have been the reason that three were still on board when the canoes finally departed, though Banks deduced they had been left behind as hostages to make sure the ship did not leave overnight. Cook, probably because he harbored the same suspicion, seems to have been irritated, and because of this—and also because there was no reason, this time, to feel guilty—the stranded Maori, though kindly treated, did not receive the same lavish hospitality as the kidnapped boys. Frank Wilkinson noted that they ate heartily of a "copper of wheat" that Cook ordered boiled and sugared (the first instance in history of Polynesians being served "stir-about," the humble porridge of British peasantry that became immensely popular in Oceania), and Munkhouse added they were given the usual seaman's ration of bread and salt meat. Like the boys, they danced and sang for their hosts, but instead of sleeping in the Great Cabin, they found a bed on a folded sail, under the scant shelter of the jutting forecastle deck.

In the morning, to their horror, they found that the ship had sailed several leagues to the south, out of their tribal territory. They wept bitterly, swearing to Tupaia that if they were put ashore here they would be eaten by their enemies. When a canoe they recognized was spied coming from the north, they leapt upon the forecastle deck, and waved vigorously. After it paddled into shouting range, they assured the stalwart, middle-aged man in charge that it was safe to come on board—that "we neither beat nor *eat* their countrymen," as Tupaia translated for Munkhouse, while the speaker demonstrated what he meant by pretending to gnaw his own flesh from the bone.

The canoe captain came on board, but only as far as the gangway, refusing all invitations to tour the ship. He readily bartered his newly made dogskin-trimmed cloak to Munkhouse, and showed off his *patu paraoa*, a flat, oval-shaped jabbing weapon with a carved handle and sharpened edges, made from a whale skull-bone. At the same time, the sailors leaned curiously over the rail to peer at the three Maori women in the canoe, as they were the first female New Zealand natives they had seen. One, Munkhouse remarked approvingly, "was jolly & had large breasts." Then the captain of the canoe took the three overnight visitors away, "much to our as well as their satisfaction," wrote Banks.

Slowly, the *Endeavour* coasted on, passing pleasantly cultivated land, and sighting two outrigger canoes, the first of that type they had seen in New Zealand. "Before noon another Canoe appeared carrying 4 people," Banks continued. It hovered within shouting distance while the man in the bow exchanged ritual greetings and challenges with Tupaia, at the same time dancing and singing and waving a green branch—conflicting messages of peace and war that confused the Europeans. Finally, according to Munkhouse, he made up his mind to paddle close and come on board, but at that precise moment a breeze blew up, carrying the ship off. Thinking the goblins were running away, the four Maori let out a derisive shout and brandished their paddles over their heads. One of them, to Munkhouse's amusement, turned his back, flicked up his garment, and pushed his naked rump at the ship, in the same sign of contempt used by the "Billingsgate ladies" of the London fish market.

This had unfortunate consequences. In the early afternoon, as the ship was rounding an island Cook called Portland, they came into shoal water, while hordes watched from the cliffs. Cook sent a quartermaster with a sounding line into the chains, but the depths he shouted back were inconclusive, varying wildly from eleven fathoms to seven, so Cook had the smallest boat lowered, to sound from closer to the surface. At this sign that the ship was in trouble, canoes put off from the shore, loaded with armed warriors thundering threats, while Munkhouse watched with scientific interest from the taffrail in the stern.

At this dangerous moment, and for no sane reason at all, the surgeon took it into his head to repay the "compliment" received that morning—before the horrified captain could stop him, he pulled down his breeches, and poked his nude bottom at the oncoming canoe. Enraged, the foremost warrior heaved his lance. When the weapon fell short, he snatched up another. Cook ordered a musket fired over their heads to prevent the small boat from being captured. Unimpressed, the Maori paddled even closer, so a cannon was loaded with grapeshot, and fired wide in warning. Stinging smoke shrouded the scene as the roar of the gun echoed from the cliffs. The warriors faltered, "and then retiring, collected themselves to hold a conference on matters of the most extraordinary nature that they would perhaps allow they had ever seen," wrote the unabashed surgeon.

While the incident had certainly given the natives something to think about, it had done nothing to further Cook's aim of making friends. He said little in his journal, but must have been very angry. That evening two canoes ventured near to the ship, one armed, and the other an innocent fishing canoe. Tupaia talked with them a long while, asking and answering questions, and the sailors threw them presents, but the Maori could not summon enough daring to come on board. After they had gone, many fires were lit on shore as a warning to the goblins to keep their distance, lighting the night eerily as the ship swung quietly at anchor.

Friday, October 13, dawned with a brisk breeze that carried them swiftly south, so that the nine canoes that stood out for them were soon left behind. The countryside they passed was populous and pleasant, but there was no sign of the safe anchorage Cook was seeking. In the evening the ship tacked for the shore, but still they could find no promising bay. Just as they were making off again, a large canoe appeared, crammed with twenty yelling warriors, but shout and paddle as they might, they could not get within a mile of the scudding *Endeavour*. And so the ship coasted through a dirty night, with the freshwater barrels emptier than ever.

The situation was close to critical. In the morning Cook ordered the ship hauled aback, and the pinnace and longboat were lowered to go inshore and search for a watering place. No sooner were they down, however, than they had to be hurriedly hoisted again, as a fleet of war canoes was seen heading their way. The admiral, described by Munkhouse as "a very aged Man," was shouting out directions, adding to the bedlam of massed yells from sixty-eight combatants: "*Haere mai, haere mai, haere ki uta hei patu-patu ake!*" they were derisively yelling, which can be freely translated as, "Come, come, come on shore, and get acquainted with our cleavers!"

It was a superlative sight, the intricately carved heads of the great canoes arrowing for them, the double rows of tattooed warriors flashing their paddles in and out of the water in perfect time. A peace-offering of a Tahitian cloak was thrown, followed by a flannel blanket, while Tupaia, standing at the stern, did his utmost to be heard above the din. Though one canoe slowed to snatch up the tapa cloak, the blanket was ignored. Attack was imminent. Cook ordered a cannon loaded and run out, and asked Tupaia to warn them what would happen if they carried on. "*Mai, mate koe!*" Tupaia cried—"Here, you will be killed!"—but he was ignored as well.

"Fire!" A mighty explosion, a billow of black smoke, and a row of waterspouts. "This had the desired effect," Cook wrote grimly. The canoes backed off, but then a large canoe arrived from shore. No sooner had the newcomers heard what had happened, "than they gave us chase," wrote Munkhouse, "paddling with all their might, thundering out their usual threats." This put new heart into the others, and soon there were seven canoes gathered under the stern of the ship. There, led by a chief who stood erect, "& brandished his paddle with the true spirit of a Veteran," the warriors staged a splendid waterborne *haka*, hammering their paddles on the gunwales of the *waka taua* in perfect unison as they shouted out their martial chant, ending with a guttural "*Hei!*"

The British seamen, greatly impressed, delivered a round of rousing cheers. Surprised, but pleased, the warriors obliged with an encore. Encouraged by this display of mutual respect, the leading canoe worked up to the side of the ship, and it was now seen that the "paddle" the chief had used to mark time was ceremonial weapon, a *tewhatewha* made of greenstone and decorated with feathers. Munkhouse likened it to a Tahitian hatchet, but the ax-like head was actually to give it weight, the edge of the shaft being the business part of the weapon. It was also a chance to admire the workmanship of the intricately carved canoe, which flew feather streamers, like the *pahi* Tupaia knew. The men began to talk trade, and might even have come on board, but then the other canoes approached with the usual threatening shouts, guns were leveled, and all the canoes dropped rapidly astern.

About noon, just as a small river had been sighted, six more *waka taua* came off from shore and gathered about a mile from the ship, where challenges were shouted again. Eventually, they paddled close enough for conversation with Tupaia. The same questions were bandied back and forth. They asked where he was from, and as always, he answered, Raiatea (in the archaic language, Hawaiki, also known to the Maori as Rangiatea). Because it had been so successful with the earlier group, he asked them to sing, and they cooperatively performed a *haka waiata*. He told them that if they came on board they would find the goblins friendly, but they would have to leave their weapons behind. Finally, some complied, but after they had received presents they went away, and still no arrangement about watering the ship had been made. Cook's quest for a safe and friendly harbor seemed doomed.

The following morning they were threatened again—by six unarmed fishing canoes! Never before, as Munkhouse remarked, had they been "insulted by such miserable raggamuffins." Enticed with Tahitian cloth, the fishermen came alongside and agreed to trade their catch, and Taiata scrambled into the chains to act as middleman, handing trinkets down, and hauling up baskets of fish. They tried to cheat by putting stones in some of the baskets, but all was still amicable when a war canoe arrived. This was captained by an old man who exchanged formal greetings with Tupaia, and crewed by twenty-two men who seemed willing to trade some weapons and clothing.

Cook bought a *taiaha*—a long two-handed weapon with an elaborately carved teardrop-shaped head at one end, and a flattened *rau* for clubbing at the other, which Munkhouse likened to a British pike called a "spontoon"—and then wanted to barter further for a white-bordered fur cloak an old man was wearing, as he was curious to know what kind of animal it came from. The old man agreed to exchange it for a length of red baize, but when the English cloth was handed down, he calmly folded it up with his cloak, and packed both away in a basket, while the canoe dropped astern. Then, as the angry Englishmen were shouting for him to come back, some of the fishermen staged a diversion by paddling up, snatching Taiata from the chains, and hauling him into their canoe.

Instant pandemonium. Everyone yelled, including Tupaia, while the canoe with Taiata fell back, and the war canoe came up between them. The gunwales of the *waka taua* were lined with warriors, ready to prevent the recapture of the boy. Tupaia shouted his warning, "*Mai, mate koe!*" but the chief told his men not to listen, saying contemptuously, "*Kahore he rakau o te hunga o Hawaiiki; he pu kakaho, he korari!*"—"The arms of these people of Hawaiki are nothing better than reeds and stalks!" And so the war canoe came on, while the terrified boy was borne away by the fishermen.

It looked very much like a premeditated plan: "Our astonishment at so unexpected a trick is not to be described," wrote Munkhouse. Cook snapped out an order for the marines to fire. A well-aimed musket mortally wounded the man holding Taiata, and the boy jumped into the water. At once, another canoe paddled up to seize him, so a loaded cannon was run out. "Fire!" roared Gore. The mighty explosion and billowing black smoke sent the canoes packing, though they retired with surprising slowness, in another demonstration of disdain.

"We saw them land and carry three men out of their Canoes," wrote Munkhouse. Two of the kidnappers had been killed. Their names were Whakaruhe and Whakaika. A third, Te Ori, was crippled for life with a ball lodged under his kneecap. But Taiata was saved. A boat was lowered and picked him up in the water. Luckily, he was a good swimmer, able to keep afloat despite being weighed down with his European clothing.

When he had recovered from his fright he took a fish to Tupaia, who told him to cast it into the sea as a thank-offering to the gods. And, in honor of the event, Cook named the nearby bluff Cape Kidnappers.

At noon on the next day, October 16, a contrary gust brought the ship aback. Cook took it as a sign, as they had arrived at latitude 40. He named the nearest headland Cape Turnagain, wore ship, turned, and headed north, steering back along the coast he had named Hawkes Bay, to Poverty Bay and beyond.

For two days the ship sailed with no incident, being well out to sea, but as Cook slanted his course toward the land again, canoes began to approach with confidence, made brave by past experience. The first had five occupants—two chiefs and their three slaves. The two *ariki* came on board with no hesitation at all, looked around the ship with great interest and attention, then announced they were staying the night. Tupaia warned them they could find themselves out of their territory in the morning, but this did not faze them, so Cook ordered their canoe hoisted. The slaves settled on the deck with the seamen, and a meal was served.

Much to the surprise of the captain and scientists, though the servants "eat most enormously almost every thing they could get" (as Banks phrased it), the two chiefs ate nothing at all—most probably because they were closely watching Tupaia, who, as usual, disdained the English food. His reputation as a noble and sage had spread, and the chiefs were careful to copy him, not knowing what rituals and customs might rule on the ship. Consequently, when their canoe was lowered in the morning, they went ashore hungry, though still pleased with their adventure. And that was the last the *Endeavours* saw of them, the ship sailing on.

Other visitors arrived, and behaved just as decorously, Munkhouse observing that it was evident their fame had reached "these good people." When Tupaia passed on a query about watering places, he was assured there was a good anchorage with fresh water ahead, and so Cook lay off and on all night, then made for two promising harbors. They could not fetch the first, the wind being contrary, but at eleven in the morning of October 20 the anchor was dropped in the fine black sand of the more northern one.

This was Anaura, though Roberts, like the other Europeans, was convinced the "bay is Caul'd by the Natives Togadoo." This may have been a mishearing of *Te ngaru*, meaning "the breakers," or picked up by mistake when the people gave the name of the southern boundary of the local tribal area, *Te Toka a Taiau*, the same rock where Cook had touched noses with the Rongowhakaaka elder. Before the ripples had stopped spreading, the ship was surrounded by canoes, and two old men came on board. They were nobles of great standing, for both were wearing aristocratic cloaks, one striped with dogskin, and the other covered with rare red parrot feathers—feathers that must have reminded Tupaia vividly of home. According to tradition, the name of the wearer, the paramount chief of the area, was Whakata te Aoterangi.

Cook gave the two men "4 yards of Linnen and a spike nail," and a meal was laid. Like the previous visitors, they did not eat. Instead, they conferred with Tupaia, who formally established his credentials, then negotiated a treaty, both with outstanding success. When it was reported that a man in one of the canoes appeared to be inciting attack, one of the chiefs leaned out the stern window to berate him severely, and when the *Endeavours* went on shore they were treated with great respect. People were careful not to crowd about them, and welcomed them to the porches of their houses, though they were uneasy about allowing men so ignorant of protocol to blunder about inside.

While Banks and Solander were exploring and botanizing, Tupaia went off to pay formal visits, just as he had at Huahine. Without a doubt, he was a welcome guest wherever he went, treated with all the hospitality due to a man of his nobility and interesting origin. After being enfolded in a flax and dog-hair cloak (*kuri purepure*), or even a cloak made entirely of dogskin (*ihupukupuku*), as befitted his status, he would have been offered the best food available at that time of the year—fish, last season's kumara, and baked fern root. If available, a dog would have been sacrificed in his honor. At last he was able to enjoy familiar food, with immediate benefit to his health. To meet with such respect, after the casually dismissive way he had been treated on board ship, would have been an even greater boon.

Banks noted that at another season there would be an abundance of "excellent vegetables," as he saw them neatly planted out. He was also delighted to discover that the Maori had toilet facilities (perhaps because rats were much scarcer). "Every house or small knot of 3 or 4 has a regular necessary house where everyone repairs," he wrote; "and consequently the neighbourhood is kept clean which was by no means the case at Otahite." (It was by no means the case in London, too.) There was also plenty of fresh water. As naturally fastidious as any Tahitian, Tupaia at last had a chance to bathe.

Typically, Banks tried to seduce the young women, finding that "the innermost veil of their modesty" was a small skirt of perfumed leaves, but that the girls were "as skittish as unbroke fillies." Pressing noses—the *hongi*—was the Maori form of kissing, and as the women decorated their faces with a red oil, which was easily transferred, the seamen found to their great amusement that it was easy to tell who had been kissing the girls. Over time, they also learned that an arrangement could be made with a young woman's family, involving presents and a great deal of politeness, and then if she was willing her favors were won—though only if her swain stayed overnight, as it was not decent for the sun to look down on the act of love. Tupaia would certainly not have needed to negotiate. As a noble priest he was considered one the *tohunga* class, a man of great *mana* with special connections to the gods, and the offer of a beautiful bedmate would have been part of the lavish hospitality.

Tupaia was back on board by the second night. The high surf made it difficult to freight the water casks, so Cook had decided to sail to the more southern cove, which seemed to be more sheltered. At one in the afternoon on October 23, the *Endeavour* dropped anchor at Uawa, which the Europeans christened "Tolaga Bay," again under the mistaken impression that it was the local name. Cook sent a squad of marines on shore with the first boat, so they could impress the locals by carrying out exercises on the beach, but the precaution was unnecessary, as they met the same friendly respect they had enjoyed at Anaura. Tupaia's treaty prevailed at Uawa, too.

And here, Tupaia rewrote history. Later, he told Cook that the Maori people knew little of their ancient religion, or the traditions of Hawaiki. Unaware of the devastation caused by the tsunami, he may have put this down to willful ignorance, but, if so, was quickly proved wrong, for they certainly wanted to learn. While Cook and Green were making lunar observations, and Banks and Solander were botanizing, Tupaia was talking to great crowds who listened with rapt attention. Banks was sufficiently aware of this to note later that whenever Tupaia "began to preach as we calld it he was sure of a numerous audience who attended with most profound silence to his doctrines."

At the time, he also remarked that Tupaia "had much conversation with one of their priests," and that they "seemd to agree very well in their notions of religion only Tupia was much more learned than the other and all his discourse was heard with much attention." This was because Tupaia told him that Maori ideas of creation and the gods were very similar to his own, but without mentioning the differences—for there was certainly room for discussion. He and the other priests must have talked of *Io*, to the Maori the greatest of all the gods, Io of the name so sacred it was very seldom spoken. While the conservative Maori, separated from the homeland, had clung to this ancient belief, the religion of Raiatea and Tahiti had moved on, elevating Ta'aroa above his brother gods, and creating Oro as the supreme deity in the great *marae* of Taputapuatea. Considering all this, it is little wonder that people listened raptly, and thought deeply about what he said, or that Tupaea family tradition has it that Tupaia progressed from *marae* to *marae* to retell the great legends and debate with their elders. Just as at Anaura, he was treated with great reverence, enfolded in valuable cloaks and gifted with ancient ornaments, formally taking custody of the powerful *mana* of these *taonga*, or treasures.

On October 26 it rained almost constantly. According to tradition, during the hardest downpours Tupaia's lectures were staged in a shallow, high-arched cavern—a nineteenth-century traveler, Joel Polack, was led to this cave and told, "*E koro, tenei ano te ana no Tupaea*"—"This, my friend, is Tupaia's cavern." Here, there is a rock drawing of a ship like the *Endeavour* being chased by canoes, which has been attributed to Tupaia himself.

As it was not right to speak of the gods in the dwelling places of men, Tupaia would have known that a cavern was appropriate for religious discourse, but he must have been puzzled by the lack of stone structures like his grand *marae* at Mahaiatea. On asking, he would have been told that for the Maori a *marae* was an open place in a village where a priest or a chief could address the people, and it is likely he was informed at the same time that though Maori had ancestral memories of stepped pyramids, they had no use for steps, for steps were where the various ranks of the priesthood stood, according to status, and in *Aotearoa*—New Zealand—these ranks did not prevail.

During more informal conversations, Tupaia talked a great deal about the ancient homeland, including hints about how much easier daily existence was in Tahiti and Raiatea, where fruits and vegetables grew freely. Once the people got over their awe of this majestic figure who had arrived so magically from the ancient homeland, Tupaia must have been besieged with questions about his present circumstances and his strange companions. Through him, Maori people had their first opportunity to examine Europeans at close quarters—he was *their* translator and interpreter, too. As an *arioi*, he was familiar with the art of caricature, so naturally enjoyed acting out the foibles of the men who had made his shipboard life so difficult, much to his listeners' amusement. Because of him, the Maori came to know Cook as "Tute," even though, unlike Tahitians, they could easily pronounce the "k" sound.

It was not Tute who became legend, however, but Tupaia himself. When the ships of Cook's second expedition arrived in New Zealand, everyone clamored for Tupaia. The news that he had died was received first with disbelief, and then with deep mourning. *"Aue, mate aue Tupaia!"*—"Departed, dead, alas! Tupaia!"—they sang in Tolaga Bay, according to a *Resolution* scientist, George Forster. This happened everywhere—as Cook observed, Tupaia's name was apparently known throughout New Zealand, and was as familiar to those who had never seen him as those who had listened to his stories. His name is still part of the New Zealand landscape. Just as Captain Cook named places after his officers, his crew, and his patrons, Maori have memorialized Tupaia by naming places after him.

For someone who had not received the respect he deserved on board the *Endeavour*, being treated with such veneration must have led to a great change of mood. Tupaia reverted to the relaxed and kindly man of the old days, when he was a wayfinder for the *arioi*. He played with children—there is a tradition that he reintroduced the bow and arrow, long forgotten by the

Maori, as a child's toy, used to whip along tops. Children were certainly called after him, his name—*Tupaea* to the Maori, "standing lightly from the sea"—being freely bestowed by him in symbolic return for the ancestor treasures he had been given. The flourishing Tupaea dynasty he founded may not have been just symbolic, though. According to Tupaea family history, it was as their biological father.

Despite his passion to get to Britain and procure arms to settle his old grievance with the Bora Borans, Tupaia must have been tempted to escape the social discomforts of the *Endeavour*, and stay with these respectful people. Intellectually, he would have felt at home here, since Uawa was the site of a great house of learning, Te Rawheoro, and a school for master carvers. His dietary problems would have been solved, for the well-tended, fertile gardens yielded an abundance of vegetables, and the fishing grounds were bountiful. Here, the houses were sturdy, warm, and dry; and the canoes were strong and richly carved. Later, when he was writing his account of New Zealand, Banks reminisced that here "the People seemd free from apprehension and as in a state of Profound peace. Their cultivations were far more numerous and larger than we saw them any where else and they had a far greater quantity of Fine boats, Fine cloaths, Fine carvd work"—in short, the people of Uawa were the most affluent of any they had seen.

Tupaia would have been very comfortable indeed. His only complaint, as he told Banks later, was that he thought the women more badly treated than their sisters in Tahiti, though they did have the advantage of being allowed to eat with their menfolk. While he would have found resistance to the introduction of the cult of Oro, he could have founded a school of navigation, reintroduced the old canoe-building methods—and even led an expedition back to Tahiti and Raiatea.

His motive for going to England was overriding, however. When the *Endeavour* set sail, Tupaia was back on board.

CHAPTER 15

❧

The Convoluted Coast
of New Zealand

Wrote Midshipman Magra, "After completing our provision of wood and water, and making an inscription on a tree a little to the right of our watering place, it being Sunday the 29th of October, at six in the morning, we sailed from Tolaga Bay, coasting to the Northward."

Within twenty-four hours they rounded a cape that Cook judged to be the easternmost extent of the land, and the day after that they were accosted by five canoes. These included an immensely large one crowded with armed warriors, who delivered a resounding *haka*, and then shouted the old derisive invitation to come on shore and be hacked to death. As Banks remarked, it was getting tiresome. Cook could not be bothered getting Tupaia to try to reason with the rascals—as he said in his journal, he was too busy with other things. So he ordered a gun loaded with round shot and fired over their heads. Stunned by the roar of the explosion and the whistle of the ball, the warrior plied their paddles with such haste to get away that Cook, abruptly amused, named the nearest bluff Cape Runaway.

On November 1, forty-five canoes approached. When they were near enough for Parkinson to notice that one, gruesomely, was baled with a human skull, Tupaia engaged the paddlers in conversation. The same questions and answers were bandied back and forth, along with his usual assurance that the goblins would refrain from firing their exploding sticks if the Maori would consent to trade in peace. And trade in peace they did, at first, having an abundance of large, succulent crayfish to sell, but then began to cheat, taking the cloth but refusing to hand over the lobsters. A fracas developed when an opportunistic fellow pulled up a line hanging off the back of the ship, and stole some laundered linen that was rinsing in the sea, and the

Joseph Banks bartering with a Maori for a crayfish. Watercolor by Tupaia.
(© The British Library Board, 15508/12)

infuriated Captain Cook drove them all away with musket balls and a four-pounder fired over their heads—though with the loss of the linen.

Tupaia, who had been entertained by the busy trade in lobsters, made a sketch of Banks trying to barter a piece of tapa for a particularly large cray-fish, held firmly by its Maori owner. It is his most famous work, because of the emotions expressed in the humorous little scene. Both figures have their legs braced, and are glaring into each other's eyes; the Maori holds the lob-ster by a string, ready to snatch it back at the first opportunity, while Banks keeps his piece of tapa just out of reach. The outcome of the battle of wills is left to the imagination of the viewer.

Many years later, Banks noted that this sketch is a caricature, which was exactly as Tupaia intended. Then the scientist dismissed it by saying "all wild people" possessed a "genius for Caricature"—for him, it was nothing remarka-ble. What he did not take into consideration was that the sketch is unique.

It is the only surviving portrait of Joseph Banks himself that was made on the voyage of the *Endeavour*.

The Europeans were getting the measure of the New Zealand natives, helped by their own stay on shore at Uawa, and Tupaia's more informed interpretations of Maori words and actions. That night, when they were off Motuhora (Whale Island), a large double canoe approached—"the first double Canoe we have seen in this Country," remarked Cook. It was not really a double canoe as Tupaia understood it, being two hulls linked closely together with boards, and was mostly remarkable because of its narrow, very graceful spritsail, which formed a long triangle between a tall mast and an equally tall spar. The paddlers spoke with Tupaia in friendly fashion, but then the mood abruptly changed. A *haka* was chanted and a few stones were thrown at the ship, and then the canoe went away. Next morning, the same canoe reappeared. Again, the paddlers talked to Tupaia, launched into a *haka*, threw rocks, then retreated after a musket was fired.

This fluctuation between amicable chat and challenge turned into a routine, described by Banks in detail at the end of the circumnavigation of New Zealand. The canoes approached at speed until in shouting distance, when a venerable, elaborately tattooed chief would stand up and lead an aggressive chant, which was "almost universally" the taunting challenge to come on shore and be killed—"*Haere mai, haere mai, haere ki uta hei patu-patu ake!*" When the *Endeavour*s made no response, the warriors paddled until near enough to speak in normal voices, and embarked on a friendly dialogue with Tupaia, asking and answering questions. Then, their curiosity satisfied, they launched into a vigorous *haka*, "after which they either became so insolent that we found it necessary to chastise them by firing small shot at them, or else threw two or three stones on board and as if content with having offerd such an insult unreveng'd left us." The sailors would pick up the stones and hurl them back, but never managed to land one on a canoe, even with the advantage of height.

There were variations. Spears might be thrown instead of stones, or the warriors might try to "bewitch" the *Endeavour*s by staring at them fixedly. This last happened at dawn on November 4, the day after the ship had come to an anchor in a fine harbor at Whitianga, which Cook christened Mercury Bay, because he intended to stay until he had made an observation of the transit of Mercury across the face of the sun, which was due on the ninth. An attack had been promised by a challenging canoe the previous evening, and the crew, blasé by now, had got up early "to see the event," as Banks phrased it. It proved to be an anticlimax. Tupaia talked to the warriors for an hour and a half, and his persuasions prevailed, for once, because instead of throwing stones the warriors traded their weapons for cloth. An attempt to cheat was stalled by shooting a hole in a canoe, muskets and cannon were fired to show off the ship's weapons, and Tupaia negotiated a peace treaty with an old chief, Toiawa, called "Torava" by Banks.

Over the following days the men fished, cut wood, and filled water barrels, and Cook and Green set up their observation post. Many Maori came on board the ship, including a small boy by the name of Horeta Te Taniwha, who reminisced much later that the old folk had jumped to the conclusion that "the people on board were *tupua*, strange beings or goblins," their reasoning being that the strangers rowed backward, facing the stern of the boat, so must have had eyes in the backs of their heads.

When the goblins first came on shore the women and children ran away, leaving the warriors to counter their magic, but when the warriors survived, they summoned the courage to come out of the trees, "and we stroked their garments with our hands, and we were pleased with the whiteness of their skins and the blue of the eyes of some of them." As time went by, Horeta Te Taniwha said, they started to have doubts about the otherworldliness of these goblins, because they seemed to be as hungry as ordinary men, enjoying kumara, fish, and shellfish.

Some collected plants, and were pleased when the children helped them, but when they asked questions everyone laughed instead of answering, because no one could comprehend the hissing noises they made. The "supreme man" of the ship had to make marks on the deck with charcoal and point to the beach before anyone understood what he wanted. "One of our aged men said to our people, 'He is asking for an outline of this land;' and that old man stood up, took the charcoal, and marked the outline of Te Ika-a-maui (the North Island of New Zealand)." Then he lay down, to demonstrate that spirits flew from the tip of the island, but the Europeans were puzzled, because no one interpreted that, either.

So where was Tupaia, who should have been there to translate? Evidently, as in Uawa, he had left the *Endeavour* to pay formal visits on the local people. He did not go far, just to an upriver encampment called Purangi, as Banks noted that he made a friend, "Tuwhatoo" (Tuwhatu) there. Purangi was very different from Uawa, because there were no proper houses, let alone gardens, the settlement being obviously temporary. The people lived out in the open despite the occasional downpour, busily drying great heaps of fern root and fish to carry into the interior, probably to stock a fort in anticipation of attack; not only was war constant here, but a new battle was brewing. While he would have been a welcome and interesting guest at the encampment, Tupaia is unlikely to have been tempted to stay in this place-especially after November 9, the day of the Transit of Mercury.

Cook, Hicks, and Green were busy at the observation post, Banks and Solander were botanizing, and Gore had been left in charge of the ship. Canoes arrived, larger and more ornately carved than any that had called here before, evidently returning from a fishing voyage, as they had a great load of fish to sell. The people seemed to be of superior rank—Parkinson, who was on the deck of the *Endeavour*, admired their bearing and the quality of their clothing.

As he went on to describe, "In one of the canoes there was a very handsome young man" who sold the clothes off his back until he had just his dogskin cloak left. Gore, who was keen to buy this, lowered a large piece of tapa on a rope in an offer to exchange, but no sooner had the Maori taken the cloth than his companions "paddled away as fast as possible, shouting, and brandishing their weapons as if they had made a great prize." Gore lost his temper—and deliberately shot the offender dead. "The name of this unfortunate young man, we afterwards learned," Parkinson continued, "was Otirreeoonooe." (Perhaps Otiriunui.) The canoes paddled frantically away, helped along by a cannonball that whistled overhead, and the shore parties rushed to the ship to see what had happened.

Gore, it seems, told the story with difficulty, because Cook instructed him to put it in writing. Banks, though he wished Gore had used small shot instead of lethal ball, philosophized that theft was a capital crime back in England, so the punishment was not particularly unjust. The Maori, too, were inclined to forget it, Horeta Te Taniwha remembering, "[T]he people said, 'He was the cause of his own death, and it will not be right to avenge him.'" They thought he should be allowed to keep "the goblin's garment which he has stolen," though—as a shroud, and so he was buried in the length of hard-won tapa.

Cook was furious. Though there is no record of what was said, according to Solander, John Gore was so distraught he took to his bed for twelve days. The young man's death had more impact on the Maori people than they would admit, too. That evening, Banks joined Tupaia to eat supper with "the Indians," and while they were feasting on fish, shellfish, lobsters, and grilled birds, a woman crouched nearby, moaning in a low, stricken tone. Tears trickled down her cheeks, and she was "cutting her arms, face or breast with a shell she held in her hand, so that she was almost coverd with blood."

There was probably more grief to come. When the ship finally weighed anchor, on November 15, Toiawa told Banks, through Tupaia, that he would have to retreat to his fort, as he expected reprisals from the friends of the man who had been killed.

The *Endeavour* coasted on, to be challenged within days in the same old way, canoe loads of warriors coming out to shout threats, converse with Tupaia, execute a *haka*, and finish up by throwing stones. The Europeans found it exasperating (though the seamen never tired of the *haka*), and Tupaia, who was doing all the talking and persuading, must have become very *hoha*, wearied with their importunity. Finally, on November 18, when his warnings about the goblins' firepower were answered with the usual, "*Haere mai, haere mai, haere ki uta hei patu-patu ake!*" he lost his temper, and treated the offenders to a long homily, reminding them in no uncertain terms that the sea was a great *marae* that belonged to them all.

Banks asked him curiously what he had said, and wrote down Tupaia's translation, because he was so astonished at the independent logic of his reasoning. "Well, said Tupia, but while we are at sea you have no manner of Business with us, the Sea is our property as much as yours." Apparently, the Maori were much less impressed, as they threw stones regardless, and had to be sent off with the usual musket shot. They must have discussed it with their elders after arriving back on shore, however, as over the following days the people in oncoming canoes called out for Tupaia by name—his fame as a *tohunga*, or priest, was spreading.

The ship dropped anchor off the mouth of a large river called Waihou, which Cook named Thames in a fit of nostalgia, and when he, with Banks, Solander, and Tupaia, explored it in one of the boats, the people were so welcoming and friendly that he decided to sail the ship upriver for some miles. The following day, while Cook was exploring further, Lieutenant Hicks, who had been left in charge of the ship, caught a young Maori in the act of stealing a half-minute "hour" glass, which was used when logging the speed of the ship. Flying into a rage, he ordered the bo'sun to have the lad triced up for a flogging—a most unwise move, as the decks were full of visitors. Hearing the hubbub, Banks came out on deck, to find the young man tied to the mainmast shrouds, the bos'un's mate ready with the cat o' nine tails, the visitors bawling for their weapons, and those weapons being handed up from the canoes.

Luckily, Tupaia was also on board. When he came up from below the Maori immediately surrounded him, shouting his name, and demanding to know why their friend was tied up. Evidently they had heard of the shooting of the thief at Purangi, because they expected the worst. He assured them the offender would not be killed, but merely given twelve lashes, and after he had explained British justice, his listeners nodded, and calmed.

Disaster had been very narrowly averted, but the flogging still went ahead. For the first time in history, Maori watched as one of their own was flogged on the deck of a foreign ship. "He endurd the punishment," wrote Banks; "and as soon as he was let go an old man who perhaps was his father beat him very soundly and sent him down into the canoes." As in Tahiti, however, public humiliation was followed by the withdrawal of supplies. The canoes retreated, and few returned, and despite promises no provisions were forthcoming.

As the ship sailed up the eastern coast of the northernmost part of the island, the people in the canoes were more elaborately groomed and more heavily tattooed, and different in that they refused to sell their beautifully wrought weapons. Rounding a headland Cook called Brett, the *Endeavour* entered a magnificent complex of islands and inlets that was fated to become famous throughout the seafaring world as the Bay of Islands. Immediately, canoes put off from the many villages, filled with well-built men who were better dressed than any the Europeans had seen. A few chiefs came on board and engaged in deep conversation with Tupaia, only interrupted when an attempt was made by one of their underlings to steal the anchor buoy. Muskets were triggered, followed by a cannon shot, which sent them all fleeing: "if it had not been for Tupia," Cook wrote with unusual appreciation, they would not have returned to the ship, but Tupaia persuaded them that if they behaved peacefully, no more guns would be fired.

Going on shore was an invitation for more hostilities. Though Cook's party included a squad of marines, Tupaia was not with them. About two hundred warriors crowded close, a *haka* was performed, and an attempt was made to seize the boats. Muskets were fired, and at least one Maori mortally wounded, but the warriors did not retreat until the lieutenant in charge of the ship fired a broadside overhead. It was a demonstration of what the circumnavigation of New Zealand would have been like without Tupaia on board.

The most likely reason Tupaia was not there is that the chiefs he had met the day before were leading him from *marae* to *marae*, to be wrapped in a ceremonial cape and formally welcomed, and to talk to the people about Hawaiki, ancient history, and the legends. As in Uawa, Tupaia found prosperous settlements, with extensive kumara gardens ready for the harvest. Again, was he tempted to escape the ship and take up a comfortable life with these people, who would guarantee the respect and reverence due to his nobility, sanctity, and special knowledge? It may be a possibility. Four days later, when the anchor was weighed and the ship's bow pointed to the outer heads, Tupaia was not on board.

The departure from the Bay of Islands was not easy. No sooner was the canvas spread than the wind dropped and the ship was becalmed. The men occupied themselves fishing to pass away the time until the offshore wind blew, unaware that the turn of the tide would carry them onto the rocks. At ten in the evening, when it became obvious they were heading for the breakers, there was panic. Orders were bawled to lower a boat to tow her off, but the boat falls snagged on a gun, and the seamen were too confused to bring the cannon in until it was almost too late. At the very last minute the boat dropped onto the water, and with energetic rowing and the help of a sudden offshore breeze, the ship's head was brought round.

It was then that someone noticed that Tupaia was not there. The boat was sent to the beach, where he had been listening to the frantic shouts over the thunder of the surf, and he was brought back on board the *Endeavour*.

Out at sea, another four days later, Tupaia proved his usefulness yet again. Some canoes were persuaded to come under the stern, so he was able to ask about the land where they were heading. The Maori readily informed him that three days' paddling led to a place called Muriwhenua, which was the northern end of the island, and after that the coast ran south. Pleased to know this, Cook told Tupaia to ask them if they had heard of any countries that might lie beyond Muriwhenua, far across the sea. "They said no," Cook noted; "but that their ancestors had told them to the NW by N or NNW was a large country to which some people had saild in a very large canoe, which passage took them up to a month: from this expedition a part only returnd who told their countrymen that they had seen a country where the people eat hogs, for which animal they usd the same name (*Booah*) as is usd in the Islands."

"And have you no hogs among you?" demanded Tupaia, knowing perfectly well that there were no pigs in New Zealand, and the paddlers admitted, "No."

"You must be a parcel of liars then," said he; "and your story a great lie, for your ancestors would never have been such fools as to come back without them."

Or so Tupaia reported to Cook, who was as impressed as Banks by his logic.

Doubling North Cape was exceptionally difficult, the ship being hammered with violent gales that did not ease until Christmas Day, when Banks shot some gannets to make a "Goose pye," and all hands became "as Drunk as our forefathers." The New Year saw them turning south on a dangerous lee shore, where the prevailing winds and currents constantly threatened to send them onto the rocks. Cook sailed cautiously but as speedily as he could down this western coast, naming a striking conical peak Mount Egmont as he passed, and negotiating Kapiti, which he named Entry Island. Then, on Tuesday, January 15, 1770, he rounded another island, called Motuara by the people who lived in the village there, and dropped anchor in Ship Cove. He had reached the bays and channels of the northernmost part of the South Island, and over the next few days was to discover that the two main islands of New Zealand were divided by a strait, which was to be endowed with his name.

Ship Cove seemed to offer everything that was needed—a freshwater stream, trees sturdy enough to provide timber for fixing the storm-battered ship, a sloping beach for careening the hull, and a remarkable abundance of fine fresh fish. Banks was disappointed to see only two new plants, but Cook could not have cared less. The people were remarkably friendly. After coming off from Motuara Island, their canoes circled the ship with the usual shouts, but after a few token stones were thrown an old man readily came on board, pressed noses with Tupaia, and accepted a few presents—including nails, which he did not seem to find a novelty.

The next day, one of the men who had come on board to trade tried to cheat, and lifted his *patu* when challenged. At once, a musket was fired (by Cook, according to Magra), and a load of small shot hit him in the knee. Everyone fled, but Tupaia persuaded them to paddle their canoes back under the stern, where he held discourse with the people "about their antiquity and Legends of their ancestors," as Banks put it, and the *Endeavours* had no trouble from then on.

This was one place, though, where Tupaia did not pay long, formal, overnight calls on the local people, perhaps because Cook made sure of it (having realized how close he had come to losing his linguist at the Bay of Islands), or perhaps because the high priest was disgusted by a discovery made here.

On the afternoon they arrived, he accompanied Banks and Cook to the shore, and their boat blundered across the floating body of a woman. There was a family on the beach, and when Tupaia asked about this, they told him it was a relation who had died, and that their custom was to tie a stone to the corpse and bury it at sea, but that the rope must have broken. While they were talking, Banks looked around, and became curious about an earth oven. Tupaia was told they were cooking a dog, and on investigation, as Magra noted, it was indeed a dog.

Meantime, however, Banks, who was poking around in some baskets, found two bones he excitedly pronounced to be human. As Parkinson wrote after hearing about this, they now had "adequate proofs that they are CANNIBALS." Though none of the Maori had ever tried to hide the fact that the custom of eating enemies was general, the *Endeavours* had dismissed it as a ghoulish story, as there had been no actual evidence. Now, melodramatically, that situation had changed.

"What bones are these?" Tupaia asked with shocked disbelief, and the family answered quite frankly, "The bones of a man."

"Did you eat the flesh?"

"Yes," they agreed.

"Have you any left?"

"No."

"Why did you not eat the woman we saw today in the water?"

"She was our sister."

"Then who is it you *do* eat?"

"Those we kill in war."

"So, whose bones are these?"

"Five days ago," they said, "an enemy canoe came into this bay and we killed seven, including the owner of these bones."

And, as the patriarch of the family further revealed, they were expecting reprisals within days.

The boat's seamen, like Cook and Banks, were listening with fascination, though of course they understood very little. Tupaia translated, and as Banks went on, the horror on the crewmen's faces was "better conceivd than describd."

The next day a small canoe arrived alongside the ship, carrying the old man who had been the first on board, whose name turned out to be Topaa. After the usual friendly greeting with a *hongi*, Tupaia immediately checked the story, having lingering doubts about Banks's identification of the bones. Topaa confirmed it, so Tupaia asked about the skulls, seeking more proof they were human.

"Do you eat the heads?" he asked.

Topaa said no—undoubtedly to Tupaia's relief, as all his life he had lived by the precept that the head was the most sacred part of the body, at times too *tapu* to be touched by either food or hands, meaning the owner had to be carefully fed by others. This principle was held by the Maori people, too, he learned. Topaa promised to bring some heads, as a testament to how reverently they were treated: "Much of this kind of conversation passd," wrote Banks (who had little idea of what was really said); "after which the old man went home."

True to his word, Topaa brought four preserved heads—*mokomokai*—to the ship. Tupaia questioned him further, most likely learning that only the heads of nobility were preserved. Those of tribal chiefs and their relatives were kept to be revered, while those of enemies were kept to be reviled, but the process was the same with both, with prayers and proper incantations at every stage. Again, Banks failed to ask what he was saying, or try to pose any questions of his own. Instead, he interrupted the dialogue between the two Polynesians—to force old Topaa to sell the head of a fourteen-year-old boy, first by bribing him with a pair of old white drawers, and then "shewing Him a musquet" when the old man tried to escape without giving up the head. It was the first instance in history of the barbarous *mokai* trade in Maori tattooed heads.

Banks would have liked all the heads, but though he kept on pressuring the old man, Topaa flatly refused to sell any more. Instead, he hurried away at the first opportunity, profoundly regretting that he had brought the *moko-mokai* to the ship. Though enemy heads might be displayed as a derisive challenge to the foe, if a truce were ever negotiated the return of captured heads would be part of the peacemaking process, and the missing head would surely be noticed.

What the seamen thought of the purchase went unexpressed—Roberts, like Pickersgill and the other young men who kept journals, was entirely preoccupied with the ghoulishly enthralling "detestable Crime" of eating people. Tupaia found cannibalism equally repellent, but for a reason the Europeans would have found difficult to comprehend. In the human sacrifice rituals he had orchestrated, an eye from the corpse was given to the *ari'i rahi*, who pretended to eat it before handing it back, a rite that symbolized the gift of the sacrifice to Oro, to whom it belonged. Human sacrifices were intensely sacred, dedicated to the gods, and according to what Tupaia had learned here, the sacred flesh was not just eaten by common men, but profaned with cooking first. While obviously this was the ultimate degradation of the enemy, it would have been difficult for him to credit that the cooking was actually a highly *tapu* process, orchestrated by priests.

Tupaia's reaction to the forced sale of the head is equally unknown, but if he found Banks's mishandling of the feathered god at Taputapuatea barbaric, the unpleasant transaction would not have changed that opinion. He must have felt grave reservations about taking such a taboo object on board the ship. Like the sacrilege at Raiatea and the comet, it would have seemed a bad omen.

Banks himself was quite unmoved by what he had done, instead observing lightly that the reason there were no visible plantations here was undoubtedly because "they live intirely upon fish dogs and Enemies."

The seamen called the harbor Cannibal Cove. Captain Cook, much more sedately, named it Queen Charlotte Sound. On January 26, he climbed a hill to take another view of the strait dividing this land from the island to the north, and came down to find Tupaia and the boat's crew chatting with a group of local Maori, who were as free and friendly as ever. Charmed by the scene, Cook wrote, "Tupia always accompanies us in every excursion we make and proves of infinate service." Though another belated appreciation, it was certainly sincere.

Four days later, Cook, accompanied by the surgeon, took Tupaia to the *pa* on Motuara Island, and asked him to explain to Topaa that they wished "to set up a mark upon the Island" to prove that the British had been here. Topaa readily agreed, and accompanied them to the highest part of Motuara after being presented with "silver, threepenny pieces dated 1763 and spike nails with the Kings broad arrow cut deep in them." The boat's crew set up a post and hoisted the Union Jack, and Captain Cook took possession of the sound "and adjacent lands in the name and for the use of his Majesty." He and the surgeon then celebrated by toasting Queen Charlotte's health with a bottle of wine, at the same time asking Topaa questions about the strait, which Tupaia translated.

Did it extend all the way to the eastern sea? Indeed it did, agreed Topaa. So what about the land to the south—was it an island itself, as Captain Cook suspected, and not part of a continent? Again, Topaa said he was right, and went on to relate that New Zealand was divided into two great *whenua*, the names of which Cook noted in his usual phonetic style as "Tovy-poenammu" (*Te Wai Poenamu*, one of the Maori names for the South Island), and "Aeheino mouwe" (*He hi no Maui*, "a thing fished up by Maui," a garbling of *Te Ika no Maui*, or "the fish of Maui," the Maori name for the North Island). Then Topaa completely misled Cook, by blithely adding that the southern island "might be circumnavigated in a few days, even in four," while Te Ika no Maui needed "a great many moons" to be circled. He was probably thinking of Arapawa, a large island on the eastern side of Queen Charlotte Sound. As Pickersgill sagely commented, the locals appeared to have a "very Imperfect knolledge" of the South Island.

When the wine was finished, Cook gave the old chief the empty bottle, "with which he was highly pleased." Topaa was beginning to find the Europeans an encumbrance, however. His people were anxious to stock their fort to get ready for the expected reprisals, and the *Endeavours*' insatiable demand for dried fish was embarrassing. On February 5, he came on board to watch their preparations for departure with half-hidden relief, and found himself cross-examined yet again, as Tupaia seized the opportunity to ask more questions.

Where had his ancestors come from? Hawaiki, Topaa replied (spelled "*Heawye*" by Banks, who was listening and taking notes as Tupaia translated)—the same Hawaiki Tupaia himself had described in stories and legends. Tupaia then asked if any ships like the *Endeavour* had called before. Though Topaa shook his head, he added that there was an old story of two large vessels, "much larger than theirs, which some time or other came here and were totally destroyd by the inhabitants and all the people belonging to them killd." Tupaia apparently knew the story already, telling Banks that this was a very old tradition, "much older than his great grandfather, and relates to two large canoes which came from *Olimaroa*, one of the Islands he has mentiond to us."

This was Banks's only reference to Tupaia's islands since leaving Tahiti—despite his early enthusiasm for Tupaia's feat of naming "above 70, the most of which he has himself been at," this tale apparently held so little interest for him that he did not make note of its similarity to stories noted on Tupaia's chart. Whether Tupaia was right, and Topaa's tradition was an ancestral memory from before the settlement of New Zealand, or if, on the other hand, it referred to the 1642 visit of a Dutch two-ship expedition, commanded by Abel Tasman, is impossible to tell. Banks was inclined to dismiss the story, remarking that "Tupia all along warnd us not to believe too much any thing these people told us." It is even possible that Topaa was merely repeating one of the anecdotes Tupaia had already related.

As Cook commented, it seemed clear that no credence could be paid, as "there knowledge of this land is only traditionary." Years later, however, he was forced to think again. When he was in command of the *Resolution* on his third expedition, and shipped a seventeen-year-old youth by the name of "Tiarooa" (Te Weheroa) in Queen Charlotte Sound, the young man told him that about three years before the advent of the *Endeavour*, a vessel the Maori knew as "Tupia's ship" had come to Cook Strait; the captain had fathered a son, now about ten years old, and the seamen had introduced venereal disease to New Zealand.

This could be a sign that Tupaia's name had become part of the mythology of the people. When Maori learned that Tupaia had died, they asked urgently if he had died of natural causes. Evidently they suspected treachery and murder—out of jealousy, perhaps, as for many Maori the *Endeavour* was "Tupia's ship," and Tupaia, not Cook, was the admiral. Was the ten-year-old son of the story a garbled memory of Taiata? If so, Tupaia's nephew had entered Maori legend, too.

"Having procured a sufficient supply of wood and water," wrote Midshipman Magra, "on the 6th of February, 1770, the wind being northerly, we left Charlotte Sound." A nasty riptide threatened to carry the ship onto the rocks, but a lucky wind and an outgoing tide brought her around. Cook shaped his course through Cook Strait, and then north to Cape Turnagain, to complete his charting of the North Island coast. South of the cape, the ship was chased by three richly carved canoes, crewed by prosperous-looking, well-dressed men, and for the first time on record they were not challenged.

Though utter strangers, the warriors came alongside and unhesitatingly boarded the ship. At once, they asked for nails, which, as Cook said, they called "<u>Whow</u> the name of a tool among them made generally of bone which they use as a chisel in making holes &C." Given nails, they were puzzled by their appearance, however, and had to ask Tupaia what they were, and whether they really did the same job as *whao* chisels; while they had heard of them, they had never seen them before. Once he had explained and demonstrated to their satisfaction, they gave gifts they had ready in exchange for the nails—as Banks observed, the first instance of organized trade the *Endeavour*s had experienced. Obviously, tales of the ship, the usefulness of nails, and Tupaia's name had reached far and wide.

Then Cook turned south, determined to learn whether Banks was right in his belief that the southern part of New Zealand was an outcrop of the Great Southern Continent, or if he and Topaa were both correct in saying it was a separate island. They coasted the eastern side, soon encountering two fishing canoes, from which they bought fish and a few wooden hooks. It was their last encounter with the Maori people. After that, they glimpsed canoes in the distance, but no one ventured near the ship, and the country they passed appeared to be sparsely populated, if at all.

On March 10, they doubled the southernmost cape, Banks ruefully noting "the total demolition of our aerial fabric calld continent." After naming a small, barren rock after Solander, Cook headed north, up the western side of the South Island, which, like the same coast of the North Island, was a treacherous lee shore. Here, in what came to be called the roaring forties, on a coast often dubbed "the jaws of hell," waves that had been driven all the way from the far side of the world, gathering immense force as they came, crashed high against cliff walls and seethed among the rocks. Yet Banks, tired of being trapped on board, wanted Cook to drop anchor.

The past four weeks had been contentious enough, with a fruitless chase after an imaginary land Gore swore he saw, and heated debates about the so-called continent, but now an open quarrel broke out. Though the officers had already likened the towering cliffs to the daunting fjords of Norway, Banks proposed that Cook should sail up one of the deep, narrow clefts, so he and Solander could go ashore and collect rocks. Cook, quite properly, refused. Not only would the prevailing wind trap the ship in the long, winding rift, but the cliffs were steep-to, so it would be almost impossible to find a secure anchorage.

And so the ship sailed on, while the botanists fumed and growled. Banks, accustomed all his life to getting his own way, harbored a deep grievance for many years to come.

On March 26 the ship was back at the northwest extremity of the South Island. Cook did not sail into Queen Charlotte Sound, but dropped anchor in a deserted cove he called Admiralty Bay. And there they stayed, to take on water and firewood, though the anchorage was exposed to the easterly winds, and not nearly as safe as Ship Cove. It was a choice that just might have been made for ulterior reasons. The stormy weeks of circumnavigating the island must have reminded Tupaia of the unpleasant passage to New Zealand, and his demeanor probably made it very clear he was not looking forward to the rest of the voyage. Cook, who had resolved to "quit this country altogether," was confident Tupaia would continue to be of "infinate service," and so it is not impossible that by choosing to stay in this uninhabited place he was making sure Tupaia had no chance to wander off, as he had so often in the past.

If Tupaia guessed he was being prevented from escaping the ship, his reaction was unnoticed. Instead, it was recorded that he and Taiata took over the smallest boat, and caught an enormous amount of fish. Then, on March 31, 1770, the *Endeavour* weighed anchor, bound east. Abandoning the search for *Terra Australis Incognita*, Cook steered for the uncharted east coast of New Holland, now called Australia.

CHAPTER 16

Botany Bay

The afternoon before they sailed, Cook and Banks began writing up their accounts of New Zealand and its people. They may have even finished the same night, because they were short and hasty affairs. Again, one man copied from the other, as the topics they covered were almost the same and in about the same order, so they either used the same draft, or looked over each others' shoulders.

Though Tupaia was mentioned often, he was never consulted. He had already played his part in translating and interpreting the Maori and their customs for Banks and Cook, as the greater richness of their journals had already testified. Since the days at Uawa, their writings had become more sensitive and reflective about the social implications of what they were seeing—because of Tupaia's interpretations and shared insight, their journals had become less presumptive and condescending, and had turned into valuable ethnographic documents.

Now, the two men described New Zealand and the Maori as seen through their own eyes, though obviously influenced by Tupaia's past commentary. The topography of the country was covered; they expressed surprise at the lack of four-legged animals, and marveled at the luxuriance of the seafood; they described the lean, active physique of the people, along with their clothing, impressive tattoos, dignified bearing, and courage, using the same admiring tones as the seamen. Cook commended the respect given to old men, and the absence of treachery once a treaty had been negotiated (though he did not mention Tupaia's mediation). The commercial possibilities of the tall timber trees and fiber from native flax were discussed. Prospects for European settlement were lauded with enthusiasm, Cook airily pointing out that as the natives were so involved in tribal wars, they would never "unite in opposing" intruders. Tupaia, if he had known about this, would have been greatly dismayed, as the logical conclusion was that if the westerners intended taking over New Zealand, they were bound to have the same ambitions for his islands.

Both Cook and Banks alluded darkly to the quarrel over Cook's refusal to sail up a fjord, Cook reiterating that it simply was not possible, not without "runing the ship into apparent danger," and Banks repeating that he was never given a chance, "to my great regret," to investigate promising territory. Whether there was another argument in the Great Cabin while this was being written is unknown, but there were definitely hard feelings. The purchase of the preserved head was described by both in different ways, Banks confessing with no apparent shame that he secured it by threatening Topaa with a musket, and Cook betraying his disgust. Banks, typically, described the process of securing a Maori girl for the night, while Cook (also typically) did not mention this at all, though he must have been annoyed that Banks set such a libidinous example to his men.

Both, however, were in perfect agreement about the magnificence of Maori canoes and decorative carving. The design of facial tattoo was admired, too, both commenting that it seemed to be added to year by year (or as marvelous feats were commemorated), since older men had the most complete and complicated *moko*. Banks, the sportsman, gave a lot of attention to Maori weapons, making two interesting and perceptive observations: first, that all the weapons were offensive, there being no defensive weapons (like shields); and second, that prized weapons were carried or worn as ornaments, "in the same manner as we Europeans wear swords." A thought was finally cast Tupaia's way when Banks noted that some of the spears were tipped with stingray stings. Tupaia's description of his wounding in the battle for Raiatea must have been grueling, for he reflected, "nothing is more terrible to a European than the sharp Jagged beards of those bones."

The Maori routine of challenging the ship was described, along with the *haka*: "This we calld the War song," wrote Banks; "for tho they seemd fond of using it upon all occasions whether in war or peace they I believe never omit it in their attacks." Both gave their views on cannibalism: "Tupia who holds this custom in great aversion hath very often argued with them against it but they always as strenuously supported it and would never own it was wrong," wrote Cook, who then theorized that the aim was to force men to fight desperately to the last. Banks, who was obviously uncomfortable with the subject despite his gruesome purchase, merely commented that "Tho Thirst of Revenge may Drive men to great lenghs when the Passions are allowd to take their full swing Yet nature through all the superior part of the creation shews how much she recoils at the thought of any species preying upon itself."

Neither had any idea of Maori religion, so repeated what Tupaia had told them, that it was very much the same as his own: they "acknowledged the influence of superior beings and have nearly the same account of the creation of the World, mankind &c. as Tupia," wrote Banks. Because he and Cook had seen no great *marae* at all, let alone anything on the scale of Tupaia's pyramid at Mahaiatea, they both came to the conclusion that the people troubled themselves little about worship, though Banks did mention seeing a shrine in a kumara plantation, which was a small area set off with stones, with a basket of fern roots suspended from a spade in the middle. He supposed the roots were an offering to the gods for the success of the crop.

Both supplied short vocabularies, Banks admitting that though Maori words and phrases were very similar to those used in the islands, he found "it very dificult to understand them till I had wrote them down," because of great differences in pronunciation, but that Tupaia, from the very first, "understood and conversd with them with great facility." The sameness of the language and traditions led both Banks and Cook to the conclusion that these people originated from Tupaia's islands—and, because of this, Cook finally wrote down as much as he could remember of what Tupaia had told him of the geography of the Pacific.

There is a strong hint that he now greatly regretted he had not embarked on "the discovery of those multitude of Islands which we are told [by Tupaia] lay within the Tropical Regions to the South of the line." Meantime, he had become convinced that no Great Southern Continent lay between the equator and that magic latitude 40° south, so he was acutely aware that all he had gained from the fruitless search was a laboriously detailed chart of New Zealand, and a gale-battered ship that was now too fragile to risk a speedy passage to England via Cape Horn. Perhaps, he meditated, he would be given a second chance—"should it be thought proper to send a ship out upon this service while Tupia lieves and he to come out in her, in that case she would have a prodigious advantage over every ship that have been upon discoveries in those seas before."

After this belated acknowledgement of Tupaia's crucial contribution to the voyage, he finally wrote down "a list of those Islands" Tupaia had named, taking the names from Tupaia's chart (mentioned now for the first and only time). This meant the list was not complete—as Cook explained, Tupaia "at one time gave us an Account of near 130 Islands but in his chart he laid down only 74." Yet, though he could not remember more names, Cook did not ask Robert Molineux to bring his journal into the cabin, perhaps because he was not aware that Molineux had written down fifty-seven island names

Tupaia had dictated to him before leaving Tahiti. If he *had* known, and had compared the master's table with his own, he would have found that Molineux had the names of at least twenty islands that were not on the chart, including "Oneewarroa"—the *Olimaroa* Topaa had mentioned when he described the visit of two large canoes. When Tupaia had dictated the list to Molineux, he had described many of the islands, and Olimaroa, he had told him, was a large, high, fertile island to the northwest of Tahiti.

Most curious of all, Cook did not call on Tupaia himself to supply the missing names. Perhaps he was too embarrassed to admit to the proud navigator-priest that he had waited so long before taking notice of the chart; perhaps he did not want to revive an old grievance, as Tupaia's change of mood when his geographical lore was not taken seriously must have been very apparent. There is also the slight possibility that Cook *did* summon Tupaia, and with a flash of haughty temper Tupaia declined to cooperate. His pride had taken a battering that would not be easily forgotten—despite the fact that Tupaia had been of "infinate service" to Cook, there was much between them that rankled.

It is much more likely that Tupaia, being out on deck at the time, was completely unaware the reports were being written. He had other things on his mind, for he was adding to his impressive catalogue of talents.

The first record of Tupaia carrying a musket was when he first went on shore at Poverty Bay. Since then, he had been far too wise to take it with him when he visited Maori, knowing he would not inspire the same trust if he were armed, and that he would quickly be robbed of it, anyway. But now those restrictions no longer held, and the weather crossing the Tasman Sea was surprisingly pleasant, so Tupaia spent the time on deck, practicing with his gun. He had natural advantages, being unusually keen-sighted. Accustomed to searching the sea and sky for navigational signs, he reported birds and flying fish and scuds of floating seaweed before anyone else saw them. Now, undoubtedly encouraged by those keen sportsmen, Banks and Gore, he was improving his aim, with the result that by the time they raised the southeast coast of Australia on April 19, Tupaia was a crack shot.

Lieutenant Hicks was the first man to sight land, but, though the point was named after him, he was not awarded a gallon of rum, perhaps because he was ineligible, being an officer, or maybe because Abel Tasman had arrived there first. Cook made a cautious coastal survey, running north after rounding Point Hicks. The landscape looked attractive, gently rolling and clothed with trees, but he was forced to pass several promising harbors because of unfavorable winds and currents.

In the afternoon of April 27, the ship was finally brought to off an open beach. Four men were observed walking briskly along the shingle, with some kind of canoe on their shoulders, but though everyone watched and waved hopefully, they ignored the ship instead of putting off for her. When the pinnace was lowered, it immediately started to founder, being leaky and rotten. After some panic and bad temper, the yawl was hoisted out, and Cook, with Tupaia, Banks, and Solander, set out for the shore, where the high surf prevented them from landing. Their last sight, as they turned back for the ship, was of the four natives running away.

It was all rather discouraging. At daylight on the 28th, however, they discovered a more hospitable bay. Molineux searched it for an anchorage, sounding the depths from a boat, watched by about a dozen tall, leanly athletic, very dark-skinned men. Some had their naked bodies painted with white stripes, and all were armed with long wooden spears; some were also carrying shorter wooden weapons that Banks likened to scimitars, but were actually *woomera*, or spear-throwers. These were Australian Aborigines, members of the Gweagal ("Fire") clan of the Tharawal tribe. Molineux and his men called out, trying to assure them that all they wanted was water, but the natives' only response was to brandish their spears.

When Molineux returned, he reported that the harbor was shallow, but navigable. The ship sailed in, passing four fishing canoes, each with one or two men inside who seemed so totally absorbed in their work that they failed to see the ship—or else deliberately ignored her, as an unwanted distraction. Feeling obscurely unsettled by this, the seamen dropped anchor abreast of a cluster of huts. A woman emerged from the woods, followed by children; more children came out of a hut; the canoes came in from fishing, and landed the men and their catch. And no one paid the ship any attention at all.

Tupaia, intrigued with this lack of response, made a pencil sketch of three oblivious Aborigines in two bark canoes, then painted it with watercolor. The work is typically energetic and evocative, but also surprisingly detailed. Tupaia's keen sight and powers of observation are obvious, as the sticks used as spreaders to keep the sides apart, and the way the canoes are tied together at each end, can be clearly distinguished. What is most compelling about the painting, though, is how vividly he captures the complete preoccupation of the fishermen. The two boys in the leading canoe watch the ship warily from the corners of their eyes, but there is no sense they have paused in their paddling. The lone fisherman in the second canoe is totally focused on the wavering shadow of the fish, absorbed to the exclusion of everything else, his fishing spear poised. Tupaia's lack of inhibition in drawing exactly what he saw is evident, too. Unlike the prudish Parkinson, he was not afraid to show the genitals of naked men.

Australian Aborigines in bark canoes. Watercolor by Tupaia. (© The British Library Board, 15508/10)

After the noon dinner was eaten, two boats were lowered, to take Tupaia, Cook, Green, Parkinson, Banks, and Solander on shore. As soon as they approached the beach, most of the people ran away, leaving two men to confront the big landing party, "each with a lance of about 10 feet long and a short stick which he seemd to handle as if it was a machine to throw the lance," wrote Banks. For the two Gweagal, it was an act of great courage. Order lived in the land, which was the spiritual home, while disorder came from the sea, threatening the status quo, so anything from the sea was a menace to be sent away, and they were just two against many. As Green observed, their lances were not even weapons, but four-pronged fishing spears instead, each spike tipped with a fish bone.

"*Warra warra wai!*" they cried, according to Parkinson—"Go away!" in the Gweagal language. Though the message was plain, their words were not. For fifteen minutes Tupaia tried to establish some kind of dialogue, but was forced to admit defeat, surely with a sinking feeling as he felt his importance slipping away. James Cook threw some nails and beads onto the sand, which the two men picked up curiously. Encouraged, Cook waved the two boats ashore, but at once the two natives pranced forward with their spears, so he fired his musket, aiming for the clear space between them.

The Gweagal men, surprised by the bang, retreated. The younger one snatched up a stone and heaved it at Cook, who triggered a second gun. Small shot spattered and struck the older man's legs. He grabbed a small shield and held it in front of his face, peering at the intruders through two eyeholes. When Cook and his party landed, two darts were hurled at them, both missing, and a third shot was fired.

The two men retreated into the trees, though slowly enough to show contempt. Cook wanted to follow and kidnap one of them, but Banks shouted a warning that their darts might be tipped with poison.

The Europeans stood irresolute, Tupaia with them. Unconsciously, he was making history again, because he was the first Polynesian to set foot on Australian soil, the herald of thousands more to come. Then the party spread out, exploring the huts, finding half-a-dozen small, wide-eyed children cowering in one of them. After giving the toddlers some strings of beads, the men looked at the canoes—poor affairs, in Cook's opinion, the worst he had ever seen, being mere pods of bark with sticks for thwarts, tied up at each end. It was easy to understand why these people had never voyaged to Tupaia's islands. Even the search for fresh water was of no avail. Giving up, Cook ordered everyone back into the boats.

In the morning, when they returned on shore, it was to find the village of bark huts deserted, and the strings of beads lying rejected on the ground. While Gore led wooding and watering parties, and found fresh water by digging holes, Cook explored the harbor in a boat, and Banks and Solander botanized. Tupaia, in his usual fashion, wandered away on his own, and had nothing to report when he returned. When everyone went back on board to eat a good meal of the fine fish that had been easily caught by casting a seine, the natives reappeared on the beach, betraying they had watched from hiding. They returned to their village, but only to retrieve their canoes. Casks sitting by the waterhole and trinkets left scattered around were left untouched.

The next days followed the same pattern. Occasionally Gweagal men approached the watering or botanizing parties, but retreated without making any response to the friendly shouts and offer of still more gifts. As Cook observed, "all they seemd to want was for us to be gone." Tupaia was tireless in his efforts to communicate—after all, when he had first met Englishmen, their speech was as incomprehensible as the sounds these natives made, so there was no need to give up easily. As part of this quest, on May 1 he accompanied Cook, Solander, and Banks on an excursion into the hinterland. They found traces of strange four-legged animals, and saw many flocks of lorikeets and cockatoos, flying in flashes of brilliant color overhead. Gifts were left in the many huts they found, but they glimpsed only one native, who, as Banks wrote wryly, "ran from us as soon as he saw us."

Returning to the shore in the evening, they encountered Gore's watering party, and the American told them they had seen a group of about twenty natives, and had tricked some into coming closer by pretending to be afraid. Those natives were still in sight. Tupaia approached them quietly, Cook and Solander trailing behind. The Aborigines merely walked away, just outpacing him. Tupaia lengthened his stride, but every time he came near, they strolled away again, staying, infuriatingly, just out of speaking distance. Finally, thoroughly tired of the pointless pursuit, he turned back, and accompanied Cook and Solander to the watering place. It was as if the natives had won some kind of battle.

As obstinate as the Gweagal men, Tupaia left the botanizing party again the next day, breaking out into new territory on his own, but returned in disgust, telling Banks he had seen "nine Indians who ran from him as soon as they perceivd him." His pockets were full of dead small birds he had shot for Banks's collection, however, and he was cradling a live rainbow lorikeet for himself. He had winged it, and when it fell to the ground he had caught it up before it could fly away.

The gorgeously colored parrot, about the length of Tupaia's hand, had a vivid indigo-blue head and lower breast, a short red beak, a large red and orange bib, and a bright green back, wings, and tail. Lorikeets make great aviary pets, being intelligent, easily taught to speak, and boisterously playful—and a pet was exactly what Tupaia made of this bird. It thrived on sugar water and scraps, and presumably learned to talk in Tahitian with a Raiatean accent, compensating for the friend he did not have on the *Endeavour*.

On May 6, they sailed away, leaving behind the body of one of the seamen, Forby Sutherland, who had died five days previously (probably of tuberculosis), the first European to be buried in New South Wales soil. Tupaia had failed to establish any kind of rapport with the natives, but Banks had gained a huge collection of plants. Cook had intended calling the bay Sting-ray Harbour, because Gore had caught several huge specimens of the stingrays that swarmed there. Indeed, the crew was feasting on stingray right now—dubiously, no doubt, as the cook had made a stew out of the tripes. In the end, however, it was decided to call it Botany Bay, on account of the immense number of new specimens Banks and Solander had found.

Cook sailed north past increasingly barren country, continuing his running survey of the coast. Though the *Endeavours* occasionally saw groups of natives on shore, none of them paid the ship any attention at all, and the surf made landing impossible. As always when the time dragged, the sailors managed to get intoxicated, and in the middle of the night of May 22, Orton, Cook's clerk, had his clothes slashed and his ears partially cropped after passing out drunk. James Cook was furious. Determined to find a scapegoat in the midshipmen's mess, he landed on Magra, though without any evidence, dividing the ship into two camps. Luckily, the very next morning he was able to bring the ship to and lower a boat to explore the shore, as a distraction to them all.

Taking the boat up a shallow, shoal-ridden salt lagoon was a sobering experience. The early air was bitterly cold, succeeded by stifling temperatures in the afternoon. The mangroves bordering the lagoon swarmed with biting ants and stinging caterpillars. Though the dry soil beyond the salty bogs yielded many new plants, large areas of ground were completely bare of trees. The sun beat down on the sere, apparently lifeless landscape. There were no natives to be seen, though there was some evidence they had been around. The party found ten small fireplaces arranged in a circle, one sheltered with a low windbreak, but there were no huts at all, leading Cook to the conclusion that the tribesmen slept unprotected, except perhaps for sheets of bark. Buzzards floated on eddies of air high above, and one of the party managed to bring one down for the cabin dinner, but there was no sign of land animals. To all appearances the natives were forced to scratch an existence out of the waters of the shallow bay, a midden near the fireplaces holding just cockleshells and fish bones.

Cook heard Tupaia murmur, "Ta'ata ino"—meaning, "These poor people are very badly off." There was no fresh water to be found; it was a relief to sail away.

Tupaia was badly off himself. Just one week later, on June 1, he complained to Banks that his gums were sore and swollen, and admitted they had been sore for a fortnight. Knowing nothing about scurvy, he did not recognize it as a symptom of the dread scourge of long voyages at sea, so had failed to mention it.

It usually takes six weeks for symptoms of scurvy to appear, which means that Tupaia had been without vitamin C (ascorbic acid) since April 1, the day the ship left New Zealand. The ship had not touched shore at all during the circumnavigation of the South Island, so he had gone short of vegetables before that, too, but the few days of fishing and gathering herbs in Admiralty Bay had provided enough of the vitamin to bring him back to health before the ship sailed west. Vitamin C, however, is not stored by the human body, any excess being excreted in the urine, so it has to be part of the daily diet. Tupaia's food had not included the vital element over the Tasman Sea crossing or the coastal survey—and, as usual, he had defied Captain Cook.

Cook's anti-scorbutic regime included a variety of foods supposed to prevent the horrible disease. As well as sauerkraut and saloup, there were porridges of wheat or dried peas flavored with portable broth (cattle offal that had been boiled down and dried), "marmalade of carrots," and malt, which was barley that had been allowed to sprout before drying. Cook placed great reliance on malt. Every morning a measured portion of this was ground up and mixed with boiling water, to make an infusion called wort, a quart of which was issued to each man. Though useful in staving off the severe constipation endemic on sailing ships, this brew held no vitamin C—in fact, the only item containing even a trace of the vitamin was sauerkraut, and someone would have to eat huge quantities of this for it to do any good. Nevertheless, by refusing to touch it, Tupaia had earned Cook's deep displeasure.

"The Surgeon immediately put him upon taking extract of Lemons in all his drink," wrote Banks. This was very sensible, lemons being a good source of ascorbic acid, but it is doubtful the extract still held any of the vitamin. Six days earlier, Banks had recorded that he and Munkhouse had examined the keg of "orange juice and brandy which had been sent on board as pre-pard by Dr Hulmes directions," and had found it good, except for a covering of mold, but that when it was put into a bottle and exposed to light, it became "ropey" and unpleasant: "On this we resolvd to have it evaporated immediately to a strong essence." Vitamin C is very susceptible to heat, and so would have been destroyed.

Whether the extract of lemon had been given the same treatment is unrecorded, but likely, because drinking it did Tupaia no good at all. As Banks wrote distractedly on June 16, Tupaia's sore, swollen gums "were very soon followd by livid spots on his legs and every symptom of inveterate scurvy." Without fresh food, Tupaia was going to die.

CHAPTER 17

❧

The Great Barrier Reef

Joseph Banks, like everyone else on board, had good reason to be distracted. Back on May 20, Captain Cook had noted that they had "discover'd a reef stretching out to the northward as far as we could see." Though he did not know it, the little ship was entering the appalling maze of the Great Barrier Reef, a vast zone of coral outcrops extending from just below the Tropic of Capricorn—latitude 24° south—to Cape York, in the far north of what is now Queensland, Australia. That day of the first sighting, he sent down a boat to sound the depths ahead, and cautiously followed with the ship, hauling aback for each warning of low water, and making sail again when five fathoms or more was signaled.

It was the start of an exhausting routine. Two boats, with Molineux in command, sailed ahead by day, constantly sounding as the *Endeavour* groped her way through the labyrinth. Luckily, the weather remained pleasant, and the winds very gentle, but the wear and tear on the nerves was brutal, only relieved when the ship anchored at night, or when Banks, Cook, and Solander made a rare excursion to the barren shore, in search of specimens and fresh water. "No signs of fertility is to be seen upon the land," Cook wrote dismally on 30 May; the ship's barrels were again very low.

On June 10, after another fruitless hunt for a replenishing stream, Cook broke his habit of remaining at anchor during the hours of dark. It was a beautiful night, lit by a full moon, and so he instructed the officer of the watch to keep the ship ghosting along under close-reefed topsails, then retired to his swinging cot. On deck, it was balmy and peaceful enough to lull the lookouts to sleep. The water was like black silk, shimmering with luminescence; the wake of the ship trailed dreamlike, punctuated with dots of glowing blue. Just as hypnotic was the regular call of the man in the chains, counting off marks and deeps as he brought up the sounding line.

"By the mark, seventeen," he chanted, just as a quartermaster's mate was about to strike six bells—11 P.M. And before he could cast the lead again, the ship ran onto the reef.

The terrible crunching, rasping noise was succeeded by violent thumps. Cook ran out in just his drawers, yelling, "All hands on deck!" Men stumbled to their stations as orders were roared to take in all sail. Up the rigging scrambled dozens of topmen, while gangs hauled at lines, and within minutes every sheet of canvas was roughly furled. With more shouted commands, boats were lowered to sound the depths all about the hull. Reports were yelled back from the rippling darkness: the ship was stuck on a broad, jagged coral head, with the nearest decent depth—about twelve fathoms—a whole ship-length away.

The tide was ebbing, pinning her to the reef. If the *Endeavour* worked back and forth on the coral, she would break up fast. More orders were barked, and men scrambled up the rigging again, to strike the topmasts and yards and sway them down to deck, to reduce the area exposed to any wind. Anchors were carried out in the boats, and carefully dropped, then the lines tautened with the capstan and windlass, to hold her fast where she lay. Meantime, everything that could be ditched was thrown overboard—ballast, cannon, barrels of old stores, even their precious fresh water. And all this time, as Banks wrote, "she continued to beat very much so that we could hardly keep our legs upon the Quarter deck; by the light of the moon we could see her sheathing boards &c. floating thick round her; about 12 her false keel came away."

Daylight was sudden, the way it is in the tropics, heralding another bright, calm day, and while they waited for the next high tide the spars and masts were lashed together to make rafts, and secured to the ship's sides to give her more buoyancy. That next high tide came at 11 A.M.—to Cook's consternation, it was lower than the night before. They heaved mightily on the anchor lines, but the *Endeavour* refused to budge. Instead, she began to leak. Everyone labored at the three pumps that could be made to work, including the gentlemen, sweating to get her as free of water as possible before the next high tide, which hopefully would be higher than the last.

At five in the afternoon the tide began to rise. At nine it was at the full, and the ship began to *float*. Soon she was on an even keel, and they could feel her new buoyancy. It was a moment of high suspense—with water rushing in, could she be safely heaved off the reef? Cook agonized that his ship would fill, and sink like a rock.

Tight-lipped, he wrote, "I resolv'd to resk all." All hands who could be spared from the pumps turned to the capstan and windlass, and eighty minutes of back-breaking labor later, off she came. Triumph was quickly succeeded by terror, as the carpenter's mate who had just sounded the depth in the hold shouted out that the leak was gaining. Every man's heart stopped for a fraction, and then started racing. Wrote Banks, "fear of Death now stard us in the face."

But the carpenter had made a mistake. He had taken the sounding in a different manner from the man he had just relieved, and the true level was no higher than the previous measurement. As Cook remembered, the realization that it was a false alarm "acted upon every man like a charm," and the pumpers worked with renewed vigor. It was time to put on sail again, and work her gently into shore: up the rigging scrambled topmen again, and masts and spars were swayed aloft by grunting gangs hauling at lines on deck. Then rolled sails were hoisted up and secured to the yards, and at eleven in the morning the ship stood slowly for the land, Molineux leading the way in a boat.

Meantime, Jonathan "Matte" Munkhouse, the midshipman who was the surgeon's young brother, had the bright idea of fothering the leak, an expedient that all the seamen had heard about, but had never seen put in practice. This involved taking a large piece of old canvas, and turning it into an oversized thrum-mat (used on shore for scraping boots, and now known as a door-mat; and used at sea for preventing ropes from chafing, now known as a baggywrinkle). This was done by bristling it with threaded hunks of rope-yarn, and sticking on clumps of wool with dung. As the ship crept landward, the great canvas, spread out on deck, was bordered on all sides with hunched men plying bodkins, creating something very strange indeed.

Then the big thrum-mat was ready. Long ropes were attached to each corner, and it was lowered over the side, and drawn along the bottom of the hull. The theory was that it would be sucked over the hole by the inrush of water, and block the leak—and to everyone's surprise and vast relief, that was exactly what happened. Within an hour the ship was pumped dry, and stayed dry when the pumps were let stand, "so that," as Banks wrote, "we were in an instant raisd from almost despondency to the greatest hopes." They could now put their minds to getting the ship to some sheltered beach, where she could be careened and repaired.

Tupaia's part in this was unrecorded. It is unlikely he did anything, save pray to the gods for relief, and grimly remember the ominous auguries of the comet, the preserved Maori head, and Banks's mishandling of the feathered god at Taputapuatea. As Banks noted, Tupaia was "now extremely ill."

The extract of lemon had failed to work, and the "bark" and "acid" the surgeon had given him were useless, "bark" being Peruvian bark, a source of quinine (a medicine for malaria), and "acid" being dilute sulfuric acid, lauded because its taste resembled that of lemons. The small, purple spots on Tupaia's swollen legs were expanding and turning black. Because vitamin C is necessary for the production of collagen, which keeps scar tissue glued, his old wounds would have started to break apart. Teeth were loosening as his swollen gums began to bleed. Soon he would die from hemorrhage of the brain. Little wonder that Banks wrote, "everybody in the Cabbin very desirous of getting ashore and impatient at our tedious delays."

The wind, which had been so light, had turned to strong gales, so Cook was forced to drop anchor at the mouth of the river Molineux had located. The fothering sail still stemmed the leak, so there was little to do but wait, and count their blessings that the storm had not sprung up while the ship was pinned to the coral. For Tupaia, the delay could have been critical. Somehow, however, he found the strength to drag himself out of bed and cast a fishing line, either from deck or out his cabin sidelight. Later, the men often hauled a seine with very poor results, but Tupaia had surprising success, catching enough for himself to eat. At six in the morning of June 17 the wind moderated at last, and the ship ran into the providential harbor. When she was still again, Tupaia caught more fish, and ate that too. And so he saved his own life.

The following evening, Banks reported with wonder that the symptoms were disappearing fast: "Tupia who had employd himself since we were here in angling and had livd intirely on what he caught was surprisingly recoverd," he wrote, though "Poor Mr Green"—who remained under the surgeon's regime of acid, bark, and sterilized extract of lemon—was still very ill. Tupaia must have eaten the fish raw, including the head and innards, as the algae in the gut and gills would have supplied the vitamin C he so desperately needed, while the uncooked fish flesh and organs would have contributed the niacin, riboflavin, and thiamin his diet also lacked, a contributing factor in sea-scurvy.

Even better was to come. While the carpentering gangs worked on the ship's hull, Gore was sent out with foraging parties, and returned with "palm cabbage" (the heart of the cabbage tree crown), wild plantains, and leaves of a kind of marsh taro, as well as reports of a mysterious animal, about the size of a greyhound, which jumped like a hare. Tupaia set up house in a small tent on shore, collected taro roots, and dug a hole for an earth oven. Lighting a fire in the bottom of this, he heated stones, and then slowly roasted the roots, wrapped well in the leaves. When he offered them around, the Europeans were unenthusiastic, as the roots were small and they preferred the leaves boiled, but Tupaia ate his own cooking with relish, and ate the boiled greens, too.

As his health recovered, he resumed his old habit of wandering off. On July 5, he accompanied Banks and Solander to the other side of the bay, where they found some washed-up coconuts that had been opened by some mysterious agency, and after informing them that the robbers were coconut crabs, Tupaia "walkd away a shooting." He said he hoped to find some local inhabitants, but returned to report that though he had been successful in sighting two of them, "digging in the ground for some kind of roots," on seeing him they had run away.

These nervous souls were coastal-living *dhulun-dhirr* ("of the sea") members of the Guugu-Yimidhirr tribe, dark, small, slender folk who painted their naked bodies white and red. They remained elusive. The next day, Tupaia accompanied Banks and John Gore on a boat excursion up the river, wandering off again while Banks botanized and Gore hunted game (the mysterious animal in particular), but all he had to report was the sight of a doglike creature (probably a dingo), which from his description Gore pronounced to have been a wolf.

The party slept very uncomfortably out in the open, tormented by mosquitoes, but were rewarded next morning by the sight of four of the mysterious animals—which, to their astonishment, fled from Banks's greyhounds by making prodigious bounds with their back legs, their little forelegs held up before their chests. In the afternoon, the smoke of a fire was glimpsed, and the three men walked toward a native camp, hoping, as Banks wrote, "that the smallness of our numbers would induce them not to be afraid of us." By the time they arrived, however, the Guugu-Yimidhirr were gone, their footprints, the fire, and the hastily abandoned remnants of a meal the only evidence they had been there at all.

Frustratingly, when the party returned to the ship, it was to hear that natives had been around—two had watched the repair work from the other side of the river. Otherwise, the good news was that one of the boats had come across an abundance of turtles, and three large ones had been taken. At last the *Endeavour*s had something substantial to eat, to eke out their rapidly diminishing stock of provisions. "This day all hands feasted upon turtle for the first time," wrote Cook with great satisfaction. Tupaia would certainly have shared in the meal, but must have kept his feelings well hidden as he watched the sailors gobble the rich, glutinous meat. In his islands, *te mau honu*, the sea turtle, was highly sacred, reserved for nobles and priests of special standing, like himself.

The Guugu-Yimidhirr were watching, too. In the morning of July 10, four natives appeared on the opposite bank shouldering an outrigger canoe, which they put into the water. Two of them bravely paddled within shouting distance of the ship, where they paused, "talking much and very loud to us," wrote Banks. Encouraged by friendly yells, they paddled closer, holding up their lances at intervals as if in warning. The seamen leaned over the rail to give them cloth, paper, beads—everything that had delighted the natives of New Zealand. Unlike the Maori, though, the Guugu-Yimidhirr were not impressed. Then, accidentally, a small fish was dropped into their canoe, "on which they expressd the greatest joy imaginable." The other two natives were fetched, and all four arrived at the European encampment, each carrying two spears and a spear-launching *woomera*.

This was Tupaia's moment. Putting aside his musket, he walked toward them. The natives braced themselves for battle, their spears lifted, but he ignored the threat. Gesturing to them to lay the weapons down, he came close, then hunkered down on the ground. Instantly understanding that he simply wanted to parley as best he could, they set their spears aside, and squatted in a row in front of him. James Cook, impressed, copied this gambit from then on, making it a habit to sit down unarmed to talk with natives, even when threatened—until the day he forgot, a lapse that led to his death.

The Europeans crowded around with little gifts, but the natives were more interested in chattering to Tupaia. They talked to him without side-comments to one another, because it would have been rude not to include him in the conversation, even when it became obvious he understood nothing or little. With the same good manners, they enfolded the Europeans into the dialogue when they saw that they were trying to communicate, too, and cooperated when Banks and Parkinson started writing down Guugu-Yimidhirr words. "*Wageegee*," one said when Parkinson pointed to his head, and, "*Tulkoore*," when he pulled at his hair; and in this fashion, with Tupaia's help, the draftsman built up an impressive vocabulary of 121 words over the next few days. Many of the nouns were for parts of the body, though there were names of plants and animals, too—the mysterious leaping quadruped was "*Kangooroo*," and Tupaia's pet bird was "*Perpore*."

Their "Voices were soft and tunable and they could easily repeat many words after us," wrote Cook. When surprised, they whistled. The atmosphere became very relaxed, disturbed only if anyone moved between the natives and their pile of weapons. By signs, the *Endeavours* urged the natives to join them for the midday dinner, but they politely declined, then clambered into their canoe, and went back to wherever they had come from.

The next day two of them returned, bringing two friends, whom they introduced by their names, one being "Yaparico." They had brought a fish, to reciprocate for the fish they had been accidentally given the previous day. With equally remarkable good manners, they withstood the Europeans' inspection of their bodies, Banks going so far as to spit on a finger and draw a wet line through one man's dust and paint, to ascertain the true color of the skin underneath. It was noticed for the first time that the septum between the nostrils was bored to take an ornament, as one of them had a bone inserted crossways across his face, which the entertained seamen likened to a spritsail yard. They were quite naked, and seemed unembarrassed about it, though it was noticed they held one hand in front of the genitals while standing still, probably because they were so conscious of the foreigners' curious stares. When the sailors started investigating their outrigger canoe with close and professional interest, they finally lost patience, pushed it off, and as Banks recorded, went away without saying another word.

The quartet put in another appearance early the next day, this time heading straight for Tupaia's tent, where they were so pleased with his welcome that one of them went off in the canoe to fetch two friends, coming back to introduce them in the same polite manner as the day before. Then they sat down and held a conversation with him, which lasted most of the morning. Obviously, there was dialogue, though Banks and Cook remained under the impression that Tupaia could not understand a word. Even if that were so (which is unlikely), a great deal was communicated. The Guugu-Yimidhirr, being accustomed to dealing with the *waguurr-ga* ("of the outside") people of the interior, were expert at sign language, and also used chirruping sounds—

Cherr, tut tut tut tut tut—to indicate emotion, interspersed with whistles.

The Europeans kept on interrupting, meaning to be friendly but only managing to be rude. Banks gave the Guugu-Yimidhirr some fish: "They receivd it with indifference, signd to our people to cook it for them, which was done, and they eat part and gave the rest to my Bitch." Drawn by the novel scene, two more native men and a woman emerged on the opposite beach. The woman was as naked as her companions. The Europeans stared at her frankly and intently through their spyglasses, and Tupaia's guests got up and left. The canoe was so small it took two trips to get all six across the river, but their point was made.

Over the next five days the Guugu-Yimidhirr, obviously displeased, almost totally ignored the *Endeavours*. Two passed by briefly during a fishing excursion, but that was all. John Gore came in from a shooting expedition, triumphantly bearing his booty, a specimen of the leaping animal. Cook and the scientists inspected it, Parkinson sketched it, and then they dressed the carcass and ate it for dinner, pronouncing it excellent. After that, they gave it the name they had heard the locals say—"*kangaroo*"—and so a Guugu-Yimidhirr word entered the English language. The people themselves, however, were almost invisible.

On July 16, the ship was ready for departure, so Tupaia set out to find his new friends while he still had the chance. Understandably, he crossed the river alone. When he came back he reported very little about what was said and done, saying only that he had seen three men. A lot more happened than he admitted, as he was carrying cooked yams—"longish roots about as thick as a mans finger and of a very good taste," according to Banks—so must have been lavishly entertained, according to local standards.

It is possible to guess more by extrapolation. A few days later, one of the seamen blundered across a group of Guugu-Yimidhirr hunters while gathering taro tops; he was very afraid, but emulated Tupaia by sitting down with them. All they wanted was to take off his clothes and examine his body, which he allowed them to do, and after he was dressed again they let him go, helpfully pointing out the direction of the ship in case he was lost. Accordingly, it seems likely that Tupaia stripped down to the *maro* he wore under his breeches, and exhibited his tattoos to his hosts, to the accompaniment of chirps and whistles of admiration and surprise.

He certainly sat down with them, and engaged in conversation. Obviously fascinated by these engaging folk, he would have been learning more all the time. By now, Tupaia had surely found out that these "*ta'ata ino*" were not "very badly off" at all, but instead were completely in tune with their inhospitable-looking country, maintenance of the status quo being their overriding aim. Like Tupaia's own people, they were intensely religious, spirituality ruling their daily lives—the Guugu-Yimidhirr may have sensed that he was a priest, one of their reasons for singling him out. Their ancestor-spirits were mythical beings who had wandered through the land in the "Dreamtime," and their heritage was rich with legends of these. Legends can be told with mimicry, laughter, and dance, as well as with words—despite Tupaia's natural gift for languages, debate about creation myths on the level of the Uawa experience was quite impossible, but a surprising amount of lore could have been imparted and understood.

Yams were a female affair, so Tupaia would have been offered the cooked yams by some women. It was an eloquent sign of the natives' trust, and respect for his stature and *mana*. After seeing these yams, Cook, Banks, and Solander made the same deduction, so that same afternoon went over the river to try their own luck. On the way, they encountered four Guugu-Yimidhirr men in a canoe, and after giving them some beads, "attempted to follow them hoping they would lead us to their fellows where we might have an opportunity of seeing their Women," as Banks confessed.

They were firmly spurned, however: "by signs made us understand that they did not desire our company."

Tupaia's visit had reassured the tribe, so the next day they visited the European encampment again. In fact, as Banks wrote, they "seemd to have lost all fear of us." One demonstrated his astonishing skill at throwing a spear, and then he and his friends clambered on board to tour the ship. The word got around: when Cook, Banks, and Solander met five unknown Guugu-Yimidhirr during a stroll in the woods, the natives showed no signs of being scared. Two wore interesting shell necklaces, but flatly refused to sell them. While barter was certainly known to the Guugu-Yimidhirr (their canoes, for instance, were made by specialist Tjungundji craftsmen to the north, and bought in a system of ceremonial exchange), anything the Europeans had to offer was culturally worthless.

When Cook and the others returned to the ship, it was to find more natives on board, inspecting twelve dead turtles Gore and his men had caught, and discussing them together. The officers told Cook that the Guugu-Yimidhirr had acted strangely, being more interested in the carcasses than anything else on the ship. The natives went away without making any fuss, though when they saw Tupaia's caged lorikeet, they tried to release it, and had to be stopped. If there had been a problem, it was over—or so everyone thought.

In the morning, ten hunters arrived, heavily armed with lances and *woomeras*. They left them in their canoe when they came on board, but their intention, it quickly became clear, was to stake claim to two of the turtles. The sea turtles were a seasonal food, long anticipated, and their tribal rights were being encroached on by the foreign invaders, who were not entitled to treat the turtles as if they were their own property. The Guugu-Yimidhirr were willing to be reasonable, and share the precious resource, but they wanted their rightful portion.

When they began to haul two carcasses over to the gangway, however, they were physically restrained by the seamen, which made them very agitated. Banks stepped forward to mediate, and the Guugu-Yimidhirr leader stamped his foot, and shoved him away. "*Aita*," they all shouted, "*aita!*"—the Tahitian word for "no," which Tupaia may have taught them. Banks, frightened, ran down to the beach. As soon as he was gone they made another attempt to take two turtles, and again were prevented. Wild with frustration, they ran about the decks, throwing gear overboard. Cook tried to appease them by offering them bread, but that made them even angrier. If the foreign invaders were starving, it would have been different, but that was obviously not the case, because they had surplus food—the bread, which the natives did not like.

Furiously, they rushed ashore, the man in the lead grabbing up a handful of dried grass as he ran. Dashing over to a fire where a pitch kettle was boiling, he lit the grass, and then ran in a huge circle about the encampment, shoving his way through the shoulder-high grass and dropping sparks as he went. With a thud, flames erupted. In a terrifyingly short time the dry, combustible area was ablaze.

Fortunately, most of the equipment had been brought on board, but a sow with her litter and Tupaia's tent were in danger. Sailors beat their way inward, and saved all but one piglet—but the fire-maker was now dashing to the side of the river where the laundry was done, and all the ship's nets and a great deal of linen were drying. Cook fired a musket—not in warning, but at the leading native. It was loaded with small shot, and the man was wounded. Blood spattered on the linen lying on the ground. Puzzled and frightened, the Guugu-Yimidhirr withdrew into the trees, and the seamen extinguished the fire.

Cook, Banks, and "3 or 4 More" (certainly including Tupaia) picked up the spears the hunters had left behind, and followed them into open country. When they were in sight, Cook's party followed Tupaia's example by setting aside the spears and quietly sitting down. The Guugu-Yimidhirr paused, then sat down too, but a good distance away. Everyone waited.

After a long interval, a little old man stood up, and came hesitantly forward. What Cook called an "unintelligible conversation" was exchanged with Tupaia, and then the old man beckoned to his friends. The hunters set their weapons against a tree, and "came to us in a very friendly manner," and once the spears were returned to their owners, all enmity vanished. The Guugu-Yimidhirr seemed as amiable as always. But they never came on board the ship again.

Wrote Banks on July 23:

> In Botanizing today . . . we accidentally found the great part of the clothes which had been given to the Indians left all in a heap together, doubtless as lumber not worth carriage. Maybe had we lookd farther we should have found our other trinkets, for they seemd to set no value upon any thing we had except our turtle, which of all things we were the least able to spare them.

On August 4, 1770, after a week of frustrating onshore gales, the *Endeavour* finally cleared the river that Cook had named Endeavour, after his ship. It was not easy, for the ship had to be warped over the bar, but he was very anxious to get to sea, as a long, dangerous passage lay ahead, and provisions were running short.

Just as before, two boats remained down, leading the way with Molineux in charge, constantly sounding as they went. It was a nerve-wracking business, as Molineux had to investigate a multitude of possible routes, all of which looked difficult and dangerous. Cook often went down in a boat himself, and every day at low tide he would climb to the masthead to judge the shoals that lurked ahead. It seems certain that Tupaia spent a lot of time in the highest rigging, too, his keen sight and experience in navigating tropical shoals being such an asset.

On August 11, they came in sight of three high islets, one abounding with so many large lizards they called it Lizard Island, and for a few glorious hours they thought they had reached the end of the labyrinth of coral. But, to Cook's mortification when he and Banks took the pinnace there, and climbed to the highest part, it was to see "a Reef of Rocks" extending as far as he could see. Then light dawned: great breakers crashed high on these rocks, which surely must come from the ocean. Salvation beckoned, after all.

Two days later, they found a passage to the open sea, and at long, long last there was deep water beneath the keel. The relief was tremendous—they had been entangled in the coral, as Cook wrote, "ever since the 26th of May, in which time we have saild 360 Leagues without ever having a Man out of the cheans heaving the Lead when the Ship was under way." Now at last they were free. Though what Banks called their "crazy ship" leaked nine inches an hour, and had to be frequently pumped, it was a minor inconvenience, compared to what they had already endured.

The reprieve was short-lived. As they found to their dismay, sailing outside the reef was far worse than creeping along within it, as the strong, prevailing, onshore gale constantly threatened to blow them onto the rocks. Laboriously beating against the wind opened up protesting planks, so that the *Endeavour* leaked at an even faster rate. Having a good breeze was vital, however, to keep the sails stiff so the helmsmen could steer the ship's head away from the reef. On the 16th, it dropped to a dead calm. Disaster beckoned. The canvas hung uselessly still, while the tide bore the ship shoreward.

Three boats were sent down, their oarsmen laboring with all their might to bring the *Endeavour*'s head around. The leaky old pinnace was in chocks on the deck, being repaired yet again; the carpenter and his mates worked frantically to get her fixed, and down she went with a full boat's crew, so that all four boats were towing. Even that did not work, so the carpenter made huge sweeps out of planks, which were rigged out the leeward stateroom windows. Men heaved at them, rowing the ship from inside. It still made no difference. Within moments the ship was just one swell away from the breakers, with nowhere to anchor because the sea was so deep.

At the very last instant a riffle of wind came flickering over the water. The weather leech of the main topgallant fluttered, and the ship finally answered her helm. As the *Endeavour* veered away a man high aloft—Tupaia?—called out that he spied a very small opening in the reef. Cook shouted through his speaking trumpet, and Hicks cast off the line of his boat, which rowed off to investigate. Back he came, with the news that though the opening was narrow, it was free of coral heads, and there was good anchorage inside. The faint wind held, and the men at the wheel, helped by two boats still towing, kept the ship's bow pointed at the passage. The flood tide carried them in, and within two hours they were lying safely at anchor.

A massed sigh of vast relief was heaved, Pickersgill meditating that it was "the narrowest Escape we ever had and had it not been for the immeadate help of Providence we must Inavatably have Perishd." Cook wrote dryly that it was a most unexpected delight to be back in the shoals, adding with unusual bitterness that such was his life—if a man left a dangerous coast uncharted and unexplored, "he is then charged with Timorouness and want of perseverance and at once pronounced the unfitest man in the world to be employ'd as a discoverer." But, if he pressed ahead into unimagined hazards and lost the gamble, "he is then charged with Temerity and want of conduct."

With that off his chest, he put his mind to what to do next, concluding he had no choice but to stay within the reef, and hope fervently they came to the strait between New Holland and New Guinea that he was convinced existed. And so the old routine recommenced, day after day after day, a man with a sounding line constantly in the chains, and the boats casting ahead as the ship slowly groped her way north. On August 21, after passing a headland Cook named Cape York, a myriad of islands lay ahead, divided by channels with a strong tide running through them. The pinnace was sent on shore to a beach where some natives were gazing in wonder. When the boat landed, they fled, so Cook and his companions, leaving a detachment of marines to carry out exercises, clambered to the top of the nearest hill.

Beyond lay clear water—the passage between New Holland and New Guinea. The east coast of Australia had been completely traversed, and Cook had discovered a new route to the Indian Ocean. It was a moment for celebration. Wrote Parkinson, watching from the ship, "they hoisted a jack, and fired a volley, which was answered by the marines below, and the marines by three vollies from the ship, and three cheers from the main shrouds." Cook had taken possession of the entire coast, "together with all the Bays, Harbours Rivers and Islands," and given it the name of New South Wales. Naturally, the ground on which he stood was named Possession Island.

Banks and Cook now commenced their accounts of "that part of New Holland now called New South Wales," as Banks called it. Again, both men copied from each other, or wrote together, discussing the topic as they went along. Otherwise, the difference from their descriptions of the South Seas islands and New Zealand is remarkable, particularly in their accounts of people. It now becomes obvious that Tupaia's interpretation was the crucial factor that turned their previous efforts into valuable ethnological documents, because without his input, the impressions and opinions of the Aborigines are wholly European—their descriptions are of people they considered primitive, written from a lofty perspective.

Though the ship's company had arrived in great need of fruit and vegetables, they had found "hardly any thing fit for man to eat"—or so Cook phrased it. His Yorkshire farming background was apparent when he added with disapproval, "the Natives know nothing of Cultivation"—a statement that might have not been strictly true, as Banks observed later on that the Endeavour River natives seemed to know exactly where to dig for yams, even when the tops had disappeared. He did not pursue the thought, but it was almost as if they had planted them.

The vegetables and fruit the *Endeavours* <u>had</u> found were listed: taro tops, a kind of purslane, a variety of wild bean, and plantains full of stone-like seeds. There were also pandanus fruits, which the natives consumed freely, judging by the remains found in their middens, but eating them made the sailors violently ill ("both upwards and downwards," wrote Banks), and killed the ship's hogs. Evidently the natives had some method of preparation that removed the poisonous element, but of course the Europeans had not been able to find out what it was. Apart from occasional captures of game, mostly kangaroos, the natives appeared to live on seafood, all of it excellent, especially the turtles, Cook pronouncing them the finest green turtle in the world.

As for the people themselves, they were "of middle Stature, straight bodied and slender limbd," with cropped black hair and beards. "Their features are far from being disagreeable and their Voices are soft and tunable," Cook added. He found it rather troubling that they all went naked. The females did not so much as "cover their privities," he firmly asserted—even though no one was ever very near their women ("one gentleman excepted"), they had seen enough through their spyglasses to be "as well satisfied of this as if we had lived among them."

Banks felt equally well qualified to make flat statements about the Aborigines (who were "but one degree removed from Brutes"), because he had seen them "either with our eyes or glasses many times." Indeed, he reckoned he could speak for the entire population of the country, basing his logic on the similarity of the natives of Botany Bay to those of the Endeavour River. They made the same kind of bark sheds (which were not long enough to stretch out in), and cooked the same kind of food in the same kind of way; both tribes singed their beards and hair, were short and slender, and kept their women out of sight. And they all went about nude, though he could not make up his mind whether it was through natural idleness, or because they had not invented clothing.

He also could not decide what their "absolute colour" might be, as they were "so completely coverd with dirt." Still more puzzling was why there were so few of them. It might be on account of the barrenness of the terrain, and the lack of fresh water, but he was inclined to think it was because they were constantly at war with each other. His reasoning for this was based on their stingray-barbed spears, which must be "intended against nothing but their own species." They seemed to have no idea of trade, for though they "readily receivd the things we gave them," they could not be made to understand that the *Endeavours* wanted something in return. On the other hand, they were certainly not thieves, and none of them had lice. "Tools among them we saw almost none," he went on, so it was a mystery how the dugout canoes he saw at the Endeavour River were hollowed out—with shells, perhaps.

Having written this sketchy account, Banks apparently remembered that he belonged to what came to be called the Age of Enlightenment, because he gave expression to elevated musing. "Thus live these I had almost said happy people," he wrote, "content with little nay almost nothing, Far enough removd from the anxieties attending upon riches, or even the possession of what we Europeans call common necessaries." Not for them the problems of increasing wealth, or the imbalance between the rich and the poor: "From them appear how small are the real wants of human nature."

Most uncharacteristically, Cook also plunged into this fashionable topic, writing, "From what I have said of the Natives of New-Holland they may appear to some to be the most wretched people upon Earth." In reality, as he mused on, they were happier than Europeans, being unencumbered with worldly possessions—"They live in a Tranquillity which is not disturb'd by the Inequality of Condition: The Earth and sea of their own accord furnishes them with all things necessary for life; they covet not Magnificent Houses, Houshold-stuff &C."

Plainly, however, these two orations were nothing more than platitudes, written for the audience back home, and neither Cook nor Banks felt the slightest inclination to trade places with these people. Cook concluded much more frankly by saying that the whole ship's company was highly delighted to quit the coral-ridden coast.

The Gweagal and Guugu-Yimidhirr, left to await the consequences of their discovery by the British, made sense of the advent of the *Endeavour* by incorporating it into their mythology, telling stories that gradually spread throughout the land. It was not Tupaia, however, who became legend. Instead, it was Cook—the symbol of dispossession, the man who brought disorder from the sea.

CHAPTER 18

❦

The Last Chapter

Obviously, Tupaia took no part in the writing of the two accounts of New Holland. If he had been present, the tone and content would have been quite different. He was not on deck practicing shooting, either. Instead, like a large number of the company, he was under the weather.

It is hard to tell what was wrong with them all, as seventeen days since leaving the Endeavour River seems too short a time for anyone to develop scurvy. Banks put it down to nostalgia, saying that the "greatest part of them were now pretty far gone with the longing for home which the Physicians have gone so far as to esteem a disease." The imminent threat of scurvy lurked in the minds of at least a few on board, however, especially the men who had sailed on the *Dolphin* with Wallis. The ship's provisions were very low, and the company had been rationed to two-thirds of the standard daily allowance. Banks asserted this did them good, as the biscuits and dried peas were crumbling, weevil-ridden ghosts of what they had been, and the salt meat was bad, having been stored for so long, but it is unlikely the men agreed.

On September 3, 1770, the *Endeavour* arrived on the southern coast of New Guinea, but those who went on shore did not bring back fruit or vegetables, as they had been driven off by the natives. Eight days later (almost six weeks after leaving the Endeavour River), the ship was off Timor, a large tropical island at the eastern end of the chain of Sunda Islands. They were coasting along with a warm, light wind, less than two miles from the shore, with a clear view of luxuriant trees. Six weeks into the *Dolphin* homeward voyage from Tahiti, Wallis had dropped anchor at Tinian, a coral island in the Marianas, and set up hospital tents on shore for the men with scurvy symptoms; they had stayed there a month, and when they had sailed everyone had been fit and well. With memories of this, the old *Dolphins* implored Cook to put in at the Timorese port of Concordia (modern Kupang). Symptoms of scurvy had appeared on board, Tupaia and the astronomer, Charles Green, being the worst cases, and they were positive that rest, fresh meat, and tropical fruit were exactly what the crew needed.

Cook flatly refused, even though they "strongly importun'd" him, being determined to press on for Batavia. Yet he had never sailed in the South China Sea, making it surprising that he did not pay more attention to men who had been there before, particularly as he had been so closely following the advice of Wallis's surgeon. His excuse was that Concordia was a Dutch settlement—"knowing that the Dutch look upon all Europeans with a jealous eye that come a mong these Islands, and our necessities were not so great to oblige me to put into a place where I might expect to be but indifferently treated," he wrote. This was completely without logic, since the Dutch were in control at Batavia, too, which brings his real motive into question.

His nerves must have been at stretching point, as creeping through unfamiliar, island-studded tropical waters was taxing enough, and the charts he had to hand were often faulty and misleading. On September 17 the ship blundered across an island—Savu—that was not laid down on the charts at all, and he gave in at last, and agreed to send a boat on shore. Gore (probably the officer who had argued most for making port in Timor) was sent in charge, and arrived back with a deceptively glowing report.

Cook agreed to drop anchor, but quickly regretted it. Solander, who could speak some Dutch, went on shore to negotiate—and so commenced a series of increasingly frustrating interviews with the extremely venal German representative of the Dutch East India Company and the bibulous local rajah, accompanied by a lot of petty bribery, several drinking bouts, and many broken promises. It would have been a comic interlude, *if* the delay had not been so critical, and *if* the result had been more than some small, stringy buffalo, a few sheep, hogs, and hens, and a lot of boiled-down palm wine, which Banks vainly hoped had anti-scorbutic qualities.

The *Endeavour* got away from this profitless place on September 21, and nine days later the southwest head of Java was raised. Captain Cook, having admitted for the first time that Tupaia was very ill, sent a boat on shore to get fruit for him, but it returned with only four coconuts and a small bunch of plantains. Though Cook did not mention it, concern was felt for his astronomer, too. Green was too sick to take his usual noon observation, so that the estimates of longitude were not nearly as reliable as they had been before. It was a very stressful time altogether, for Cook was about to rejoin civilization, which meant the job of producing letters and reports to send by the first homebound ship.

On Sunday, September 30, 1770, he confiscated the logbooks and jour-nals the officers, petty officers, and seamen had been writing—"at least all that I could find"—and cautioned them all not to say anything to anyone about where they had been. He did not find all the books. James Magra kept his hidden, and when he got back to London it was rushed illicitly into print; though the author's identity was kept anonymous, the publish-ers blandly assured the public that he was "a gentleman and a scholar." Another who was not forthcoming was Banks's footman, James Roberts. He had lost interest in keeping his journal up to date some months back, the last entry being written on Sunday, May 14, 1770, "on the coast of New Hollang," but was reluctant to hand it in, as it was his only evidence he had been some years at sea, which he would need if he applied to be a midshipman.

Having collected what he could, Cook concentrated on beating against strong currents and dodging islands, reefs, shoals, canoes, and other inbound ships, to fetch the port of Batavia. It was almost as arduous as grop-ing a way through the Great Barrier Reef, but a lot more spectacular for the men on the deck—who certainly did not include Tupaia. After nine weeks of almost no fresh food, he was growing weaker and more scurvy-ridden, every day closer to death.

It was not until October 10, by the logbook, that the *Endeavour* arrived off the rectangular network of walls, courts, colonnaded buildings, and canals that made up the city of Batavia. As the ship dropped anchor a boat called, carrying an officer who wanted to know who they were, departing almost immediately after getting a brief and unsatisfactory reply. "Both him-self and his people were almost as Spectres," wrote Banks—quite a contrast to the *Endeavours*, "who truly might be calld rosy and plump, for we had not a sick man among us."

It was the first instance of what was to become a systematic lie.

James Cook was in the throes of writing up his account of the voyage. A fleet was due to sail for London on October 24, and one of the captains had agreed to carry a package. A copy of his journal, a letter to the Royal Society, a book of astronomical observations, and charts of the South Seas, New Zealand, and the coast of New South Wales had all been packed, and now he was composing the long report to the Admiralty that would go with it. But what to write?

Cook's problem was that in his honest estimation he had not accom-plished very much. His charts were ground-breaking and brilliant (for quite some years, his charts of the New Zealand coast were more detailed and reli-able than those of the coast of Britain), but he regarded this as simply doing his job as a cartographer. The difficulty, for him, was that he had been "employ'd as a discoverer"—and, indeed, had boasted to the London newspaper *Gazetteer* just one week before he sailed that his aim was to find "new discoveries in that vast unknown tract"—but in the end he had discovered nothing of great significance.

"I have made no great discoveries," he apologetically repeated later, in a letter to a friend. He had made painstaking surveys of Tahiti, New Zealand, and the east coast of New Holland, but those were countries people knew about already. Though he had tried much harder, he had done no better than Wallis—in fact, where discovering was concerned, he had not done as well, for Wallis was able to claim the "discovery" of Tahiti. It was a moment for great regret that he had not given in to Tupaia's urgings, and sailed west in the tropics to "discover" the multitude of islands Tupaia had promised, a reflection that could have caused some bitterness.

Additionally, much of the credit for what he *had* accomplished belonged to others. James Cook had established the precise latitude and longitude of a large part of the world—but this was largely due to the meticulous observations and calculations of his astronomer. A huge amount of scientific information had been collected, along with hundreds of drawings and thousands of specimens, but Cook was perfectly well aware that Banks and Solander would claim the honor and glory as soon as the ship got home. He gave them due recognition in his report, and gave credit to the ship's company, too: "In Justice to the officers and the whole crew," he wrote, "I must say that they have gone through the fatigues and dangers of the whole voyage with that cheerfulness and alertness that will always do honour to British Seamen."

But Tupaia's name was never mentioned, not even once.

Cook, most probably, did not fully realize that their very survival was due to the protective mantle the noble priest had cast over them all. But surely, even if he did not understand that Tupaia had protected them from their own ignorance, he must have privately admitted that Tupaia had been a magnificently competent interpreter, translator, advisor, and intermediary. But he was not generous enough to put it down on paper.

Instead, as the next phrase in Cook's report hinted, the high priest had become an embarrassment. "I have the satisfaction to say that I have not lost one man by sickness during the whole Voyage," he famously wrote. The log reveals that the ships' company had, in fact, lost five men—Reading of overindulgence in rum, Sutherland of consumption, and three hands drowned. And that did not include the three passengers who had died—two of Banks's servants had succumbed to hypothermia in freezing Cape Horn weather, and Buchan had died in a fit. As well as that, Zachary Hicks, Cook's senior lieutenant, was close to death from the tuberculosis he had brought on board.

James Cook, however, did not have ordinary accidents or sickness in mind. What he meant was *scurvy*. After ten weeks without daily fresh food, all his men must have had symptoms, and Tupaia and Charles Green were definitely laid low. But Cook was determined to ignore that. Ambitious for his future, he had made up his mind to become known as the man who had conquered scurvy at sea.

As soon as the anchor was dropped, Banks and Solander left the ship to live on shore. They tried out the inn sponsored by the Dutch East India Company, where all strangers were supposed to stay, but found it so unsatisfactory that Banks rented the house next door. After moving in, he hired two carriages, and then sent for his books and Tupaia, "who had till now remain on board on account of his Illness which was of the Bilious kind, and for which he had all along refusd to take any medecines."

This "Bilious" complaint was scurvy, obviously, exaggerated by Tupaia's lifelong dependence on vegetable food. Cook half-admitted it, writing in his journal about the same time, "I had forgot to mention that upon our arrival here I had not one man upon the Sick list, Lieu^t Hicks Mr Green and Tupia were the only People that had any complaints Occasion'd by a long continuence at sea." The pretence that scurvy had not affected anyone on the *Endeavour* was becoming well established, however.

So what were the medicines Tupaia had refused to allow the surgeon to administer? If he was being treated for scurvy, they would have been the same lemon, bark, and acid that had failed him on the Australian coast, so he would not have seen the point of bothering. If, on the other hand, he was being medicated for problems with his stomach (called gastrodynia), the potions would have ranged from relatively harmless Epsom salts (magnesium sulfate) to emetics like ipecac and purges such as jalap, administered with calomel, which was a chloride of the deadly metal, mercury. This unpleasant regime of vomiting and purging would most probably be accompanied with blistering, which was the raising of painful blisters on sensitive areas of the skin with Spanish fly (cantharides) or Burgundy pitch. Surgeons of the time had great faith in violent medical treatment, mostly because it was not fully understood that the human body either dies or recovers of its own accord. When, by some miracle of physical fortitude, their patients survived, the doctors gave the credit that properly belonged to nature to their medical skills. Tupaia, who had recovered in the past from at least one life-threatening wound, had good reason for believing he knew better.

Arriving in the city, with its completely foreign sights and sounds, was a miraculous cure, mainly because it lifted his spirits so. For Tupaia, exploring Batavia was like an early realization of a dream. While he had little idea of what he would find in Europe, here were the strange and wonderful scenes he had endured so much to experience. Where he had had been weak, listless, and depressed (classical symptoms of scurvy), he was now highly animated, while, as Banks commented with amusement, "his boy Tayeto who had always been perfectly well was almost ready to run mad."

Everything was novel and exciting—horses, houses, carts, soldiers in blue and white, slaves dragging carts or shouldering heavy burdens on poles, statues of Olympian gods and goddesses with strangely protruding eyes, gaily dressed gentlemen and women in costumes from all around the world. Told that these last were wearing national dress, Tupaia sent for his tapa cloth robes, and he and Taiata shed their heavy European clothes, to become tropically Tahitian again.

This led to an interesting encounter. When Tupaia was walking in the street with Banks, a man ran out of his house and eagerly accosted them, asking if Tupaia had been in Batavia before. Banks shook his head, surprised, then wanted to know why he had asked such an odd question, to be told that a man who strongly resembled Tupaia had arrived in Batavia about eighteen months earlier. He had come on a ship belonging to a French expedition commanded by Louis de Bougainville.

With a flash of brilliance, Banks surmised the answer—this Polynesian traveler who looked so much like Tupaia was none other than "Otourrou the Brother of Rette Chief of Hidea." Ahutoru, the Tahitian who had made up his mind to sail to Europe and find out what Frenchwomen were like, had been a sensation in Batavia, obviously. And so the mystery of the ships that had anchored off Hitia'a was solved. Banks even heard the story of Jeanne Baret, who dressed as a male servant and "Followd a young man sent out in the character of Botanist." There was still the problem of Tupura'a's misidentification of the flag, but Banks explained it to his own satisfaction by surmising that Bougainville had been sailing under false colors.

Banks paid for three meals a day for a table of five—himself, Tupaia, Solander, and two others who may have been his clerk, Spöring, and Dr. Munkhouse. The surgeon should have been back on the ship keeping a professional eye on the men, but, as he had demonstrated in Tahiti and New Zealand, he preferred exotic scenes and sights to the mundane job of medicine. Taiata, always considered by the Europeans to be Tupaia's servant, would have eaten in the kitchen with Banks's footmen, James Roberts and Peter Briscoe.

The meals were strangely cooked, and often had odd ingredients—Banks was once promised a meal of roast monkey, but when he found the poor pinioned creatures in the courtyard, his heart was touched and he released them all. Despite this, much of what Tupaia ate was surprisingly familiar to him—bananas, coconuts, plantains, yams, pork, chicken, and fish. There was rice and soft European bread instead of the much-missed breadfruit, which did not grow well here, but there were also exotic, delicious fruits—mangosteen, pineapples, rambutans—and vegetables that reminded his European companions of home—French beans, asparagus, lettuce, parsley, potatoes, spinach, cucumbers, celery. Unconsciously admitting that Tupaia was suffering from scurvy, Banks wrote, "We were now able to get food for him similar to that of his own country and he grew visibly better every day." The longer they stayed in Batavia, he optimistically thought, the more Tupaia would improve.

He could not have been more mistaken. The locals had repeatedly warned them about the unhealthiness of the climate, something that should have been abundantly apparent from the stink of the meandering canals, which were laden with refuse, dung, and dead animals. Taiata caught a cold that turned into pneumonia (probably malaria with pulmonary complications). All the Europeans, including the two footmen, were seized with classic intermittent malarial fever. Tupaia, with his "broken constitution" (as Banks put it), was the worst affected, though his symptoms were not described.

In England, when Banks gave Tupaia's pet bird to his friend, Marmaduke Tunstall, he told him that Tupaia had typhus. This is unlikely, however. Typhus is transmitted by body lice, and is a disease of cramped, filthy, crowded conditions. At sea, it was known as ship-fever, and on land, as jail-fever—in England, more people died in jails of typhus than were executed for their crimes, and the Royal Navy had at times been forced to take battleships out of commission because so many crew died of the same disease. Cook kept a meticulously clean and airy ship, and Tupaia was not living in crowded conditions; if he had the gangrenous rash that is typical of typhus, it was probably due to scurvy. The other indicators of typhus, which are severe headache and high fever, are symptoms of typhoid fever, too—and this is a much more likely diagnosis, as typhoid is carried by polluted water. A body severely weakened by scurvy did not have the resources to fight such a serious disease. Once again, as Banks wrote, fears were felt for Tupaia's life.

On October 18, after a great deal of negotiation, Cook finally managed to have his ship booked in at the shipyard. The ship went first to Kuyper Island, where his men broke out all her stores and ballast and stowed everything in the many warehouses that lined the waterfront. Then the *Endeavour* was towed to the yard, which was on the nearby island of Onrust. The men stayed behind on Kuyper, living in a tent village—not a good decision. The ship was in even worse condition than feared, so was going to be under repair for an extended time, and living out in the open in marshy land did not augur well for the general health, especially as the rains of the seasonal monsoon were due.

Yet Tupaia asked to be moved to this tent village, telling Banks he wanted to "breathe a freeer air clear of the numerous houses which he believd to be the cause of his disease by stopping the free draught." His real reason—the one he did not voice—could have been the instinctive realization he was about to die. When a person expired from disease in his home islands, everything about the deathbed was burned—furniture, bedding, clothing, hangings, anything that could have been touched by the evil spirits that had brought an end to his life. That was not possible in the Batavia house.

On October 28, 1770, he sailed to Kuyper with Taiata and Banks. The first sight of the circular island, with its two pier heads, many warehouses, and slimy surrounding water, would not have been encouraging. Because of the wild dogs that ran loose at night, the locals who worked here chose to live on Onrust. There were large tamarind trees, though, offering a welcoming shade, and Tupaia chose a spot where the winds blew freely, and he could look out to sea. His tent—the same one that had been saved from the fire at Endeavour River—was set up for him. Ominously, the canvas village nearby was filled with sick seamen from the *Endeavour*, ailing with typhoid, or malaria, or both.

Banks stayed two days to make sure the two Polynesians were comfortable, then "left Tupia well satisfied in Mind but not at all better in body and returnd to town." Back in Batavia, he immediately fell ill of malaria again, probably because he had been bitten by *Anopheles* mosquitoes on Kuyper. At the same time, Dr. Munkhouse's citywide jaunts were brought to an abrupt halt by a feverish dysentery that defied all the local physician's remedies. Solander, whose malaria had worsened, declined to let the doctor treat him, probably because he saw what was done to Munkhouse—until he became too delirious to resist, and was purged, bled, and blistered himself, to within an inch of his life.

Banks, though he was dosing himself with bark, was soon too weak to crawl down the stairs. "In the afternoon of this day poor Mr. Monkhouse departed the first sacrifice to the climate," he wrote, when he was well enough to hold a pen. He dated this retrospective entry November 5, perhaps taking it from the ship's books, where Munkhouse's death was logged on the sixth. Cook noted on November 7 that he had the "Missfortune" to lose his surgeon, adding that Munkhouse would be succeeded by his mate, William Perry, "who is equally well if not better skilld in his profession."

This slightly cynical note turned to anger when Cook found that Munkhouse had not just neglected to keep the required journal of the "Tryal" of sauerkraut as an antiscorbutic, but had also sold or given away the ship's remaining stock of apothecary supplies, as the medical chest was found to be empty. Because of the climate, the surgeon was buried the same day. Solander attended the funeral, but Banks was too ill to get out of bed. Finally, in desperation, the rich young scientist spent several hundred pounds to buy two Malay "wives" with their retinues of slaves, and fled with his friend to a house in the hills, where the air was healthier.

On Kuyper Island, Sydney Parkinson was watching helplessly as Taiata burned up with fever, often crying out, *"Taio mate ua!"*—translated by Parkinson as, "My friends, I am dying." When the boy passed away, he sent a message to Banks. "This day received the disagreeable news of the death of Tayeto," Banks noted, in an entry dated November 9; "and that his death had so much affected Tupia that there was little hopes of him surviving many days."

For Tupaia, Taiata's death was devastating. Parkinson could do nothing for him—"he was quite inconsolable, crying out frequently, Taiyota! Taiyota!" Tupaia had often found fault with the boy (though no more so than any conscientious teacher or father), but was obviously very fond of him. Their family link was close, probably that of uncle and nephew, though Taiata called him by the name of *metua*—father, a title of affection as well as respect. Even more critically for Tupaia, Taiata was his repository of knowledge. They had spent countless hours together on the deck of the *Endeavour*, talking about the arching of the stars and the interruptions in the waves and winds; like his mentor, Taiata would have been able to point a finger unerringly in the direction of Tahiti, because he had been taught so well.

In Tahiti and Raiatea, a very learned man who was about to pass away summoned his chosen heir and acolyte, and with their heads close together they would share his last breaths, and so, symbolically, the transfer of precious knowledge was confirmed. But Tupaia's heir, his nephew-son, his acolyte, was gone; the vessel chosen to hold his vast fund of lore was lost. Later, when the Maori heard of Tupaia's death, they cried, *"Aue Tupaea!"*-"Alas! Tupaia!"—but now it was Tupaia's time to mourn, *"Aue, aue Taiata."* As Parkinson recorded, he was tortured with regrets that he had been foolish enough to leave Tahiti.

According to Banks, Tupaia's mental and physical agony lasted two days. "We receivd the news of Tupia's death," he wrote; "I had given him quite over ever since his boy died whom I well knew he sincerely lovd."

The entry was dated November 11, 1770.

Whether the date was right is open to question. Banks was too ill to write on the actual day, and it is hard to tell if he got the date correct when he caught up his journal later. While Lieutenant Hicks's logbook confirms that

Taiata died on November 9, Tupaia's passing is not recorded. Roberts, who added notes about the crew on the first page of the journal he kept hidden from Captain Cook, bracketed Tupaia and Taiata together as "inhabats of King georges Isl, Dead at Coopins Isld Tobia 9th Tiato 7th Dec 1770." This puzzling memorandum of their deaths in the following month, December, is confirmed by the muster book, which was kept by Captain Cook, and logs Taiata as "DD" (discharged dead) on December 17, 1770, and gives December 20, 1770, as the date of Tupaia's death.

Why such strange differences between the muster book and the ship's logbook? Banks, who logged November as the month of Tupaia's death, was not back on board until Christmas, and could easily have become confused. On the other hand, Cook could be wrong. He was very busy with the ship, which was hove down on November 9, to reveal damage far worse than anyone had ever imagined. Men were falling ill all the time: "We are now become so sickly that we seldom can muster above 12 or 14 hands to do duty," he wrote on November 14, and this despite the extra hands (including John Marra) he had shipped in the middle of October.

It was a consistent mistake, though, if it was indeed an error. When Cook signed off the two-month October-November muster roll on November 30, to all appearances the two Polynesians were still alive, though Dr. Munkhouse had been logged as dead. At noon on both December 8 and 17, they were again ticked present. It was not until the following week, after both Tupaia and Taiata had been marked "DD," that the number of supernumeraries is logged as two less.

Was Cook right, meaning that Hicks was mistaken when he logged Taiata's death on November 9, and Banks was equally in error when he noted Tupaia's passing on November 11? The logbook, kept conscientiously at noon each day, is more likely to be correct. It also has to be borne in mind that if Taiata and Tupaia died in early November, it was just four weeks since the ship had arrived in Batavia, not long enough for Tupaia to fully recover from severe scurvy. Alternatively, if Tupaia passed away in the third week of December, seventy days after the ship arrived, no one could possibly believe that scurvy played any part at all.

So, did Cook fudge the muster book entries? Was it a convenient mistake? If he was influenced by his ambition to be known as the man who had conquered scurvy, the error was very convenient indeed, because his unblemished record meant great accolades, in the end. On November 30, 1776, he was awarded Sir Godfrey Copley's medal for his success in the prevention of scurvy, an achievement remembered long after his own death: in *The Medical and Physical Journal* of 1799, James Cook was hailed as the man who had carried his crews through a variety of climates "without losing one man by disease," a feat considered more useful to mankind "than all the discoveries he ever made."

There is nothing in Cook's journal to indicate what really happened, because he did not get round to mentioning Tupaia's death until December 26, as they were leaving Batavia. After pointing out that it had been quite an accomplishment to lose only seven men, considering the climate, he listed those deceased: "the Surgeon three Seamen, Mr Green's Servant and Tupia and his servant, both of which fell a sacrifice to this unwholsom climate before they had reached the Object of their wishes."

Tupaia's death, he admitted, "indeed cannot be said to be owing wholly to the unwholsom air of Batavia, the long want of a Vegetable diat which he had all his life before been use'd to had brought upon him all the disorders attending a sea life." But, having said that, he went on in a tone that seethed with remembered exasperation, writing, "He was a Shrewd Sensible, Ingenious Man, but proud and obstinate which often made his situation on board both disagreable to himself and those about him, and tended much to promote the deceases which put a period to his life."

In short, because Tupaia was so arrogant, he had not listened to dietary advice, and had refused to take his medicine. And, added to that, he was not liked.

This, surely, must be one of the most uncharitable obituaries ever written. Not only was the summing up petty, but it was a gross injustice. The *Endeavour* voyage had been blessed with the most intelligent and eloquent Polynesian intermediary in the history of European discovery: that Cook's and Banks's *Endeavour* journals are great travel stories with remarkable insight, destined to be everlastingly popular, is directly due to Tupaia. The story of that voyage should be that of *three* extraordinary men, not just two, but Cook's moment of malice and the silence that followed have ensured that until very recent times Tupaia has been almost invisible.

"They were both buried in the island of Eadam," wrote Parkinson. This was Edam island, now known as Damar Besar. The cemetery there was the closest graveyard to Kuyper—more evidence that Cook's muster book is wrong, as the *Endeavour* sailed back to the port of Batavia on December 9, so was swinging at her anchors eleven miles away from Edam on the dates Tupaia and Taiata officially died.

In Tupaia's time, Edam island was reached by a single pier, and from there a path led through a forest of enormous, sacred Indian fig trees to the luxuriant gardens of the Dutch governor's weekend mansion. Nearer the waterfront was a rope-works, manned by white convicts and commanded by a sea captain. The cemetery where Tupaia and Taiata were laid to rest was shadowed by great trees, and dominated by the sepulcher of a sultan's wife who died there in 1751.

Few signs remain. The Dutch mansion was destroyed by the British in 1800, and the Japanese cleared the island to set up gun emplacements during World War II. Edam has reverted to snake-ridden jungle, and there is no trace left of their graves.

When Cook claimed he had escaped lightly by losing only seven men, he came to bitterly regret his words, for twenty-eight more died on passage from Batavia to England. Sydney Parkinson, the gentle Quaker artist who could be considered one of Tupaia's few friends, passed away in a fever on January 27; two days later Charles Green, who had taken such trouble to teach Tupaia English grammar, followed him to a watery grave. Banks, who was suffering "the pains of the Damnd," made little comment, but Cook—who undoubtedly remembered that Green was the *other* man who had developed severe scurvy—gave vent to remembered irritation, writing that the astronomer "had long been in a bad state of hilth," and his careless and dissolute habits had "brought on the Flux which put a period to his life."

The trade winds arrived at the start of February, bringing hope that the plague was coming to an end, but on the sixth the dead surgeon's young brother, Jonathan "Matte" Munkhouse, expired, and Henry Jeffs, the butcher whose flogging had so greatly distressed Tupura'a and Tomio, passed away three weeks later. On April 15, as they were sailing out of Cape Town, Robert Molineux died, earning his own tart entry in Cook's journal—though he was a young man of promise, he had "unfortunately given himself up to extavecancy and intemperance which brought on disorders that put a pirod to his life." His fellow old *Dolphin*, convivial Richard Pickersgill, took his place as master. On May 25, Zachary Hicks finally succumbed to tuberculosis, and old *Dolphin* John Gore was promoted to senior lieutenant, and his friend and shipmate from the first *Dolphin* voyage, Charles Clerke, became his junior.

Joseph Banks and Daniel Solander recovered their health, though Solander had a relapse in Cape Town. They dabbled in some collecting at St. Helena, but their hearts were not in it: they were preparing themselves for arrival in London and the honor and glory they quite confidently (and justifiably) expected. James Cook had to do his planning, too. Formal presentations at Court should be accompanied by gifts to royalty of exotica collected in the Pacific—but natural history specimens were not quite appropriate. Instead, native artifacts, called "artificial curiosities," would be perfect—Tahitian ornaments, images, and clothing, Maori *hei tiki*, *taiaha*, *mere pounamu*, and cloaks.

Not considered as valuable as beetles, bird skins, and dried flowers, these arti-facts would be ideal for presents for friends and donations to museums, too. And so the afterquarters were ransacked.

Sydney Parkinson had collected many little curiosities for his beloved cousin, Jane Gomeldon; Dr. Munkhouse had bartered a length of tapa cloth for a dogskin-trimmed cloak. The owners were not alive to claim them, so no one objected if they were taken, though after Banks got to London Par-kinson's brother, Stanford, made an embarrassing fuss, particularly when it was found that Sydney had not been paid his promised wage, and his jour-nal had disappeared. But there was no one to protest about the cloaks that had enfolded Tupaia as he talked of legends, creation myths, and Hawaiki to enraptured crowds in New Zealand, or the precious *taonga* he had been entrusted on dozens of *marae*. There were personal belongings, too—his chest of keepsakes, including tapa beaters and sacred feathers, his long box holding tapa garments, carved images, Taiata's flute, their pillow stools, his ceremonial stool, his tiny feather-gods.

No one knows what has happened to them. Only his artwork is recog-nized now. The rest was either given away by Cook and Banks, or retained by Banks, to be auctioned after his death. A greenstone *hei tiki* pendant, so precious that it would have been entrusted only to a man of the highest *mana*, was presented by Cook to King George III in 1771, and is now in the British Museum—but no one knows its history. Without doubt, the *taonga* entrusted to Tupaia can be seen in a number of institutions today, but no one knows their origin.

Nick Young, the boy who had first raised New Zealand, was the first to spy the outpost of England. The *Endeavour* dropped anchor in the Thames two days later, on July 13, 1771. It was exactly two years since Tupaia had sailed from Tahiti, but no one noticed the coincidence.

Commentary and Acknowledgments

❧

I know the exact date I first became intrigued with Tupaia. It was August 5, 2006, when I read an article by Greg Ansley in the *New Zealand Herald*, headed "Rewriting our history," and with the grabber line, "Most of the credit for Captain Cook's remarkable first voyage ought to go to a Polynesian navigator, according to new research." The story stemmed from an interview with Dr. Paul Tapsell, who theorized that for the Maori Tupaia was the leader of the expedition, not Captain Cook, and that the prized artifacts taken to England and distributed by Cook and Joseph Banks were most probably presented to Tupaia, the man of greatest prestige on board.

Moved by the powerful argument, I cut the story out, and kept it in a folder. I must have talked about it often, as in February 2008 a friend remarked rather pointedly that no one had written a biography of Tupaia yet. Rising to the implied challenge, I headed for the Alexander Turnbull Library, the National Library of New Zealand, and the Beaglehole Library at Victoria University, to read everything about the *Endeavour* voyage, Cook, Banks, early Tahiti, and—of course—Tupaia, that I could find. I owe a debt to the librarians at all these places, and am particularly grateful to Nicola Frean, Beaglehole Librarian, for her continued enthusiasm.

Once I found the biography was feasible, Creative New Zealand responded with a substantial grant. Travel to Tahiti, Australia, London, and Connecticut was very generously funded by the Stout Trust. This book would not have been possible without the financial assistance of both these bodies, for which I am most grateful. A six-month associate-ship with the

Stout Institute of New Zealand Studies at Victoria University was also help-ful, as it gave me access to collections overseas that otherwise would have been difficult.

I owe a debt, too, to the staff at the Mitchell Library and the Australian Maritime Museum, New South Wales, Beinecke Rare Books Library at Yale, the New York Public Library, the British Library, the National Maritime Mu-seum, and the Public Records Office in London. I am grateful to the Alexander Turnbull Library for making it so easy to obtain the Cook and Banks illustrations, and to my husband, Ron Druett, for his meticulously researched ship plans and map of the Pacific. Paul Tapsell merits immediate gratitude for his huge enthusiasm for the voyage that he unwittingly launched me upon, and the fascinating discussions we have shared. The many individuals who have been most helpful with advice, information, and comments will see their names in the following commentary; I am immensely grateful to them all.

This commentary also explains sources. The major books used are listed in a separate bibliography, while references to chapters, journal articles, and unpublished manuscripts are in the body of the commentary. The chapter order of the book is followed, but at times the commentary is sub-divided so topics can be treated separately. When using Tahitian and Maori words, I have opted to use forms in commonplace use—how they appear on signposts, for instance. Therefore I have chosen not to use the macron or to double long vowels, and have used the glottal stop as little as possible.

INTRODUCTION

Tupaia's famous sketch of Joseph Banks bartering for a crayfish is with his other artwork at the British Library (Add 15508); I thank Auste Micku-naite for his helpfulness in obtaining the rights to reproduce six of these sketches, plus Tupaia's chart.

Carter's attribution to Tupaia was on the basis of a letter written by Banks to a fellow member of the Royal Society, Dawson Turner, dated December 12, 1812. The context is the difficulty in getting payment for a farm (the lawyer handed over the deed without making sure of the money first), which reminded Banks of his problems in dealing with the Maori. Carter's conse-quent "Note on the Drawings by an Unknown Artist from the Voyage of HMS *Endeavour*" is 133–34 of Lincoln.

George Forster called Tupaia "an extraordinary genius": McCormick, 295–96.

CHAPTER 1: IN THE BEGINNING

Tupaia's early history

Wilson (1799) provides an early missionary view: 330 (birth, infancy), 340–42 (birth rituals and the sanctity of the baby), 347 (infanticide). Henry (275) also discusses infanticide. Wilson (1799) reports Tupaia excelled in "information and sagacity": x. Also see Oliver (1974): 27, 54.

Learning was by rote, usually in chant form. Henry describes schooling, 153–56; also see 188 (circumcision), and 287–89 (tattooing). Ferdon devotes a whole chapter to rites of passage, "From Birth to Death," 138–52. Henry, 230–41, has a long description of *arioi*. She describes the ranks: 234–35; the style of Tupaia's tattooing places him in the *taputu* group. I thank Charles Chauvel for the comment that the *arioi* movement reached its greatest flowering then. For a description of Taputapuatea *marae* in Raiatea see Crawford, 54–55. Also see De Bovis, 15, 43–44; for *arioi*, see 35–36.

Arioi voyages: Ellis, 183–95; Henry, 230, 238–40. Ellis (192) states women ate with men during *arioi* feasts. Tupaia's kindliness as a typical master navigator is extrapolated from Gladwin, 126.

The background to Tupaia's early life is detailed in an unpublished manuscript written by a missionary, Rev. R. Thomson, which he called "History of Tahiti" (London Missionary Society archives, Mitchell Library, Sydney, ms 660): see 10–17. Tupaia also told his tale to Magra (61–66), and Molineux, who summarized it in his journal, July 13, 1769. Johann Forster, (III: 524) notes Tupaia may have been named "Parooa" (Paroa), changing his name to Tupaia (meaning "beaten") after his loss to the Bora Borans; this is also mentioned by Sparrman: 63.

For the medical treatment of Tupaia's wound, see a paper by Beall, Bricker, Crawford, and De Bakey, "Surgical Management of Penetrating Thoracic Trauma" in *Chest* (official publication of the American College of Chest Physicians), v.49, no.6 (1966): 568–77. Banks's description of Tupaia's wounding and his scar is cited in Oliver (1974): 478. Marra (179) was told such a wound was usually mortal, but repeats (234) that Tupaia was completely cured.

For religion see de Bovis, 25 (human sacrifice), 36–39 (*arioi*), 44–47 (feathered gods), 55 (coronation of a new high chief). The creation of a *to'o* or feathered god, and the interchange of feathers is described in Alain Babadzan's chapter, "The Gods Stripped Bare," in Colchester: 26–38. Another description is Henry, 157–69; for the creation of a new lappet for the *maro ura* and its attachment: *ibid* 188–89; for human sacrifice: 196–98. Also see Roger G. Rose, *Symbols of Sovereignty: Feather Girdles of Tahiti and*

Hawai'i, Bernice P. Bishop Museum, Hawaii: Pacific Anthropological Records, no. 28, 1978.

A thoughtful discussion of Tupaia's escape is in Hank Driessen's chapter, "Tupa'ia, the Trials and Tributions of a Polynesian Priest" in Herda et al.: 67–86, esp. 68–69. Driessen suggests Maua traveled separately from Tupaia, but Thomson (16) was told by Tahitian informants they voyaged in the same canoe.

For events after Tupaia arrived in Tahiti, also see Driessen (chapter in Herda), 73. Oliver (1974), 1199–1200, describes the history of Amo and Purea; he notes several times Tupaia was their counselor, e.g. 27, 32, 1202. Adams, 9–51 passim, conveys the background of this period of Tupaia's life, including genealogies of Amo and Purea. Dening (2004: 170–75) encapsulates Tupaia's story as theater; he does the same for Purea in his paper, "The Hegemony of Laughter: Purea's Theatre" in Frost and Samson, 127–46. To paraphrase his own words (175), the tales he tells are often wrong in detail, but he is always creative and thought-provoking.

Polynesian voyaging

The childhood experiences of a master navigator come by extrapolation from Lewis, 314–15. The life of a Polynesian fisherman is described by Gordon R. Lewthwaite in, "Man and the Sea in Early Tahiti: A Maritime Economy through European Eyes," *Pacific Viewpoint*, 7 (1), 1966: 28–53, esp. 28, 33–34.

For the time line of Polynesian voyaging see Irwin, 6–10; Lewis, 315–17; and Finney (1979), appendix III, 292–302, esp. 296; also Finney (1994), 10–13, and 288–303. Prickett, 16–17, has a useful summary. David Lewis, in his chapter, "The Pacific Navigators' debt to the ancient seafarers of Asia," in Gunson (1978), 46–66, makes interesting deductions about the evolution of Lapita canoes. Also see Roger C. Green's chapter, "Lapita," in Jennings, 27–60, esp. 45–47. Kenneth P. Emory, "The Societies," also in Jennings, 200–221, gives archaeological evidence.

How the South American sweet potato (*Ipomoea batatas*) arrived in Polynesia is a mystery; it became an important root crop in Rapa Nui and New Zealand, where taro would not easily grow. The Polynesian name is *kumara*, while the Peruvian name is *kumar*; the first European to identify it as "sweet potato" was John Gore, master's mate on the *Dolphin*, June 20, 1767. Ferdon (52) notes that the legend Maui used a large land mass to the east to break off pieces to form islands indicates early knowledge of South America. Te Rangi Hiroa (Sir Peter Buck) describes Maori voyaging traditions in his paper, "The Value of Tradition in Polynesian Research," *Journal of the Polynesian Society*, 35 (1926): 181–203.

For the timing of the outward expansion and details of trade, see Finney (1973), 14–15. Banks, July 12, 1769, noted that Tupaia "came of a family well-known for its skill in navigation." Greg Dening, in a chapter called "Voyaging the Past, Present, and Future," in Nussbaum, 319–23, includes an evocation of the responsibilities of a Polynesian navigator. Scarr, chapter five, "Destinies Ashore" (44ff) describes reasons for voyaging, and associated rituals. The story of the *African Galley* is in Lincoln Paine's encyclopedia, *Ships of the World* (New York: Houghton Mifflin, 1997): 32.

CHAPTER 2: THE *DOLPHIN*

Journals and logbooks of the *Dolphin* voyage, 1766–68

Logbooks and shipboard journals come in set forms. The deck-log was a formal affair, each page ruled up for hourly notations of wind, weather, course sailed, and the position of the ship, plus remarkable events such as punishments, sickness, accidents, or death. Usually there was a note of food served out to the crew, partly to stave off future complaints. In port, work done on board and provisions procured on shore were also recorded. The log might be kept by one man, or the hourly notation might be made by whoever was "on watch" (was in charge of the deck at the time-officers, just like seamen, stood watches). The sea-day started at noon and ended at noon, when the date changed, becoming twelve hours ahead of the civil day, though the logkeeper might correct this when the ship was in port.

Shipboard journals (occasionally, confusingly, called "logbooks" by their owners), were more like diaries, as interesting events were described in detail, and the lines dividing up the page could be ignored. A journal where the account was written on the same day, or soon afterward, can be very useful indeed, especially if the writer has added personal comments and observations. The longer the delay between the event and its recording, the more likely the journal has become colored by vagaries of memory, the illumination of hindsight, or conversations with shipmates. The researcher has to make constant value judgments.

A basic source was the daily logbook kept by Captain Samuel Wallis, a scrawled, spontaneous account now held at the Mitchell Library, New South Wales, Australia (J27951). Probably on the homeward passage, Wallis created a revised journal by transposing, adapting, and lengthening logbook entries. This was a "public" journal, destined for publication. Soon after James Cook arrived home from his *Endeavour* voyage (July 13, 1771), the Admiralty commissioned a very popular book editor, John Hawkesworth, to produce a three-volume record of eighteenth-century British discovery voyages (see bibliography), and Wallis's revised journal was a major reference. It is now held at the Public Record Office (PRO) London (Adm 55/35), with penciled notes by Hawkesworth in the margins. (For an interesting overview, see Lamb's chapter, "John Hawkesworth, the Unfortunate Compiler," in Lamb, Smith, and Thomas: 73–75.)

Before Wallis handed it over, a copy was made, evidently for his own use; this is now at the Alexander Turnbull Library in Wellington (qMS-2114), and is interesting because of additions in Wallis's script, including a list of artifacts handed over to the Admiralty. Otherwise it is identical to the public journal.

That there are two Wallis accounts—the rough logbook and the revised journal—presented problems, as the differences between them are striking, particularly in Tahiti. Wallis was very ill when he wrote the logbook (meaning a lot could be missing), while his public journal was written to put his actions in the best light possible (meaning it may not be dependable). For instance, it is likely he magnified his association with "the Queen," to add legitimacy to his "possession" of Tahiti.

Accounts written by the sailing master, George Robertson, vary too. The most important collection is held at the PRO as Adm 51/4539. This includes an informal diary, written on the spot. There is also a public journal that is a revision of this, probably in imitation of Wallis. A lot of subjective material is added to this public journal (including sexual adventures coyly described as happening to "my friend"), along with retrospective comments that make it evident it was written after arrival in London. Robertson was a vivid writer, and it is a racy and fascinating read. Though never mentioned as a source, it was used by Hawkesworth, as there are penciled notations in the same hand as those in the Wallis public journal. It was eventually (1948) edited by Hugh Carrington, and published by the Hakluyt Society. A modernized version appeared later, edited by Warner. Where I used the published version, I chose Carrington (1948) as being more accurate.

To complicate matters still further, there are more Robertson versions. Another box, Adm 51/4540, holds his very interesting journal on HMS *Swift*, beginning March 1, 1763, ending May 29, 1766, and encompassing the wreck of the ship, followed by a neat transcription of the *Dolphin* diary. Some sentences are corrected, and there is the occasional added detail, but on the whole they are the same. Another Robertson account is a long appendix to Wallis's public journal (the one with annotations by Hawkesworth). After ending on May 19, 1768, and signing it "Saml Wallis," the captain added several pages of navigational observations. Then Robertson took over the book to write descriptions of landfalls, including a seven-page description of Tahiti, basically an abstract of his journal, but with additional material. It is signed "George Robertson."

Also at the PRO are logs and journals kept by other men. Adm 51/4538 includes two deck-logs, one entirely in the hand of William Clarke, first lieutenant, and the other in various scripts (including Robertson's). There is also a journal by Clarke, but apart from a few longer entries at Tahiti, it is as brief as the deck-logs, probably because of his ill health. Others, kept by Francis Wilkinson, William Luke, Humphrey West, "Mr Douglas Carpenter," and Benjamin Butler, are boxed together as Adm 51/4541; and those by George Pinnock, Henry Ibbott, Tobias Furneaux, and Hambly are collected as Adm 51/4542. Pinnock's begins on "July ye 16th 1766 at Deptford," and ends at Tinian, where he writes "Finis." Ibbott's begins July 15, 1766, and ends December 10, 1767, at Batavia. It includes a long description of Tahiti and the people, which must have been written over several days, because it is dated July 4 but includes things he learned later, such as the method of making tapa. Lieutenant Furneaux's log is made up of technical entries, while Hambly's is very brief, with the occasional blank page, as if he meant to write more when he got around to it. Box Adm. 51/4543 has equally uninformative logs kept by Francis Pender, Samuel Horsenail, and Thomas Coles (though Pender has rousing descriptions of the battles). Adm 51/4544 has a journal kept by John Nichols, and two more by George Pinnock and Humphrey West, with very similar entries to their previous records.

There is also a journal kept by John Gore. When Wallis collected the logs, Gore flatly refused to hand his over. "Mr Gore Mate of this Ship was the only person that took any umbrage at it," wrote Wallis in his logbook. Evidently, he gave in and let Gore keep it, as the journal is now held at the National Library of Australia, Canberra (MS 4), and is not part of the Admiralty holdings. I am grateful to the librarians who interloaned a microfilm to me. It is hard to tell why Gore made a fuss, as it contains no indiscretions. It ends October 16, 1767, leaving Tinian, and is signed "J^{no} Gore, Master Hunter."

The *Dolphin*'s arrival

The various predictions of the coming of European ships are in Henry, 4–5, 9–10, 430–31. Also see Dreissen's paper, "Outriggerless Canoes and Glorious Beings," in *Journal of Pacific History,* vol. 17 (1982): 3–27; also

Niel Gunson's "Cover's Notes on the Tahitians" in *Journal of Pacific History,* vol. 15, Oct. 1980: 217–24; on p. 220 Gunson comments that navigators looked for the reflection of lagoons in clouds, which, by extrapolation, can be applied to the cloud of sails on a ship.

"We are now in the Greatest hopes of Seeing the Southern Continent," wrote Robertson on first sighting (June 19, 1767, Adm 51/4540). In his addendum to Wallis's public journal (Adm 55/35) he wrote "all the full Grown Men and Women Paint there Arms, Legs, and thighs, with a Black sort of Stuff." His story of the men grunting like hogs, etc., is in his public journal and does not appear in the earlier records. Wallis, in his logbook, simply says that they showed the shipboard animals to the natives. Wilkinson, however, notes on June 20 that they imitated the sounds. Wilson (1799): xi, confirms Tahitians knew about iron after the wreck of Roggeveen's ship. The story of the goat scaring the islander appears only in Wallis's public journal.

The order of events as the ship skirted the coast is taken from Wallis's logbook, with additions from Robertson's public journal. Wallis provided details of the conflict in Matavai Bay omitted by Robertson, so his account is the basis of this story. The feather amulet—'ura-tatae—is described by Oliver (1974): 75–76, and Henry, 13. Also see Ferdon, 64. John Nicholls described seeing "Quantities of stones" in the canoes, and was another to describe the shot woman (July 24, 1767). While the mention of conch-shell trumpets might seem anachronistic, as the usual belief is they were introduced to Tahiti after European arrival, Wallis's list of Tahitian artifacts delivered to the Admiralty included a "Conque."

CHAPTER 3: THE RED PENNANT

The identity of the chief or priest who led the assault is unknown. Thomson (35–36) offers the possibility it was Amo, also strongly implied by Wilson (1799): x. Thomson describes Amo watching the ship from concealment on the hill (a crucial word is missing, so it might have been a rock, though more likely a tree), which indicates he was afraid of being recognized by the Europeans. That Amo survived is another factor: while it would be easy for the Tahitians to name a dead man as the misguided priest or ill-advised chief who led the attack, it was not diplomatic to point the finger at someone who was still alive. Certainly, no living chief (or high priest) would confess to taking a leading part in the debacle.

For offering riches with one hand and death with the other, see Thomas (2003): 80. Wilkinson described the marines going "through their excises with the gratest regularity, the Indians facing of them within pistol shott of them after which the Lieutent advanced with an English pendent and took possession of the isl[d.]." For the events that followed, I used all accounts written by Robertson and Wallis, plus Hawkesworth, 271–73. Details vary: Wallis said the old man came to the ship on his own, while Robertson says he came with a friend. As Wallis is likely to have risen from his bed to receive the emissary, I used his version.

While in his public journal Robertson says the pennant was removed by the Tahitians right away, his logbook says they "carried it off at night." An illustration of the pennant can be seen in plate II 24 (67) of Wilson (1986). Its resemblance to the *maro 'ura*, once the white square with its cross is removed, is striking. For a thought-provoking discussion of the role of ritual in the planting of this flag see Dening (1992), 198–202.

The alleged attack on the watering party is based on Wallis's logbook, with added details from Furneaux, Nicholls, and Robertson. All shipboard accounts tell the same basic story, that the Europeans were facing another attempt to seize the ship. The Tahitian view of the tragedy is taken from Thomson, 34–36. Banks wrote, "They have often described to us the terror which the Dolphins guns put them into and when we ask how many people were killd they number names upon their fingers, some ten some twenty some thirty, and then they said worrow worow the same word as is usd for a flock of birds or a shoal of fish" (July 3, 1769). Marra (216–17) itemizes the cruelty of the destruction of the canoes.

Interpretations of Purea's role vary. Thomson (36) says she was at Matavai Bay at the time, but it seems likely that if she had been there, she and Tupaia would have made the initial peacemaking approach. For the incorporation of the cross of St. George into the canoe's streamer, see Dening (1992): 207; deciphering the *maro ura* like a book is in Henry, 189.

CHAPTER 4: THE QUEEN OF TAHITI

Wallis's logbook notes "the old man" (Fa'a) had returned from his jaunt "up the country" (July 6, 1767). Fa'a's account would have reached Purea and Tupaia, triggering the return to Matavai Bay.

For the significance of the presentation of tapa, see Serge Tcherkézoff's illuminating chapter, "On Cloth, Gifts and Nudity: Regarding Some European Misunderstandings During Early Encounters in Polynesia," in Colchester, pp. 51–58; for the manufacture of tapa, see Ferdon, pp. 111–17. Robertson described the trading procedure and the restriction on crossing the river in his revised journal (Robertson 1948, 168–70). The quotes come from Wallis's logbook, June 29–30, 1767. Robertson's story of the "Dear Irish boy" is in his public journal, July 6, 1767; there is no such mention in his logbook. Scarr (73) notes islanders found Europeans foul-smelling. Sparrman (69) commented islanders were fascinated by white skin. Quotes from Ibbott are taken from a discursive page dated July 4, obviously expanded later. Wallis first noted prying off cleats for the nails in his public journal, July 11, 1767.

Adams (50) recorded Purea taking over the *fare hau*. Henry points out (15) Purea was advised and seconded in all her actions by Tupaia; there is nothing in the *Endeavour* accounts, or records kept on Cook's later voyages, to indicate she was naturally so resourceful. Wallis noted the method of buying trees for firewood in his logbook July 9, the same day he described Jonathan's first visit, but did not mention either in his revised journal. Robertson mentioned the wood-cutting in his revised journal on the same date (Robertson 1948, 183), but delayed describing Purea's interference and Jonathan's visit until the following day's entry, when he devoted a great deal of detail to both (Robertson 1948, 186–89). His logbook and addendum to Wallis's revised journal note the same events, much more briefly, on the same dates. Confusingly, Wilkinson's description of seeing the "large house" and the visit of the "Queen" on board "with some of her Attendance" are both dated July 16, so must be retrospective. The christening of "Jonathan" appears only in Robertson's public journal (Robertson 1948: 188–89). Wallis noted, "This man we called Jonathan," in his rough log, but did not mention it in his revised journal, which is probably why it does not appear in Hawkesworth. Dening (e.g., 2004: 172–73) avers Jonathan and Tupaia were the same man. However, Robertson testified that after Jonathan's July 13 visit "we neaver saw nor heard anything more of him," and Tupaia certainly called on board after that date. None of the old *Dolphin*s identified Tupaia as Jonathan on their return to Tahiti—yet Wilkinson was one of those who dressed Jonathan in European clothes.

In his addendum to Wallis's revised journal, Robertson notes briefly on July 14, "This Day the Queen came off to see the Ship for the first time," but does not mention it in any of his own logs. Consequently, the description of her experiences on board comes from Wallis's logbook and journal, which are both dated July 13, and tell the same basic story. The difference between his dating and Robertson's is easily accounted for by the 12-hour difference between sea-time and shore-time. Years afterward (1785), the *Dolphins*' colorful descriptions of their queen provided the inspiration for a theatrical costume for a pantomime, "Omai, or a Trip Around the World." The character of Purea, "Obereyan Enchantress," was sketched by either de Loutherbourg, designer of the pantomime, or John Webber, who had been the artist with Cook's third expedition. Webber definitely advised on the details of the costume.

CHAPTER 5: THE STATE VISIT

That Wallis visited "the Queen's House" the very next morning occurred *only* in his revised journal. In his logbook, the entire entry following her visit to the ship reads: "AM the weather so bad could send no Boat onshoar, the Natives came down to the Watering Place and Cut the Bank of the River and made a New Channell, as the water has Risen very much on the flat ground—this forenoon came of two Chiefs & brought with them some Roasted Pigs & fruit, gave them presents in return." His visit is not described in his logbook until July 22, 1767, and then in almost the same words as those in the public journal for July 13–14.

The difference is puzzling. There is a good chance that July 22 is correct, and Wallis brought the date of his visit forward when he revised his journal, knowing that delaying such an important event would not look good on his record. None of the other journal-keepers mention the visit to the *fare hau*—not even Clarke, who was supposed to be there—so there is no confirmation of either date. Because Hawkesworth made the July 13 date standard, it is the one I have used.

Wallis's beautiful scale drawing, "A Ground plan, & Elivation of the Queens House at King Georges Island, in the South Seas, taken in July 1767," is held with his logbook at the Mitchell Library, Sydney. The anecdote about the surgeon removing his wig is given in Hawkesworth (291), and must have stemmed from a personal communication, as it is not mentioned in any of the records.

Wallis's logbook entry for July 18, 1767, reads, "this day the Queen shewed herself again she having been absent some days," while his revised journal merely mentions she came to the beach. Robertson described entertaining the Tahitian nobles in the gunroom in his logbook entry for July 18. In his revised journal a much more detailed recounting is dated July 19, for the morning events (the feast at the *fare hau*) and July 20, for the afternoon events (Purea's visit on board). It is also here that Pickersgill is named as Gallagher's companion on the stroll. This is the first mention of "the Queen" in any of Robertson's own records, save a July 14, notation in his addendum to Wallis's journal, where he describes her attendants being dressed in white. The story of the breakfast, Robertson's visit to the *fare hau*, and his flirtation with Purea comes entirely from Robertson's revised journal.

For the *tapu* nature of the head, see Steiner, 45–46. *Tabu*, which the English adopted as "taboo," is a Tongan word; the Tahitian word, like the Maori, is *tapu*. Adams (51) details the disastrous implications for Amo, Purea, and Tupaia of Wallis's failure to visit Papara.

For a discussion of John Harrison's method of finding longitude by using a pre-publication copy of Maskelyne's tables, see Richardson, 29. Robertson's angry tirade about his shipmates' suspicions of Purea's "Treacherous designe" is in his addendum to Wallis's revised journal. Wilkinson's comment about "the Indians suspecting we Ware going away" is dated July 26, 1767; in the same entry he described weighing the sheet anchor and setting up the topgallant masts and yards. The stream anchor had been weighed on July 24. Pinnock's entry about the gunner was dated July 26.

Wallis's journal states that the queen came on board while the ship was getting underway, but in his logbook he is definite that she did not: "the Queen kept in her Canoe at the gunroom Port, & wept very much." None of the other logbooks or journals mention her boarding the ship at this time, so it seems likely Wallis's memory was faulty.

CHAPTER 6: TUPAIA'S PYRAMID

The war chant at the start of this chapter comes from Henry, 305.

L'Étoile was rated at 480 tons, while *La Boudeuse* was 550 tons; *Dolphin* was 508 tons, and about the same length as *L'Étoile*. Because Ahutoru was so remarkably familiar with Europeans, their dress, and their food, he could have been "Jonathan," but of course it is impossible to be sure. Jeanne Baret's story is told by John Dunmore: *Monsieur Baret, First Woman Around the World 1766–68* (Auckland: Heritage Press, 2002). Magra (65) says Purea sent women on board the *Dolphin*. The anecdote about Bougainville's cook is in Sparrman (72). I am grateful to Anne Salmond, who shared a prepublication draft of *Aphrodite's Island* with me; my description of the Bougainville visit was greatly assisted by reading chapter four of this draft, "Happy Island of Cythera." Another important source was Dunmore (2005 and 1965). For Tutaha's visit to Hitia'a see Wilson (1799): xi.

Robertson noted they dressed two chiefs "in the European manner" (July 13, 1767) in all accounts, but named Jonathan as one of the chiefs in only his revised journal (Robertson 1948: 193).

A long account of the building of a *marae* is in Henry, 131–38; for a particular description of Mahaiatea *marae*, see 139–41; also Thomson, 26–28. See Adams, 29, 41–46, esp. 42, for the likely impact on Tutaha and other rival chiefs. For the attempt to break the *rahui*, and the developing feud, see Henry, 69, and Adams, 59ff. See Scarr for an interesting discussion of rival feasts in Melanesia, 44ff.

See Oliver (1974): 375–408 for the art of warfare; and 1223–25 for the Paparan war. Ellis: v. II, 509–10 describes battle at sea. Henry has a good description of wreaking revenge, 310–16. Wilson (1799: xiii) says Tupaia escaped before the war began. My account of Tupaia's pact with Tutaha is extrapolated from his own account to Magra; also Adams, 7–10, 41, 71.

CHAPTER 7: THE *ENDEAVOUR*

Records kept on the *Endeavour*

There are several extant copies of James Cook's logs and journals, described in detail in Beaglehole (1955) cxciii–ccxxvii. I started out by using the Beaglehole edition of the Canberra-held journal (MS 1), but then turned to the online transcript of the same journal (with some amendments and additions from the Mitchell-held ms), painstakingly created by David Turnbull, which can be found on the "South Seas Voyaging Accounts" Web site; this was because I wanted a fresh look, unfiltered through the mind of an editor. The Banks and Parkinson journals are on the site as well, along with the relevant part of Hawkesworth, so that a day's accounting is easily compared. After skimming through the other logs, I returned to Beaglehole (1955), when I could make best use of his fine footnoting and commentary.

The official ship's log, apparently kept by Hicks and Wilkinson, is at the British Library (Add. Ms 8959). There is also a log kept by Hicks at the Alexander Turnbull Library, Wellington (qMS-0954). Gore's journal (Adm 51/4548/145–6) is in two scripts, so some might have been written by his servant, Nathaniel Morey. It begins July 31, 1768, working down the Thames. Title page is "On Board His Majesty,s Bark Endeavour, Lieutenant James Cook Commander," and (significantly?) he always refers to Captain Cook as "Mr Cook."

Robert Molineux's two journals, rewarding because of very interesting Tahiti entries, are both at the PRO (Adm 51/4546/152 and Adm 55/39 26). Less useful is the sketchy log kept by Midshipman Jonathan Munkhouse (Mitchell Library, MSS 5994). Midshipman John Bootie, (PRO, Adm 51/4546) either copied from his shipmates, or they copied from him, because the phrasing is so similar, though his style is more educated than most. He wrote some unique entries in New Zealand; and July 15, 1769, has an unusual note: "Evil communications corrupt good manners N. Young is a son of a Bitch."

Charles Clerke (PRO, Adm 51/4548) was another copyist; his ends June 8, 1770, for no apparent reason, as there are plenty of pages left. Richard Pickersgill (PRO, Adm 51/4547) is interesting in that his style and enthusiasm for writing developed as the voyage went along, though his spelling did not improve. Francis Wilkinson's journal, in the same box (PRO, Adm 51/4547), is neat and very professional, also indicative of growth in character. It ends August 3, 1770, at the Endeavour River, no reason given.

I have made good use of the journal kept by James Roberts, Banks's footman, because it is an unusual voice from the lower deck. Much of it is copied from Pickersgill (evidently from dictation, as the spelling differs), and it was kept with the aim of proving he had time at sea. It becomes intermittent about May 1770, perhaps because he had a difference with Pickersgill. It ends Sunday, May 14, 1770, "on the coast of New Hollang." Roberts did not hand his journal in to Cook, as Cook demanded only those journals kept by officers and petty officers. It is now at the Mitchell Library (CY Safe 157).

For Banks (like Cook, a major source), I used the "South Seas Voyaging Accounts" Web site, following it up with a careful reading of the Beaglehole (1962) edition. His journal is held by the Mitchell Library (Safe 1/12–13). An interesting letter from Banks to Count Lauragais, 1771, describing the voyage is also at the Mitchell Library (CY 1559). Two documents written by Dr. William Munkhouse are in a folder of miscellanea, held at the British Library as Add 27889, and misleadingly titled "Cook's Second Voyage, Fragments." The archivist appears to have been misled by the fact that it includes a draft of a long letter urging the Admiralty to buy the *Resolution*. Everything else is to do with the *Endeavour* voyage. By use of extrapolation and logic, Beaglehole identified the author of the account of the first weeks in New Zealand (October 6–21, 1769) as Munkhouse, and though the other, labeled "Government," an account of social stratification in Tahiti, is not in the same hand, the writer must be Munkhouse, as he describes events after he picked a flower at a *marae*, an incident described by others as happening to him. His medical journal has disappeared.

Charles Green's journal (PRO, Adm 51/4545) is in a large book signed by John Ibbetson, secretary to the Board of Longitude, but is indubitably the astronomer's work. It includes a running account of his voyage with Maskelyne to Barbados and back in 1763–64, which is very amusing. The account of the *Endeavour* is in a much smaller script. Observation figures, kept conscientiously, and notes about "assistants" testify to his efforts to teach lunars, and occasional entries display a dry, acerbic humor. There are twelve blank pages between July 12 and 13, 1769, as if he intended to write a description of Tahiti. It ends anchoring at Batavia, October 3, 1770.

No journal kept by Solander survives—if he kept one at all. He did, however, gossip after he got home, and Dr. Charles Blagden noted interesting tidbits. These are held as the Blagden papers, Osborn collection, Beinecke Rare Books Library, Yale. Ms. file 1354 has interesting jottings from Solander's travels, including stories told by the seamen, the gossip about "Shyboots" Parkinson, Cook's jealousy of Gore, and how "wives" were bought by Banks in Batavia. Box 5, folder 49, has a vocabulary of Tahiti that continues on shipboard, when Solander coaxed significant words out of Tupaia.

The only surviving account kept by Parkinson is the journal printed by his brother. Almost as useful is the anonymous publication of James Magra's journal. Both writers were very interested in Tupaia, and went to great trouble to record what he told them about his early history.

Dolphin's arrival home and *Endeavour's* Voyage to Tahiti:

Wallis made the decision to abandon the hunt for the phantom continent on August 15, 1767, indicating in his revised journal that he had accomplished enough by discovering a good source of "the refreshments that may be had for any future expedition," and that it was "most prudent and more for the benefit of His Maj's Service to make the best of my way to Tinian, Batavia & to Europe."

Other papers running the sensational story (after *Lloyd's*) were *The St. James's Chronicle* (May 24–26), *The London Chronicle* (May 24–26), and *The Gazetteer and New Daily Advertiser* (May 26–27). It was still running as late as July: *Scots Magazine,* vol. XXX, July 1768, pp. 378–79. Glyn Williams's paper "The *Endeavour* Voyage: A coincidence of motives" (Williams 2005: 3–18) is an excellent recounting of events after the *Dolphin* arrived home.

For contemporary documentation of the sailors' strike, see *Scots Magazine,* vol. XXX, June 1768, 328–30. The *Dolphin* was most probably laid up ("mothballed," in modern terminology) because the next muster for her was not until April 1770, and she was broken up soon after that. The pay rates of the men, and the fate of Robertson are described by Carrington (Robertson 1948): xxxviii–xlii. Careers of Furneaux, Molyneux, Pickersgill, and Gore are summarized in Robson 2004: 105, 106–7, 151, 178. Francis Wilkinson, who went on to write a beautifully penned log of the voyage of the *Endeavour*, is a shadowy, undocumented figure, apart from the brief notation on the muster roll that he was born in Chatham in 1747.

The absence of George Robertson from the crew list of the *Endeavour* is notable, particularly as he had trained three of the old *Dolphins* who were given berths. He was still on the *Dolphin,* in charge of the anchored frigate as shipkeeper, though it seems likely he applied for a post on the *Endeavour*, as in 1771 he wrote a letter to Banks, begging him to find him a position on the *Resolution.* He had a black mark on his record, as not only had he led the *Dolphins'* protest, but it was obviously he who defied orders by talking to the reporters. For Hawkesworth, it was a plus, as it was probably now that Robertson rewrote his journal; they certainly talked, as Hawkesworth picked up anecdotes that were not in any of the records, such as the gossip about the Tahitians' stunned reaction when the surgeon removed his wig.

For descriptions of the remodeling of the *Endeavour*, and its accommodations, I referred to Villiers (77–82 in particular), but relied largely on Parkin's impressive account, which is accompanied by wonderfully detailed drafts. For ranks and ratings, and boys on board, see Rodger, 15–29, 37–45, 68–69.

Hough says (101) that by the middle of May Banks's constant companion was Tupaia, who was at the gate of the fort every morning after breakfast, ready to assist in conducting trade. Paul Tapsell described Taiata's relationship to Tupaia in a personal communication. Typically, Cook took the trouble to find out the Tahitians' names when he was noting his new recruits in the muster book. The following day (April 19) he wrote that "Lycurgus, whose real name is Tobia Tomita came with his Family . . . to live near us." Banks did not find out Tupura'a's name until April 27, when he wrote, "This day we found that our friends had names . . . for the future Lycurgus will be calld *Tubourai tamaide*. . . ."

CHAPTER 8: RECOGNIZING TUPAIA

For evidence that priests had clean-shaven chins, see Parkinson's sketch of a Raiatean priest (British Library Add 10497, f.6). Munkhouse's treatise headed "Government" is in British Library folder Add 27889. Banks noted that Tahitians who became drunk were disgusted with themselves in "Manners & Customs of S. Sea Islands": 109; Sparrman confirms this (86). Dreissen's paper, "Dramatis Personae of Society Islands, Cook's 'Endeavour' Voyage 1769" (*Journal of Pacific History*, v.17, no.4 (1982): 227–32) was very helpful for identifying Tahitian participants in Tupaia's story. Carter (82) quotes Solander's names for the various mistresses of the officers.

Wilson (1986) describes French and Spanish flags of the time, 53–55, 60–62, 74–76. Lummis (43) says that the first case of venereal disease was reported five days after the arrival of the *Endeavour*; by the time they left half the crew was infected. Wallis, accused, emphatically denied it had been introduced by the *Dolphin*. In Robertson's public logbook, the page at the bottom of the July 9, 1767, entry is marked in red "No Venereal Disease."

For expert commentary on Tupaia's art, see: Keith Vincent Smith, "Tupaia's Sketchbook" *eBritish Library Journal*, article 10 (2005): 1–6; and Glyndwr Williams's chapter, "Tupaia, Polynesian Warrior, Navigator, High Priest—and Artist," in Nussbaum, 38–51. It should be noted that while seaman John Marra called Tupaia "an excellent artist" (Marra, 219), he meant a "sea artist" or skilled navigator: see, for instance, *The compleat sea artist, or, the art of navigation*, (1684) by Samuel Sturmy, editor of *Mariner's Magazine*. Joppien and Smith discuss Tupaia as "Artist of the Chief Mourner," p.60. Also see Salmond (2003): 56ff; Thomas (2003): 75–77. Smith (1992: 56) comments that studies were made on the spot; he also remarks on Parkinson's unpreparedness to take on figure drawings (82–83, 89, 98, 193–94); and his prudery (96). I am grateful to Rudiger Joppien and Glyndwr Williams for their interest and advice. I thank Caroline Hutton for sharing her study of the costume of the chief mourner.

CHAPTER 9: TUPAIA'S MYTHOLOGY

The Creation Chant comes from De Bovis, p. 45.

Ferdon describes the interesting background to rats on Tahiti, pp. 196–97.

Ellis claimed Tahitians were reluctant to talk of their gods, and described what myths he knew, v. 2: 40–41, 191–95. Cook's rough notes of Tupaia's Maui stories and his account of the creation myth are held by the British Library (Add. Ms. 27889). Moerenhout (I: 439) notes that Ta'aroa was so far above the affairs of the world that he took no part, and consequently was not worshipped. Also see Oliver (1974): II, 890ff.

Wilson (1799: 207–8) describes Tupaia praying at Mahaiatea. I am very grateful to John Mitchell, who devoted much time and enthusiasm into studying Tupaia's creation story. In conversation, we came to the conclusion that the various "Hina" were all incarnations of Hina, who according to de Bovis (40) was considered the wife of Ta'aroa, and goddess of the Earth.

It is impossible not to wonder what would have happened if it had been Wallis, not Cook, who had carried Tupaia to England. Born 1728 in the parish of Lanteglos-by-Camelford, Cornwall, Wallis was a son of minor gentry, and is unlikely to have been able to afford the upkeep of an exotic guest; otherwise it can be reasonably argued that traveling with him would have been the better option. And for the *Dolphins*, having an intelligent and articulate Tahitian with them would have brought them popular attention, forcing the Admiralty to publicly recognize the value of the first European discovery of Tahiti.

According to Sparrman (83) Tupaia's major reason for sailing was the desire to wreak revenge on the Bora Borans.

CHAPTER 10: RETURN TO RAIATEA

Backsight was an important area of Polynesian navigation, as the outline of the departure island altered according to the direction the canoe was steering. Tupaia crouched on the sill of the stern windows to check the outline of Tahiti against the image in his mental library, knowing precisely how Tahiti should look if the ship was steering the correct departure course. See Gladwin, 165–68. Though Banks's description of Tupaia praying for a wind is dated July 14, and Parkinson included his comments in a portion of his journal that covers July 13–15, both entries are obviously retrospective, as it is apparent that Tupaia made a habit of this—until the day he realized the Europeans regarded it as hocus-pocus. Undoubtedly he continued to pray, in a private corner of the open deck.

Tupaia's story about the Bora Borans was recorded by Parkinson (73) and Magra (60–63). According to a list Banks made (see Dreissen, "Dramatis Personae . . .", 232), Tupaia's estates in Raiatea were extensive: they included "Oaheuti" (Vaihuti), "Matawai" (Matavai), "Owaeiao (o Vaiaao valley), "Malahei" (Marahi Point), "Ohetuna" (o Fetuna), Tioroa, "Outurata" (o Uturata), "Otuatau" (perhaps a *motu* off Tahaa), "Ohatemu" (o Faatemu Bay), "Oayenae" and "Oahapapalha" (o Haaparara Bay).

CHAPTER 11: TUPAIA'S MAP

There are several excellent discussions of Tupaia's chart, which is pictured and described in David, Joppien, and Smith, xliv, 130–31; the editors theorize that the arrangement of the islands is in concentric circles from Tahiti corresponding to sailing time.

Robert Langdon has made a special study of the captions and ship sketches. See: "Of Time, Prophesy and the European Ships of Tupaia's Chart," in *Journal of Pacific History,* vol. 19 (1984): 239–47; and "The European Ships of Tupaia's Chart, an Essay in Identification," in *Journal of Pacific History,* vol. 15 (1980): 225–32. Other interpretations of the captions come from Duff, 17–18. More details came from reading Dreissen's paper, "Outriggerless Canoes and Glorious Beings," in *Journal of Pacific History,* vol. 17 (1982): 23–27.

Gordon Lewthwaite gives a geographer's perspective in, "Tupaia's Map: The Horizons of a Polynesian Geographer," *Association of Pacific Coast Geographers Yearbook 28* (1966): 41–53; and "Puzzle of Tupaia's Map," in *New Zealand Geographer,* v. 26, no. 1 (1970): 1–19. David Turnbull discusses Cook's strange lack of interest in finding out precisely how Tupaia navigated in his chapter in Lincoln (117–32), "Cook and Tupaia: A Tale of Cartographic *Méconnaissance?*" His powerful argument is repeated in Ballantyne (225–45), "(En)-Countering Knowledge Traditions: The Story of Cook and Tupaia." Also see Finney (1992): 7–10; and Scarr: 52–53. Coote (20) comments that Cook and Banks never reached a full appreciation of Tupaia's skill and knowledge.

Cook's list is in Beaglehole (1955): 291–93. For interpretations of the island names and their locations, see Hale, 122–25; J. Forster, Chapter VI, esp. 306–15; also Duff, 17–18. An exciting new interpretation has been made by Anne di Piazza and Erik Pearthree, "A New Reading of Tupaia's Chart," *Journal of the Polynesian Society*, v. 116, no. 3 (Sept. 2007): 321–40. A meditative overview is given by O. H. K. Spate, in his chapter, "The Pacific as an artefact," 32–45 of Gunson (1978).

For Marra's comment on Tupaia's expertise, see Marra (219), who mentions Tupaia's map (41); and also (89) refers to the captions. For the interesting detail of the two-headed dragon, I am grateful to Michael Reps. Also see Thomas (2003): 134. That Tupaia could point unerringly to the position of Tahiti was recorded by Johann Forster (531) and Marra (217). Lewis (38) describes island-hopping. My discussion of Cook's moment of insight is a combination of Cook's journal entry for August 15, 1769, and pages 38 and 43 of his description of King George's Island. George Forster's reporting of Tupaia's comment about the king having too many expensive offspring is quoted in Oliver (1974): 953. For the background to Tupaia's drawing of war canoes see Oliver (1974): 404.

CHAPTER 12: LATITUDE FORTY SOUTH

O'Brian (105), pictures the next four weeks as a time of reflection, "as there were not a great many birds or sea creatures to observe", when Banks, "no doubt influenced by Linneaus's rule that the naturalist should report upon every aspect of a foreign people, spent much of his time reflecting on his recent experience, discussing many aspects of it with Tupia, and setting his ordered thoughts down on paper."

For the gossip about Tupaia, see Marra: 219–20. The routine in the Great Cabin was described by Banks in a letter to Alströmer, November 16, 1784: see Duyker and Tingbrand: 410–14. Solander's jolly relationship with the crew is detailed in his letter to John Ellis, December 1, 1768, quoted in Duyker, 110. Dr. Charles Blagden, a close friend, jotted down Solander's stories, now held at the Beinecke Rare Books Library, Yale; Solander's Tahitian vocabulary is in the same collection. I am grateful to the librarians for making this interesting archive available. The story of "Patini" who sailed with American crews comes from the crew cards in the New Bedford Free Public Library, and I thank Paul Cyr, librarian, for his helpfulness.

Solander also described John Gore's vast experience in a letter written at Rio de Janeiro, December 1, 1768: Duyker and Tingbrand, 281. I am very grateful to Solander's biographer, Edward Duyker, for his friendly interest and advice.

For background on the other civilians who shared the afterquarters with Tupaia, I used John Robson's encyclopedia, and also his Web site, "The Men Who Sailed with Captain James Cook," at quicksilver.net.nz. I also thank John Robson for his helpful personal communications. For Parkinson, see Carr passim. For the technical details of calculating longitude by the lunar distance method, see Howse, pp. 194–97. For the story of Maskelyne's tables, see ibid., pp. 63–67. James Roberts complained about the awful conditions in his diary entry for September 23, 1769.

Listing the possessions Tupaia probably carried with him relies partly on Henry's description of the *haanatoroa*, or uniform of a priest, (152). Gladwin described the provisioning of a voyaging canoe: 50–51.

Wallis's logbook provides a fascinating day-to-day account of the medical and dietary care of his men. Wine was considered better than grog, which was spirit (brandy in the *Dolphins*' case) mixed with water, because wine was acid, and acid was supposed to prevent and cure scurvy. (Wine is acid because of its tartaric acid content, and has no vitamin C, but Wallis was acting by the best principles he knew.) An interesting exposition on the preparation and medical uses of "salep" or saloup was published in *Scots Magazine*, vol. XXX (1768, but dated Oct. 29, 1767): 8. Hutchinson's letter, dated May 16, 1768, is included with the first volume of the *Endeavour* log held at National Library of Australia, Canberra (MS 1).

Richard T. Mihaere discusses *whakama* in McCall and Connell, 67–68.

CHAPTER 13: YOUNG NICK'S HEAD

For the great tsunami see McFadgen: 221–37. It may coincide with the deluge of Tahitian and Raiatean legend: Henry, 445–52. For background to contacts with Maori during the circumnavigation of New Zealand, I referred often to Anne Salmond's remarkable book, *Two Worlds* (Salmond 1991), and thank her for her interest and help.

Mere and *patu* were used in close-quarter fighting. Though often called "clubs," they were not bludgeons; instead, the warrior hacked with the sharpened edge at the strike zone, usually the temple, jaw, or ribs. Once lodged, a powerful flick of the wrist wreaked the maximum damage. The *mere pounamu* was partly revered because of the immense labor involved in the chipping and polishing, and also because greenstone was relatively rare; the weapon also took on the prestige of past owners, attaining great *mana* as it was handed down from generation to generation. The value of a cutlass was given as eight shillings, two pence, in the estate papers of Captain

Ebenezer Ellinwood, of Beverly, Massachusetts, 1771: Essex County Records.

Pickersgill remarked on the bravery of the Maori, writing regarding the retrieval of the *mere pounamu* "this Peice of courage is unparrelled and is greatly to be admird." It is customary to give November 15, 1769, as the date Cook took formal possession of New Zealand, but Parkinson's earlier description is persuasive: see W. Colenso, "On the Day in which Captain Cook took Formal Possession of New Zealand," *Transactions and Proceedings of the Royal Society of New Zealand,* v. 10 (1877): 99–105. The three kidnapped boys were named by Archdeacon W. L. Williams (393) in his paper, "On the Visit of Captain Cook to Poverty Bay and Tolaga Bay," *Transactions and Proceedings of the Royal Society of New Zealand,* v. 21 (1888): 389–97. Munkhouse wrote the names of their gods phonetically as "*Torònomy—Tahòugoona—Ohyere.*" Hicks (qMS-0954) confirms the three boys slept "in the great Cabbin"—another indication Tupaia had a berth in the afterquarters.

CHAPTER 14: BECOMING LEGEND

Salmond (1991) evocates the background to the interactions at Uawa: 169–79. Colenso described Tupaia's cave and the drawing in, "A few remarks on a cavern . . ." *Transactions and Proceedings of the Royal Society of New Zealand,* v. 12 (1879): 147–50. In a footnote to p. 148 Colenso gives the name of the high chief who received Cook as "Whakatataraoterangi"—his grandson, Te Kaniotakirau ("Kani") was the man who showed Tupaia's cave to Polack, and swore to him the drawing was Tupaia's. That Tupaia left Banks and Solander to their own devices while he visited *marae* is confirmed by the fact that Banks acquired a carved panel, or *poupou*, which he evidently prized off a half-finished building on Te Pourewa Island. If Tupaia had been there, he certainly would not have permitted the sacrilege. See Salmond (1991): 173. Wilkinson, October 21, 1769, confirms that Taiata accompanied him.

Both Magra (78–79) and Banks (Account of New Zealand: 207–8) described the system for obtaining female companionship. Wilkinson wrote (October 21) that many men had more than one "wife." That Tupaia would have been welcomed with lavish hospitality (including the offer of an aristocratic bedmate), was confirmed by Pei Te Hurinui Jones, in "A Maori Comment . . ." *Journal of the Polynesian Society,* v. 66, no.1: 132–34; and Mathew Tupaea, in a personal communication. I am most grateful to Bronwyn Tupaea Judd and the Tupaea family for their interest and comments. Gudgeon, "Mana Tangata," *Journal of the Polynesian Society,* v. 14, no.2 (June 1905): 49–66, discusses *mana* and *marae*; his comparison of stepped platforms with Maori *marae* is on p. 52. For the prosperity of this area, see Salmond (1991): 178. Also see Simmons: 350–51.

Bayly (Cook's astronomer, second expedition) recorded (April 9, 1773) Tupaia had become legend (quoted in McNab: 202, 205); Bayly also noted the word "ahou" for garment had entered the Maori language. Cook's observation that people everywhere had heard of Tupaia is in his *Resolution* journal, June 3, 1773: Beaglehole (1961): 170. Sparrman (37) recorded a *waiata* for Tupaia. That Tupaia reintroduced the bow and arrow was postulated by E. Tregear, "The Polynesian Bow," *Journal of the Polynesian Society,* v.1, no. 1 (1892): 56–59. An inspiration was Paul Tapsell's chapter, "Footprints in the Sand," in Hetherington and Morphy: 92–111, which argues powerfully for the presenting of precious *taonga* to Tupaia.

CHAPTER 15: THE CONVOLUTED COAST OF NEW ZEALAND

Horeta Te Taniwha's account of the shooting by Gore is quoted by Salmond (1991): 198–99. Duyker (1998) points out (163) that Solander, because he was aided by Tupaia, recorded Maori plant names with remarkable accuracy, confirmed by an article by Hatch (*Tuatara* v. 11, no. 2 (June 1963): 66–71, asserting that Tupaia's presence was both "providential" and "invaluable."

I am most grateful to Hilary and John Mitchell for their enthusiastic support during the research for this chapter, the Queen Charlotte Sound area in particular. John Mitchell provided the interesting comment that Maori there seemed to know about nails already. Tupaia's conversations are my loose versions of what he himself reported; it was Magra who said the dead woman was a sister (96). Australia's Governor Darling tried to suppress the *mokai* trade, calling it "barbarous," but it remained active into the early nineteenth century, greatly affecting Maori custom. Because a head with an elaborately detailed *moko* was extra-valuable, its owner became a moving target, so having a facial tattoo became much less popular (James Belich, personal communication). I thank John Mitchell for his enlightening thoughts on cannibalism and *tapu* involved with preparation of the corpse.

Burney (49) noted Maori questioned how Tupaia died: "seemed to suspect we had put him to death." Molyneux spelled Olimaroa "Oneewarroa," described by Tupaia as one of several large, high, fertile islands to the west and northwest of Tahiti (probably the Tongan group); it is not in Cook's list or on Tupaia's chart. The story about "Tupia's ship" comes from Belich (20); it is also mentioned by Beaglehole (1961): 73.

CHAPTER 16: BOTANY BAY

An excellent analysis of the Banks and Cook reports as ethnographic accounts is in Salmond (1991): 265–95.

Descriptions of first contacts with Aborigines were inspired by Duyker (1998), particularly 179; and Keith Vincent Smith's, "Confronting Cook": *eBritish Library Journal*, 2009, article 4: 1–5. Rosemary Hunter, in Attwood, 3, describes the concept of disorder coming from the sea.

The charming story of Tupaia's pet lorikeet was first told by Whittell (81), quoting George Allen of Darlington, purchaser of the Tunstall collection. More details come from Olsen: 16–19. I thank Nick Burningham for his interesting communication about Tupaia's habit of wandering away from the Europeans.

Cook's notes concerning his anti-scorbutic dietary supplements are included in Add Ms 27889 (British Library). Much more effective was his habit of scavenging herbs from shore. It should be noted that keeping a clean, dry, airy ship, and having a three-watch system (where the men worked four hours and had the next eight hours off) were effective, too, as grueling work and grim conditions sap the body's resistance to scurvy. See Brett Stubb's paper, "Captain Cook's beer: the antiscorbutic use of malt and beer in late 18th century sea voyages," *Asia Pacific Journal of Clinical Nutrition* 2003: 12 (2): 129–37.

CHAPTER 17: THE GREAT BARRIER REEF

Ferdon (96) says that fish were eaten raw, gills, guts, and all, confirmed by Sparrman (89). This means gill and stomach contents were consumed, with their valuable vitamin and dietary fiber content undamaged by cooking. This would account for Tupaia's miraculous recovery.

First contacts with natives of the Endeavour River are well described by Duyker (1998): 198–201. Interesting background to the local dialect is discussed by John B. Haviland in his contribution ("The Language of Cooktown") to Shopen, 164–69. Also see: Lippmann (19–23).

CHAPTER 18: THE LAST CHAPTER

Cook admitted he had made no great discoveries in a letter to Mr. Walker of Whitby, quoted by Wood, 115.

For sharing of the last breath see Henry, 290. The lack of a vegetable diet was indeed a crucial factor in Tupaia's premature death. James Watt's chapter "Medical Aspects and Consequences of Cook's Voyages" (Fisher and Johnston: 129–57) points out there was more scurvy than Cook admitted, giving Green and Tupaia as examples (139).

Descriptions of Edam come from *The Jakarta Post*, "An Unforgettable Trip to Bidadari and Damar islands," June 2, 2000, and "Let there be light,"

November 19, 2008; see also John Joseph Stockdale, *Sketches, Civil and Military, of the Island of Java* . . . (London, 1812), 126–27; John Pinkerton, *A general collection of the best and most interesting travels* . . . (London, 1808), 214–15.

Parkinson described collecting small artifacts for his cousin, Jane Gomeldon, in a letter to her written at Batavia, October 16, 1770: see Beaglehole in Banks 1962: 57–62; and Carr, xii–xiii; the dogskin-trimmed cloak is the one Munkhouse bought on October 12, 1769. Adrienne Kaeppler's paper, "Enlightened Ethnographic Collections" in Kaeppler et al., has a list of "curiosities" Cook donated to the Admiralty (56), and discusses the significance of artifacts collected on the first expedition (55–58). Coote has details of Banks's "curiosities" now held by the Pitt Rivers Museum, University of Oxford (which may include Taiata's flute); Coote's paper, "Joseph Banks's Forty Brass Patus" (*Journal of Museum Ethnology,* no. 20, March 2008: 49–68), 59, comments that Banks was "often frustrated" by his inability to get hold of *taonga.*

Which brings us full circle to the *New Zealand Herald* interview that inspired this book (August 5, 2006), and Paul Tapsell's convincing argument that Banks's Maori treasures were in fact presented to Tupaia, in recognition of his extraordinary status as the high priest and master navigator of the *Endeavour.*

Bibliography

Adams, Henry. *Tahiti*. Edited by Robert E. Spiller. Memoirs of Arii Taimai, the last chiefess of Papara (and Purea's great-niece), as told to Adams through Marau Taaroa, "last queen of Tahiti", who translated. Paris: privately printed, 1901.

Attwood, Bain, ed. *In the Age of Mabo: History, Aborigines, and Australia*. St. Leonard's, NSW: Allen & Unwin, 1996.

Aughton, Peter. *Endeavour, the Story of Captain Cook's First Great Epic Voyage*. London: Cassell, 2002.

Ballantyne, Tony, ed. *Science, Empire and the European Exploration of the Pacific*. London: Pacific World Series (Ashgate), 2004.

Banks, Joseph. Endeavour *Journal of Joseph Banks*. Edited by J.C. Beaglehole. Sydney: The Trustees of the Public Library of New South Wales in association with Angus and Robertson, 1962.

Banks, Joseph. *The Journal of Joseph Banks in the* Endeavour. Facsimile of the journal with a commentary by A. M. Lysaght. Adelaide: Rigby, 1980.

Beaglehole, John Cawte. *The Life of Captain James Cook*. London: A & C Black, 1974.

Beasley, A.W. *Fellowship of Three*. [John Hunter, James Cook, Joseph Banks] Kenthurst, NSW: Kangaroo Press, 1993.

Begg, A. Charles, and Neil C. Begg. *James Cook and New Zealand*. Wellington: Government Printing Office, 1969.

Belich, James. *Making Peoples, a History of the New Zealanders*. Auckland: Penguin, 2007.

Buck, Peter (Te Rangi Hiroa). *An Introduction to Polynesian Anthropology*. Honolulu: Kraus reprint, 1945.

Burney, James. *With Captain James Cook in the Antarctic and Pacific, the Private Journal of James Burney, Second Lieutenant of the* Adventure *on Cook's Second Voyage.* Edited by Beverley Hooper. Canberra: National Library of Australia, 1975.

Carr, D. J., ed. *Sydney Parkinson, Artist.* Honolulu: University of Hawaii Press, 1983.

Carter, Harold B. *Sir Joseph Banks 1743–1820.* London: British Museum, 1988.

Colchester, Chloè, ed. *Clothing the Pacific.* Oxford, UK: Berg, 2003.

Cook, James. *The Journals of Captain James Cook on His Voyages of Discovery.* (Vol. I, *Endeavour.*) Edited by J.C. Beaglehole. Cambridge, UK: Hakluyt Society, 1955.

Coote, Jeremy. *Curiosities from the* Endeavour, *A Forgotten Collection.* Whitby: Captain Cook Memorial Museum, 2004 (exhibition catalogue).

Corney, Bolton G. *The Quest and Occupation of Tahiti by Emissaries of Spain during the years 1772 to 1776.* 3 vols. London: Hakluyt Society, 1913.

Crawford, Peter. *Nomads of the Wind, A Natural History of Polynesia.* London: BBC Books, 1993.

David, Andrew, Rudiger Joppien, and Bernard Smith. *Charts and Coastal Views of Captain Cook's Voyages.* (Vol. I, *Endeavour.*) London: Hakluyt Society, with Australian Academy of the Humanities, 1988.

Dawson, Warren R. *The Banks Letters.* London: British Museum, 1958.

De Bovis, Edmond. *Tahitian Society Before the Arrival of the Europeans.* Translated and edited by Robert D. Craig. Honolulu: Institute for Polynesian Studies, Brigham Young University, 1976.

Dening, Greg. *Mr Bligh's Bad Language.* Cambridge, UK: Cambridge University Press, 1992.

Dening, Greg. *Beach Crossings, Voyaging across Times, Cultures and Self.* Melbourne: Miegunyah Press, 2004.

Druett, Joan. *Rough Medicine, Surgeons at Sea in the Age of Sail.* New York: Routledge, 2001.

Duff, Roger, ed. *No Sort of Iron, Culture of Cook's Polynesians.* Christchurch: Art Galleries and Museums Association of New Zealand, 1969.

Dunmore, John. *Storms and Dreams: Louis de Bougainville, Soldier, Explorer, Statesman.* Auckland: Exisle, 2005.

Dunmore, John. *French Explorers in the Pacific.* 2 vols. London: Oxford University Press, 1965–69.

Duyker, Edward. *Nature's Argonaut: Daniel Solander 1733–1782.* Melbourne: Miegunyah Press, 1998.

Duyker, Edward, and Per Tingbrand, eds. and trans. *Daniel Solander: Collected Correspondence.* Melbourne: Miegunyah Press, 1995.

Edwards, Philip. *Story of the Voyage, Sea-Narratives in Eighteenth-Century England.* Cambridge, New York: Cambridge University Press, 1994.

Ellis, William. *Polynesian Researches*. London: G. Robinson, 1782.

Evans, Jeff. *Maori Weapons in Pre-European New Zealand*. Wellington: Reed, 2002.

Ferdon, Edwin N. *Early Tahiti, As the Explorers Saw It, 1767–1797*. Tucson: University of Arizona Press, 1981.

Finney, Ben R. *Polynesian Peasants and Proletarians*. Cambridge, MA: Schenkman Publishing, 1973.

Finney, Ben R. *Hokule'a, The Way to Tahiti*. New York: Dodd, Mead, 1979.

Finney, Ben R. *From Sea to Space*. Palmerston North: Massey University Press, 1992.

Finney, Ben R. *Voyage of Rediscovery, A Cultural Odyssey Through Polynesia*. Berkeley: University of California Press, 1994.

Fisher, Robin, and Hugh Johnston, eds. *Captain James Cook and His Times*. London: Croom Helm, 1979.

Forster, George. *A Voyage Round the World in His Britannic Majesty's Sloop* Resolution, *Commanded by Captain James Cook, during the Years 1772, 3, 4, and 5*. London: B. White, J. Robson, and P. Elmsly., 1777.

Forster, Johann Reinhold. *Observations Made During a Voyage Round the World on Physical Geography, Natural History and Ethical Philosophy*. London: G. Robinson, 1778.

Frost, Alan. *The Precarious Life of James Maria Matra, Voyager with Cook; American loyalist; servant of empire*. Melbourne: Miegunyah Press, 1995.

Frost, Alan, and Jane Samson, eds. *Pacific Empires: Essays in Honour of Glyndwr Williams*. Vancouver: University of British Columbia Press, 1999.

Furneaux, Rupert. *Tobias Furneaux, Circumnavigator*. London: Cassell, 1960.

Gladwin, Thomas. *East Is a Big Bird: Navigation and Logic on Pulawat Atoll*. Cambridge, MA: Harvard University Press, 1970.

Gunson, Niel, ed. *The Changing Pacific: Essays in Honour of H. E. Maude*. New York: Oxford University Press, 1978.

Hale, Horatio. *Ethnology and Philology*. Philadelphia: C. Sherman, 1846.

Hawkesworth, John. *An Account of the Voyages Undertaken by the Order of His Present Majesty for Making Discoveries in the Southern Hemisphere*. London: Strahan and Cadell, 1773.

Henry, Teuira. *Ancient Tahiti*. Honolulu: Bernice Bishop Museum Bulletin 48, 1928.

Herda, Phyllis, Michael Reilly, and David Hilliard, eds. *Vision and Reality in Pacific Religion, Essays in Honour of Niel Gunson*. Christchurch: Macmillan Brown Centre for Pacific Studies, 2005.

Hetherington, Michelle. *Cook & Omai, the Cult of the South Seas*. Canberra: National Library of Australia, 2001.

Hetherington, Michelle, and Howard Morphy, eds. *Discovering Cook's Collections*. Canberra: National Museum of Australia Press, 2009.

Hooper, Steven. *Brief Encounters: Art of Divinity in Polynesia 1760–1860*. Wellington: Te Papa Press, 2006.

Horwitz, Tony. *Blue Latitudes, Boldly Going Where Captain Cook Has Gone Before.* New York: Henry Holt, 2002.

Hough, Richard. *Captain James Cook: A Biography.* London: Hodder & Stoughton, 1994.

Howarth, David. *Tahiti, a Paradise Lost.* London: Horvill, 1983.

Howe, K. R., ed. *Vaka Moana: Voyages of the Ancestors, the Discovery and Settlement of the Pacific.* Auckland: David Bateman with Auckland Museum, 2006.

Howe, Kerry R. *Where the Waves Fall, A New South Sea Islands History from First Settlement to Colonial Rule.* Sydney: Allen & Unwin, 1984.

Howse, Derek. *Greenwich Time and the Discovery of Longitude.* Oxford, UK: Oxford University Press, 1980.

Irwin, Geoffrey. *Prehistoric Exploration and Colonisation of the Pacific.* Cambridge, UK: Cambridge University Press, 1992.

Jennings, Jess D., ed. *The Prehistory of Polynesia.* Cambridge, MA: Harvard University Press, 1979.

Joppien, Rudiger, and Bernard Smith. *The Art of Captain Cook's Voyages.* (3 vols.) Melbourne: Oxford University Press, 1985–87.

Kaeppler, Adrienne, et al. *James Cook and the Exploration of the Pacific.* London: Thames & Hudson, 2009 (Exhibition catalogue).

Lamb, Jonathan, Vanessa Smith, and Nicholas Thomas. *Exploration and Exchange: A South Seas Anthology 1680–1900.* Chicago: University of Chicago Press, 2000.

Lewis, David. *We, the Navigators, the Ancient Art of Landfinding in the Pacific.* Honolulu: University Press of Hawaii, 1972.

Lincoln, Margarette, ed. *Science and Exploration in the Pacific: European Voyages to the Southern Oceans in the 18th Century.* London: Boydell with National Maritime Museum, 1998.

Lippmann, Lorna. *To Achieve Our Country: Australia and the Aborigines.* Melbourne: Cheshire, 1970.

Lummis, Trevor. *Pacific Paradises, the Discovery of Tahiti & Hawaii.* London: Sutton, 2005.

Macarthur, Antonia. *His Majesty's Bark* Endeavour. Sydney: Angus & Robertson with the Australian National Maritime Museum, 1997.

Mackay, David. *In the Wake of Cook: Exploration, Science & Empire.* Wellington: Victoria University Press, 1985.

Magra, James, aka James Matra (anonymously published). *A Journal of a Voyage round the World, In His Majesty's Ship* Endeavour. London: Becket and De Hondt, 1771.

Marra, John. *Journal of the* Resolution *Voyage in 1771–1775.* New York: Da Capo, 1967.

McCall, Grant, and John Connell, ed. *A World Perspective on Pacific Islander Migration.* Australia: University of New South Wales Centre for South Pacific Studies, 1993.

McCormick, E. H. *Omai, Pacific Envoy.* Auckland: Auckland University Press, 1977.

McFadgen, Bruce. *Hostile Shores: Catastrophic Events in Prehistoric New Zealand and their Impact on Maori Coastal Communities.* Auckland: Auckland University Press, 2007.

McNab, Robert, ed. *Historical Records of New Zealand.* Wellington: Government Printer, 1908.

Mitchell, Hilary, and John Mitchell. *Te tau ihu o te waka, a History of Maori of Nelson and Marlborough.* Wellington: Huia Press, with Wakatu Incorporated, 2004.

Mitchell, T. C., ed. *Captain Cook and the South Pacific.* Canberra: Australian National University Press, 1979.

Moerenhout, Jacques-Antoine. *Voyages aux îles du Grand Ocean (Travels to the Islands of the Pacific Ocean)* (translated by Arthur R. Borden). Lanham, MD: University Press of America, 1993.

Nussbaum, Felicity A., ed. *The Global Eighteenth Century.* Baltimore: Johns Hopkins University Press, 2003.

O'Brian, Patrick. *Joseph Banks: A Life.* London: Collins Harvill, 1987.

Oliver, Douglas L. *Ancient Tahitian Society.* (3 vols.) Honolulu: University of Hawaii Press, 1974.

Oliver, Douglas L. *Return to Tahiti: Bligh's Second Breadfruit Voyage.* Honolulu: University of Hawaii Press, 1988.

Olsen, Penny. *Feather and Brush: 300 Years of Australian Bird Art.* Melbourne: CSIRO Publishing 2001.

Parkin, Ray. *H. M. Bark* Endeavour, *Her Place in Australian History.* Melbourne: Miegunyah Press, 1999.

Parkinson, Sydney. *A Journal of a Voyage to the South Seas in His Majesty's Ship the* Endeavour. London: Stanfield Parkinson, 1773.

Prickett, Nigel. *Maori Origins, From Asia to Aotearoa.* Auckland: David Bateman with Auckland Museum, 2001.

Reed, A.W. *Taonga Tuku Iho, Illustrated Encyclopaedia of Traditional Maori Life.* Revised by Buddy Mikaere. Auckland: New Holland, 2002.

Richardson, Brian W. *Longitude and Empire: How Captain Cook's Voyages Changed the World.* Vancouver: University of British Columbia Press, 2005.

Rigby, Nigel, and Pieter van der Merwe. *Captain Cook in the Pacific.* London: National Maritime Museum, 2002.

Robertson, George. *The Discovery of Tahiti. A Journal of the Second Voyage of H.M.S.* Dolphin *Round the World Under the Command of Captain Wallis, R.N., in the Years 1766, 1767 and 1768, Written by Her Master George Robertson.* Hugh Carrington, ed. London: Hakluyt Society, 1948 (second series, No. XCVIII).

Robertson, George. *An Account of the Discovery of Tahiti, from the Journal of George Robertson.* Oliver Warner, ed. London: Folio Press, 1955.

Robson, John. *The Captain Cook Encyclopaedia.* Auckland: Random House, 2004.

Rodger, N. A. M. *The Wooden World, an Anatomy of the Georgian Navy.* London: HarperCollins, 1986.

Salmond, Anne. *Two Worlds: First Meetings between Maori and Europeans 1642–1772.* Auckland: Penguin, 1991.

Salmond, Anne. *Trial of the Cannibal Dog: Captain Cook in the South Seas.* London: Penguin, 2003.

Salmond, Anne. *Aphrodite's Island.* Auckland: Penguin, 2009.

Scarr, Deryck. *A History of the Pacific Islands: Passages Through Tropical Time.* New York: Routledge, 2000.

Sharp, Andrew. *Ancient Voyagers in Polynesia.* Sydney: Angus & Robertson, 1963.

Shopen, Timothy, ed. *Languages and Their Speakers.* Philadelphia: University of Pennsylvania Press, 1987.

Simmons, D. R. *The Great New Zealand Myth: A Study of the Discovery and Origin Traditions of the Maori.* Wellington: Reed, 1976.

Smith, Bernard. *Imagining the Pacific in the Wake of the Cook Voyages.* Melbourne: Miegunyah Press, 1992.

Sparrman, Anders. *A Voyage Round the World with Captain James Cook in HMS* Resolution. London: Robert Hale, 1944.

Steiner, Franz Baermann. *Taboo.* London: Cohen & West, 1956. This valuable study has been reprinted as, *Taboo, Truth, and Religion,* in volume 1 of the *Selected Writings* of Franz Baermann Steiner series. Edited by Jeremy Adler and Richard Fardon. New York: Berghahn Books, 1999.

Strang, Herbert. *Captain Cook's Voyages.* Oxford University Press, 1923.

Thomas, Nicholas. *In Oceania: Visions, Artifacts, Histories.* London: Durham, 1997.

Thomas, Nicholas. *Discoveries: The Voyages of Captain Cook.* London: Penguin, 2003.

Thrower, Norman J. W. *Captain James Cook and His Voyages of Discovery in the Pacific.* Los Angeles: University of California Library, 1970 (exhibition catalogue).

Villiers, Alan. *Captain Cook, the Seamen's Seaman.* London: Hodder & Stoughton, 1967.

Whittell, Hubert Massey. *The Literature of Australian Birds.* Perth: Paterson Brokensha, 1954.

Williams, Glyndwr. *Buccaneers, Explorers and Settlers: British Enterprises and Encounters in the Pacific 1670–1800.* London: Variorium Collected Studies (Ashgate), 2005.

Williams, Glyndwr, and Alan Frost. *Terra Australis to Australia.* Melbourne: Oxford University Press, 1989.

Wilson, James. *A Missionary Voyage to the Southern Pacific Ocean, Performed in the Years 1796, 1797, 1798, in the Ship* Duff. London: T. Chapman, 1799.

Wilson, Timothy. *Flags at Sea.* London: National Maritime Museum, 1986.

Wood, G. Arnold. *The Voyage of the* Endeavour. Melbourne: Macmillan, 1944.

Index

⚬≈⚬

Note: page numbers in italic denote figures.

About the Author

JOAN DRUETT is an independent maritime historian and writer, who lives in Wellington, New Zealand. She has published many award-winning maritime studies, including *In the Wake of Madness* (2003) and *Island of the Lost* (2007), and is also the author of the popular Wiki Coffin mystery series.

BAN 5116